SPECIAL   EDUCATION

SPECIAL EDUCATION

Children with Learning Problems

ROGER REGER

WENDY SCHROEDER

AND

KATHIE USCHOLD

New York

OXFORD UNIVERSITY PRESS

London · Toronto   1968

This is intended to serve as a text for those interested in the formal education of children who deviate significantly in a negative direction from the average in their learning patterns or in their general behavior. These children frequently are called emotionally disturbed or minimally brain injured, but whenever possible we have purposely stayed away from using such labels. Our concern is with the labeling of programming and technology rather than with the labeling of children.

Our intended audience includes both those responsible for establishing and administering special education programs and those who are or will be teachers in such programs.

We have—perhaps too rashly—prepared a book that attempts to describe how and why to establish and carry out a particular kind of educational program. It is a kind of plan book. The format reflects this purpose. The first part is devoted to critical discussions about the nature of special education. The section following is concerned with specific curriculum materials, techniques, and methods of evaluating problems—practical matters—that should be especially useful to teachers.

We admit this is a book of opinions; no pretense is made that anything described has been verified by scientific evaluation. We reflected upon the wisdom of this and concluded that if we, or anybody else, waited for scientific evidence no book of this kind would be forthcoming for many years.

The source of our opinions is varied but primarily stems from experience with problem children in the public schools. Of particular importance to us has been experience with what we have called a "Program for Children with Learning Problems," conducted under the auspices of the Board of Cooperative Educational Services of the First Supervisory District Schools in Erie County, New York.

We have attempted to stay close to home in describing the familiar and to refrain from extending ourselves into areas where we lack first-hand observations. We believe, nevertheless, that our descriptions can be generalized to school situations that might have characteristics quite different from ours.

We place a great deal of emphasis on individualized programming, a term that is quite popular but seldom understood in educational circles today. We discuss the kinds of things teachers might do with children, including specific outlines of techniques, materials, and sources for implementing action in the classroom. Our intention in part is to provide enough information so that a teacher who had never before worked with the kinds of children we describe could refer to this text as an aid in knowing specifically what to do from one day to the next.

The sophisticated reader perhaps will find many occasions to disagree with us. We believe it makes sense to have a clear understanding and definition of the problems we are facing before attempting to prepare answers. In devising questions we have drawn more from educational philosophies and curriculum theories than from such sources as the medical literature. The result is that our questions, and thus our answers, are formulated in a somewhat different manner than has been traditional in the field of special education.

Typically those concerned with special education have emphasized *antecedents*—causation, history, and diagnosis. While we do not neglect antecedents, our emphasis is on *consequences* because we believe that labels do not explain, that understanding should not be substituted for action, and that our ultimate concern is what happens to children.

R. R.
W. S.
K. U.

February 1968

Acknowledgements

We would find it difficult to work on a book without being aware that we are immersed in a supportive environment that favors initiative and new ways of looking at old problems. To a large extent these conditions exist because of our superintendents, Dr. Justus A. Prentice and Mr. Ernest H. Hoeldtke.

Contents

Part I

INTRODUCTION AND COMMENTARY

In this first section are discussed some of the issues related to the nature and process of what we call special education. In the first chapter a brief outline is presented of the setting that provided the immediate stimulus for the book. It is observed that the book is not a description of a single program although many recent experiences are reflected.

Chapter 2 reviews the responsibility of the schools for deviant behavior among children. The following chapter begins a specific discussion of the nature of special education, what makes it "special" and what changes might be made in our thinking.

The nature of *handicap* is reviewed in Chapters 5 and 6, and in Chapters 7 and 8 the discussion deals with the kinds of people who work with our children. The last chapters look at the way we decide *who* should do *what* in our school programs and review some old problems in special education: How can one manage children effectively, and what reasons are behind our methods?

1

Introduction: The Setting and the Program

The intention in preparing this book is not simply to describe a special education program. The intention is, rather, to use the various special education programs the authors have been associated with as reference points for general observations.

Nevertheless, we do want to offer a brief outline of the setting and the program that provided the major source of observational material for us. Specific aspects of the program are described in Reger (1967) and in additional forthcoming journal publications.

THE COOPERATIVE BOARD—"BOCES"

A publication, *Cooperative Programs in Special Education*, edited by Lord and Isenberg (1964), briefly outlines the major ways in which smaller school districts pool their resources to provide services to meet their special educational problems. Boards of Cooperative Educational Services—often called "BOCES" (pronounced "bo-cees")—are described by Griffin and Langworthy (1964).

A cursory observation of Cooperative Boards in New York State suggests that each has its own *modus operandi,* so the references made here to "the Cooperative Board" apply only to the Board of Cooperative Educational Services in Erie County, New York. Although a Cooperative Board is a unique organization in many ways, in other ways it is similar to other administrative structures seen in school systems in other states.

Administrative Structure

Eighteen school districts in suburban Buffalo, with school populations ranging from about 1500 to about 10,000 children, participate in the Cooperative Board. The total public-school enrollment is approximately 80,000 children in the eighteen school districts. In the same geographic area about 25,000 children attend non-public schools, primarily Catholic. Several school districts in the area that would be eligible for "membership" in the Cooperative Board have chosen not to belong to the organization. The Buffalo City School District does not belong.

The Cooperative Board has a superintendent, a deputy superintendent, and four directors. The directors are responsible for the areas of special educational services, data processing, curriculum development, and vocational and trade technical education. A Board of Education, with five members elected at an annual meeting, is the legal policy-making agent for the Cooperative Board.

The Cooperative Board can own property; it sets salaries, employs and supervises teachers and other staff members, provides transportation when requested by local school districts, and in many other ways is similar to local school districts.

A unique feature of the Cooperative Board is that the chief school officers of the participating school districts are the real locus of power, even though legally all authority rests with the various Boards of Education. Regular meetings are held, at which decisions are made that determine the operational basis for the Cooperative Board.

Financing

This is more complicated than will be implied here, but basically the local school districts pay all the expenses for the operation of the Cooperative Board's special education (and other) programs. No state aid money is directly paid to the Cooperative Board. The local school districts receive all state aid payments and no special financial provisions are made for special education programs in New York State. The Cooperative Board can receive special grants from the state and federal governments for various projects but these typically are for short periods of time.

The formula for determining the cost of special education programs operated by the Cooperative Board is relatively simple. A budget is prepared itemizing all costs of administration, supervision, space rental, staff members, and supplies. The total cost is then divided by the numbers of children in the programs and the schools are sent a bill for payment based on the numbers of children they have in the programs. No school district pays for services not received, so if a budget item does not materialize into a service the local school district is not billed for that particular item.

Program Operation

All the participating school districts make provisions for handicapped children through the Cooperative Board. However, several school districts operate their own local programs for some of their handicapped students. For example, one district has all its children classified as mentally retarded placed in programs operated by the Cooperative Board but all its children classified as emotionally disturbed are in locally administered classes. To illustrate further the flexibility of the operation of the programs, this particular school district requests that some of its children classified as emotionally disturbed be included in summer programming offered through the Cooperative Board.

By the beginning of the 1965-66 school year there were nineteen special classes established in what was labeled "A Program for Children with Learning and/or Behavioral Problems." The following year saw a total of thirty-nine classes in operation. Children were considered eligible for this program if they were declared by local school district personnel to exhibit significant learning and/or behavioral problems. No children were screened by Cooperative Board staff and placements were made by an administrative assistant on the basis of age and nearness to home. Of the 175 children placed in this fashion, only one or two were found to be misplaced and the reasons for this were in the relationships among the children themselves once they had been placed and could not have been predicted ahead of time.

The maximum class enrollment the first year was ten children but this was later reduced to eight children. It was found that ten children presented too difficult a task for teachers.

Three teacher aides were employed the first year but this was later reduced to one aide. It is interesting to note that among those not close to the program, one major solution proposed for many problems that arose was adding teacher aides. However, teachers who used aides found they had to spend as much time with the aides as with the children.

CHILD BEHAVIOR CONSULTANTS

During the 1966-67 school year funds were made available through the Elementary and Secondary Education Act of 1965, Title III, for a project called "The Training and Utilization of Child Behavior Consultants in the Schools." The project started with a small planning grant that was used to provide a six-week orientation course during the summer prior to the beginning of the school year. The major task for the twenty-one personnel in the summer program was to define a role for themselves.

An attempt will be made here to outline briefly what child behavior consultants *should* do rather than what they actually *did* during their first year in the project. This is because, as was anticipated, in the first year many mistakes were made.

Each child behavior consultant works with a defined population, and this population is as similar as possible to the population typically placed into special classes. Such a procedure makes it easier for school personnel to understand the program and it also makes sense to those responsible for preparing and defending budgets.

Thus, each child behavior consultant works with no more than eight children for 60 percent of his time; 30 percent of his time is devoted to working with either the same children or with other children on an informal, crisis, or unscheduled basis; and the remaining 10 percent of his time is devoted to working with other staff members.

The eight children assigned for 60 percent of the child behavior consultant's time are selected by the building principal, the program director, the regular classroom teachers, and the child behavior consultant. The children assigned can be taken off the assignment list at any time and new children added. The basis for assignment is that the children are deemed to have significant learning and/or behavioral problems, or it is predicted that such problems will arise if assistance is not provided.

The task of the child behavior consultant is not confined to remedial reading and arithmetic; it includes all aspects of a child's behavior in school. He can work with children who seem to be headed for difficulty; it is not necessary to wait until the child is a casualty that he demonstrate that he is emotionally disturbed, brain injured, or mentally retarded before he can receive help. Because much of the assistance provided in special education programs today comes too late, the work of the child behavior consultant offers opportunities to undertake preventative programming.

This thumbnail sketch has omitted many details but should provide enough information to allow a general picture to be formed of the setting that provided a base for many of the authors' observations about children and about educational programming.

REFERENCES

Griffin, F. E., & Langworthy, H. W. Boards of Cooperative Educational Services in New York. In Lord & Isenberg, 1964, pp. 46–50.

Lord, F. E., & Isenberg, R. M. (Eds.) *Cooperative Programs in Special Education.* Washington, D.C.: National Education Association, 1964.

Reger, R. A program for children with learning and behavioral problems. *Psychology in the Schools,* October 1967, 4, 317–24.

The Schools and Deviant Behavior

While the focus of this book is on educational programming the intention also is to point out that the schools can, and in fact do, provide most of whatever remediative or corrective work is done for children who exhibit significant learning and/or behavioral problems—the so-called emotionally disturbed and minimally brain injured. The school is increasingly taking over many functions usually considered the responsibility of other elements of society.

It has long been assumed that "society" has assigned roles to different social agencies, each of which in the past has carried out its functions fairly well. Reveries portray the family, the church, the neighborhood, and the city each playing a distinct part in the upbringing of children and, in the good old days, doing an adequate job. As society has become more sophisticated it has become correspondingly more aware that not all social agencies have been carrying their share of the burden. Many see this as a problem of decreasing acceptance of responsibility on the part of lagging agencies: they *used to* do certain things but today no longer are measuring up.

Referral Without Consequences

We find several stages in the development of assigning responsibilities for deviant behavior. Thirty years ago children were being identified in the schools as needing help because for some unknown reasons they were unable to learn, or they were extremely disturbing to themselves and others. These children were then sent—or "referred"—to outside agencies.

After what was typically a long wait the referral was acted upon to the extent that an appointment date was set and the child and his parents were "seen." This usually meant having the child go through a series of psychological tests and having the parents answer a number of questions. The result most often was a "report"; this document went to the schools and contained information about early feeding problems and toilet training, along with information the schools originally had sent to the agency as part of the referral data. The only thing finally added of any apparent consequence was a "diagnosis." The net result was that the schools, the parents, and the child had gone through a process, usually at considerable expense to the parents, that had no practical implications.

What could the schools do with a diagnosis? Sometimes a child would be referred because he was unable to read, even though he was in the fourth grade. To be told that the child had a diagnosis of "primary reading disability" or "dyslexia" perhaps sounded impressive and informative, but in fact the schools knew whatever this meant in the first place.

"Referral," then, became notorious for being nothing more than having a label, a fancy medical term, applied to an already known problem. Further, the result often was increased confusion rather than clarification. "I knew the child couldn't read, but what is this business about 'dyslexia'—what does it mean?" The helping agency apparently suffered under the impression that labeling was explaining, but the child was the loser because the school could do nothing with the label; it had no bases for action. If anything, the school now felt completely helpless because the problem had been defined in terms not relevant educationally.

Referrals With Consequences

As special education programs developed around the country, the focus shifted several years ago. Schools that sent children to outside agencies for information and other types of assistance, and formerly received what was in effect a worthless document, now received sanctions for placement into special education programs. The document had consequences for action. Many educators began once again to have faith in the usefulness of the referral system. Help was being provided because something could be done with the label—and the child who was its carrier.

Referral to Placement

But once again questions arise. If a child, known to have educational problems, is referred for a neurological, psychiatric, or "total team" evaluation, and the only result is a recommendation for a placement into a special class, educators are again beginning to wonder why they should go through the referral process just to be told what they already know. The process has gone full cycle. What educators want, after all, is a neurological examination with a report on a child's neurological problems, if any. A recommendation for placement into a special class hardly sounds like the report of a neurological examination.

It does help, of course, for an educator to have somebody besides himself express the opinion that a child should be placed into a special class. For the child who is not there, special classes are seen as something to avoid if at all possible. For the child who is there we find ourselves talking out of the other sides of our mouths. Nevertheless, if a parent questions why his child should be placed into a special class it is easier to say, "Because the doctors found he may have a neurological problem" than it is to say, "Because his teachers and I feel he has an educational problem that we cannot resolve if his present placement is continued."

If the several steps just sketched no longer existed there would be no need for this kind of commentary other than for historical interest. But there are many schools, and there are many obliging non-school agencies, who are willing to allow these practices to continue. In fact, much heat can be generated by suggesting that schools can, and indeed should, make educational placement decisions without benefit of a sanction from a non-school agency. Clements (1967), in a paper ironically titled "Come to the Wedding," joins his plea for greater agency-school cooperation with the observation that education is a "tragedy" which "feeds on a system which is addicted to mediocrity and inflexibility; impervious to the individual differences and needs of the children; trapped in time-worn tradition . . . " (p. 134). He notes that there is "a small group of upper-echelon educators who are shamefully obvious in their anti-medical attitude. One can then presume their abhorrence of the multidisciplinary approach to deviant children" (p. 136). Clements then suggests that "We stand at the portal of a new era in child guidance and for this we owe a debt of gratitude to the concept of 'learning disabilities' (minimal brain dysfunction) for the major role it has played" (p. 134).

Contributions of Specialists

There is a vast difference between obtaining a medical or other kind of non-educational evaluation of a child for the purpose of knowing more about the child, and on the other hand obtaining such an evaluation for the sole purpose of making educational placement decisions. For example, a medical evaluation should be made to discover if any medical problems exist that can and should be given medical treatment. If a parent came to school for a conference and was told by the child's teacher that the child seemed somewhat listless lately and should be sent to a local hospital for a six-week rest and put on a specific kind of medication, the teacher would likely be considered ready for retirement due to a sad case of senility. The teacher could argue that a similar treatment program was frequently used for many children who showed similar behavioral signs. Such an argument probably would only hasten the teacher's permanent departure and produce an even more embarrassed school administrator.

If a parent goes to a non-school agency, however, and is told that his or her child should be in a special class—and perhaps even told the specific kind of educational material or method that should be used—this often is taken as a wise, responsible recommendation.

The School's Responsibilities

The school is an agency of society that is taking on increasing responsibility for more of a child's life than ever before. The important issue today no longer is whether the schools should be taking on these responsibilities; the really important question, and the one to which this book is addressed, is: How can the schools most effectively carry out their increasing responsibilities?

The assumption is made that children and parents do not bear the full brunt of responsibility for being, or having, problems vis-à-vis the school. It is easy to say a child *could* learn *if* he behaved himself and *if* his parents were more cooperative. It is easy because the buck has been passed and nothing more needs to be done. Responsibility for the problem has evaporated as fingers wag with "should-if" and "could-if only" admonitions. But the fact that the child still is not learning and that his parents still are not cooperative suggests that a more responsible form of action must be taken.

REFERENCES

Clements, S. D. Come to the wedding! *Academic Therapy Quarterly*, Spring 1967, 2, 134–8.

3

Special Education

What is *special* education? At first glance this question perhaps has such an obvious answer it appears trivial. Everybody knows, it might be assumed, that special education is programming for handicapped children.

But two questions loom before those who seriously reflect upon this matter. The first is: What is "special" about special education? The second question is: What is "handicap"?

A closer examination reveals that asking "What is special education?" is not at all trivial. We will explore the first question in this and the following chapter and turn to the second question in Chapter 5.

Current Practices

The development of current concepts and programs that fall under the classification of special education will not be discussed here. Reference can be made to other sources (Baker, 1959; Barbe, 1963; Bowers *et al.*, 1967; Cruickshank, 1967; Cruickshank *et al.*, 1961; Dunn, 1963; Frampton & Gall, 1956; Haring & Phillips, 1962; Jordan, 1962; Kirk, 1962; Magary & Eichorn, 1960; Morse, Cutler, & Fink, 1964; Pritchard, 1963; Trapp & Himelstein, 1962; UNESCO, 1960). Additional recent descriptions of special programs for children classified as emotionally disturbed or brain injured can be found in Aserlind, 1965; Bebb, 1967; Camp & Lathen, 1967; Edgington, 1967; Heckelman, 1966; Rinsley, 1967; Rubin, Simson, & Betwee, 1966; Safford & Watts, 1967; Smith, 1967; Templeton, Sperry, & Prentice, 1967; Thomas & Foley, 1967; and Turner & Claman, 1967.

Our impression is that current conceptions and practices in special education should be re-examined. It frequently is reiterated that not enough is being done for handicapped children. We agree wholeheartedly with this but in our opinion the solution does not lie in doing more of what typically is being done today; rather, the search for solutions should focus on conceptual and qualitative areas.

If one takes available figures on the prevalence of problems usually defined as within the province of special education it would be easy to conclude that anywhere from 15 to 30 percent or more of the school-age population should have "special educational treatment." This treatment, most often, is defined as placement into special classes. If we really had all the special educational programming (i.e., special classes) we desired, would we really want to take this route—to do more of what we presently are doing?

Preventing Curriculum Change

Special educational programming faces a critical danger today in becoming the vehicle for preventing change in the general curriculum. It is becoming increasingly easier, as programs multiply and our alertness to problems sharpens, to remove children who do not fit the general curriculum rather than to think in terms of making changes in the general curriculum to accommodate the child. If a school believes that its curriculum program is adequate it will never be proven wrong as long as any child who is unable to fit the pattern is removed and placed into a special educational program. If a child and his curriculum are not aligned with each other, we can label the child and remove him.

Schools and their curriculums do not fail; only children fail. We as special educators step in with our curriculum deodorizers and spray everything with a heavy mist of fancy words inappropriately borrowed from medicine and everybody breathes a new aroma of pseudo-understanding. "No wonder that child couldn't read; he's brain injured!" And the reason the child was called brain injured was that he could not read.

Should we place all children who score below a certain cut-off point on an intelligence scale into special classes? Should all children classified as emotionally disturbed be similarly placed? Or all children considered brain injured—even those who demonstrate the ability to achieve high standards although they may be slightly cerebral palsied (and thus brain injured)? Should the economically disadvantaged, the visually or aurally impaired, the gifted, be placed into special classes as they exist today?

Few would assert that this is appropriate. But today we are somewhat fixed in a straitjacket because our conceptual reach has been limited. We have promoted the notion that a special class is medicine for curriculum-versus-child ills. In practice we do not place children into special classes because they are mentally retarded, emotionally disturbed, or brain injured. One of our problems is that we do not recognize this.

Dunn (1963) suggests that "as far as the schools are concerned, a pupil is identified as mentally retarded only when he is both low in measured intelligence and impaired in learning ability. It must be pointed out that, if IQ scores were used as the sole criterion for identifying the mentally retarded, about 16 percent . . . of the population would be more than one standard deviation below the mean in measured intelligence and would have to be classified as mentally retarded" (p. 56).

It is interesting to note that if one were to examine the process used by the schools, as intimated by Dunn, the conclusion could be reached that the most significant "cause" of mental retardation is formal education. IQ scores are not enough to classify a child as mentally retarded; the child also must repeatedly fail in school ("impaired in learning ability"). Many psychologists in schools have observed that some teachers refer many children for psychological testing while some teachers never refer children; some principals encourage teachers to refer children and others discourage teachers from doing so. The entire curriculum of one school can be such that few children fail—become classified as mentally retarded—while another school can be oriented in such a way that many children do not fit into the program offered. A public school that sees its mission as preparing children to become trained as rocket-makers and shop-owners probably is going to find many of its students having "learning problems."

PLACING CHILDREN

If, as suggested, we do not really place children into special classes because they are mentally retarded (or brain injured, etc.), what then are the reasons for placing children into special classes? The process of such placements is an interesting phenomenon to observe with an objective but somewhat critical eye.

In summary, the process is something like this: A child is found to have problems vis-à-vis the curriculum. He then is "tested," or "evaluated," for the purpose of obtaining what is called a diagnosis; this is done either by local school personnel or, as noted in the last chapter, by an outside agency.

The diagnostic process basically consists of after-the-fact labeling because the problems *always* have been identified before the diagnostic sessions ever begin. The circular nature of the process is presented in Figure 1: observed behavior (hyperactivity, impulsiveness) causes a referral for an evaluation and, during the evaluation, becomes the basis for making a diagnostic statement (brain injury);

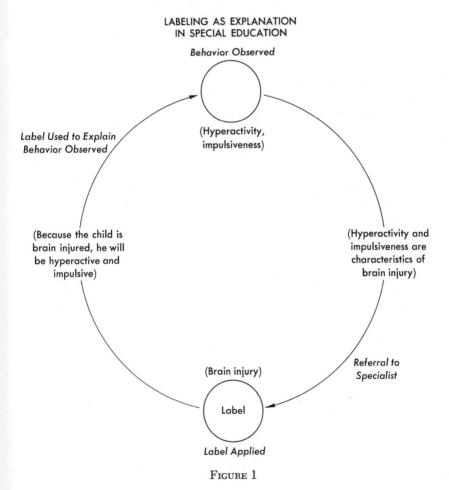

LABELING AS EXPLANATION
IN SPECIAL EDUCATION

Behavior Observed

(Hyperactivity,
impulsiveness)

Label Used to Explain
Behavior Observed

(Because the child is
brain injured, he will
be hyperactive and
impulsive)

(Hyperactivity and
impulsiveness are
characteristics of
brain injury)

(Brain injury)

Referral to
Specialist

Label

Label Applied

FIGURE 1

the diagnostic statement, in turn, implies certain inner mechanisms are involved in the observed behavior and the result is that, in this illustration, brain injury is felt to explain the observed behavior. Hyperactivity is said to be a characteristic of brain injury; if a child is brain injured, this explains why he is hyperactive.

The label applied to the child serves as a sanction for administrative action, meaning placement into a special class or into some other special program. The whole procedure tells us nothing about a child that we did not already know because nothing was added to our fund of knowledge about the child, and we have no information about what to do with the child after placement changes are made. Moving a child from one classroom to another is an administrative action; it is not an act of understanding or explanation.

An Example

Let us discuss an example for illustration. A child is found to be very slow in learning. The teacher says she does not understand the child. Translated, this usually means she does not understand why this child cannot do what most of the other children in her class can do. There is concern on the part of the teacher about whether she is at fault in not being able to "reach" the child, or whether the child is not capable of being "reached." Again, to translate this concern, the teacher has dichotomized the problem into a "me or him" issue, and if it is "he" she wants absolution because her performance as a teacher is on the line.

After the problem reaches a certain stage it becomes necessary to settle the dichotomized issue and an evaluation is sought. This certain stage might be extremely destructive behavior in the classroom, accusations and other pressures from parents, or repeating a grade for the second time. *Whatever the reason, the existence of the problem already has been established.*

It would be very helpful at this point to think of the problem in terms of "the child, the teacher and the curriculum," because this possibly could help in devising some immediate answers directly related to the problem. But this is not what typically happens.

An evaluation is performed for the sole purpose of attaching a label to the child which can sanction an administrative decision, to make a change in placement. If the child scores below a certain level on an intelligence scale he is called mentally retarded and is then placed into a special class for the mentally retarded. But even so it does not matter how the child scores on an intelligence scale; because the existence of the problem has been established it is the responsibility of the labeling agent to classify the child with one diagnosis or another. The diagnostician can choose from an ever-increasing selection of labels: mental retardation, emotional disturbance, social maladjustment, brain injury (also called perceptual handicap, educational handicap, learning disability, minimal brain dysfunction, etc.).

Diagnosis Versus Understanding

One of the gross fictions associated with the diagnostic process is the belief that some kind of understanding of the child is achieved. It is true that if the child scores low on an intelligence scale and thus is called mentally retarded the teacher will feel a sense of relief. She will even say that she now understands why the child is very slow in learning. Everybody, in fact, might feel they have found what are considered the basic causes of the child's problems. But no basic causes have been found and no understanding has been achieved. A stereotype has been formed which, if anything, deters understanding.

Dybwad (1967) offers an example of what often happens. "In country after country all that needed to be known was that there was mongolism and immediately one knew, 'they can't learn to read or write, they can't work a full day, they can't do this, they can't do that.' Because they couldn't learn we naturally didn't teach them; because we didn't teach them, naturally they didn't learn, and thus went the vicious circle" (p. 24).

It is curious that administrative decisions in education about children with problems often cannot be made on the basis of relevant educational data. A child cannot be exempted from school in many instances because he is destructive and potentially harmful to himself and other children. He must be classified as emotionally disturbed; his destructive behaviors are considered symptoms of the emotional disturbance. A child cannot be provided with an educational program on the basis of his observed slower learning characteristics. He must be classified as mentally retarded; his learning characteristics are considered symptoms of the mental retardation.

Staats and Staats (1963) provide another illustration: "The teacher who observes eight-year-old Jimmy constantly fighting with other children is concerned with understanding or explaining his behavior in order that she might attempt to change it. For a school psychologist to say that Jimmy is constantly fighting because he is a hostile-aggressive child may sound very impressive, but it really adds no new knowledge, for if we ask how one knows that this is a hostile-aggressive child, the reply is that he is always fighting. The term 'hostile-aggressive,' then, is only another name for 'one who is always fighting.' It does not explain the behavior or indeed add any new information, if the only ways of observing 'hostility' are in the behavior itself. In the end, the statement that 'Jimmy fights because he is hostile-aggressive' proves to be a tautology: 'Jimmy fights because he fights'" (p. 16).

The unfortunate consequences of this kind of prelogical thinking are that specialized programming is not based primarily on children's learning characteristics or their destructive or hyperactive behaviors, but primarily on the basis of stereotypes of mental retardation, brain injury, and similar labels. Observed characteristics are considered of secondary importance while presumed basic causes are emphasized.

FOLLOWING PLACEMENT

After a child is placed into a special class he finds himself with a teacher trained to understand him and meet his unique needs. Is this really true?

Disabilities and Teaching Specialties

If a child is classified as mentally retarded or emotionally disturbed, in the most progressive school districts today he will have a teacher who went through a college program that prepared him to teach the mentally retarded or the emotionally disturbed. It is of interest to observe that if the teacher trained to work with the mentally retarded child finds what he feels is an emotionally disturbed child in his class (usually, a child who is difficult to control), he will protest that he is not qualified to teach that child. A similar complaint will be raised by the teacher of the emotionally disturbed who feels he has a mentally retarded child in his class.

The teacher who "specializes" in special education has been trained to understand and provide for the specific needs of certain children. However, for the most part the teacher's training was focused on stereotypes of children rather than on real children. The teacher learned "how to teach reading to the mentally retarded," "how to teach music to the mentally retarded," and "arts and crafts for the mentally retarded." "The" mentally retarded child for many special education teachers fills fifteen chairs in the classroom.

Further, many teachers have been trained to teach children rather than to provide the conditions for children to learn. Teachers are expected to "teach [at] children reading" rather than to encourage children to learn to read. Learning often seems almost incidental to the teaching process.

It is difficult to understand why there must be a different technique based on such categories as mental retardation, emotional disturbance, brain injury, and so on. Every child has unique learning patterns which may or may not be related to medically defined conditions of disability. If a teacher understands the processes involved in learning to read, and understands that each child will display a unique pattern that might require individualized approaches to learning to read, he should be able to assist almost any individual in learning to read.

Contrary to popular opinion, there is not *a method* of teaching reading to brain-injured children or to any other children. There are a variety of ways of assisting brain-injured children to learn to read. The way each child learns is not primarily related to the actual (or supposed) brain injury, but to the observable needs of the individual child.

It might appear that we are advocating "throwing everybody together" for grouping purposes. That is, if we are saying that each child is different and has unique learning patterns and instructional needs, then why make any pretense about a rationale for grouping children?

We are saying that grouping children on the basis of medically derived disability labels has no practical utility in the schools. Children should be grouped on the basis of their educational needs, and these needs may be defined in any number of ways. The notion that simple labels, applied by high-status authorities from outside the school, should serve as a basis for grouping children is basically nothing more than a refusal to accept responsibility for making educational decisions. It is educational laziness.

For example, if the condition of blindness presents an educational handicap for certain children there might be some reason for grouping these children together. But if a blind child can manage quite effectively in a regular curriculum program, perhaps with the assistance of an itinerant teacher, it is foolish to assume there is some overpowering but irrational force dictating that the child *must* be placed into a special class for the blind.

It is necessary for the schools to look at *educational handicap* rather than physical, emotional, or mental disability. A physical disability may or may not present an educational handicap; the two are not necessarily identical (Dolberg & Lenard, 1967). Brabner (1967) observes that "one must distinguish in physically disabled persons between the physical defect and the handicap—a distinction rehabilitation counselors are keenly aware of—rather than assume that the physical impairment is causing the handicap" (p. 150).

Fisher (1967) sums up the problem: "We seem to be possessed with categories and organizational designs which entrench the categories. Are we so sure that special classes, broken down into categories—slow learners, neurologically impaired, etc. are doing the job? While the process may be administratively convenient, there is no doubt that the procedure has made special education special, isolated it and in so doing perpetuated the isolationism and attending mysticism which has stood in the way of special education development" (p. 10).

REFERENCES

Aserlind, L. Summer laboratory school. *The Winnower*, September 1965, 2, 34–8.

Baker, H. J. *Introduction to Exceptional Children*. Third Edition. New York: Macmillan, 1959.

Barbe, W. B. *The Exceptional Child*. Washington, D.C.: Center for Applied Research in Education, 1963.

Bebb, B. (Report:) From the U.S.A.: Children with special learning problems. *Forward Trends*, Summer 1967, 2, 94.

Bowers, J. E., Clement, J., Francis, M. I., & Johnston, M. C. *Exceptional Children in Home, School and Community*. Second Edition. Toronto: J. M. Dent, 1967.

Brabner, G. The myth of mental retardation. *The Training School Bulletin*, February 1967, 63, 149–52.

Camp, W. L., & Lathen, L. A successful classroom program for emotionally disturbed children. *The Training School Bulletin*, May 1967, 64, 31–8.

Cruickshank, W. M. *The Brain-injured Child in Home, School, and Community*. Syracuse, N.Y.: Syracuse University Press, 1967.

Cruickshank, W. M., Bentzen, F. A., Ratzeburg, F. H., & Tannhauser, M. T. *A Teaching Method for Brain-injured and Hyperactive Children: A Demonstration Study*. Syracuse, N.Y.: Syracuse University Press, 1961.

Dolberg, M., and Lenard, H. M. The concepts of disability and handicap revisited. *The Cerebral Palsy Journal,* March–April 1967, 28, 3–6, 9.

Dunn, L. M. (Ed.) *Exceptional Children in the Schools.* New York: Holt, Rinehart & Winston, 1963.

Dybwad, G. Education for the ineducable—an international paradox. *Forward Trends,* Spring 1967, 11, 19–27.

Edgington, R. Public School programming for children with learning disabilities. *Academic Therapy Quarterly,* Spring 1967, 2, 166–9, 196.

Fisher, H. K. What is special education? *Special Education in Canada,* June 1967, 41, 9–16.

Frampton, M. E., & Gall, E. D. (Eds.) *Special Education for the Exceptional.* Boston: Porter Sargent, 1956.

Haring, N. G., & Phillips, E. L. *Educating Emotionally Disturbed Children.* New York: McGraw-Hill, 1962.

Heckelman, R. G. A lesson plan for educationally handicapped children in learning disability groups. *Academic Therapy Quarterly,* Fall 1966, 2, 18–22.

Jordan, T. E. *The Exceptional Child.* Columbus, O.: Charles E. Merrill, 1962.

Kirk, S. A. *Educating Exceptional Children.* Boston: Houghton Mifflin, 1962.

Magary, J. F., & Eichorn, J. R. *The Exceptional Child.* New York: Holt, Rinehart & Winston, 1960.

Morse, W. C., Cutler, R. L., & Fink, A. H. *Public School Classes for the Emotionally Handicapped: A Research Analysis.* Washington, D.C.: NEA, Council for Exceptional Children, 1964.

Pritchard, D. G. *Education and the Handicapped: 1760–1960.* New York: Humanities Press, 1963.

Rinsley, D. B. Inservice residential treatment of the adolescent. *The Psychiatric Quarterly,* January 1967, 41, 134–43.

Rubin, E. Z., Simson, C. B., & Betwee, M. C. *Emotionally Handicapped Children and the Elementary School.* Detroit: Wayne State University Press, 1966.

Safford, A., & Watts, C. A. An evaluation of a public school program for educationally handicapped children. *California Journal of Educational Research,* May 1967, 18, 125–32.

Smith, S. A. An educational program for emotionally disturbed children. *Psychology in the Schools,* July 1967, 4, 280–83.

Staats, A. W., & Staats, C. K. *Complex Human Behavior.* New York: Holt, Rinehart & Winston, 1963.

Templeton, R. G., Sperry, B. M., & Prentice, N. M. Theoretical and technical issues in therapeutic tutoring of children with psychogenic learning problems. *Journal of Child Psychiatry,* July 1967, 6, 464–77.

Thomas, Y. A., & Foley, R. E. Special class for behavior problems. *The Instructor,* October 1967, 77, 23–4.

Trapp, E. P., & Himelstein, P. (Eds.) *Readings on the Exceptional Child.* New York: Appleton-Century-Crofts, 1962.

Turner, R. M., & Claman, L. Teaching strategies in a public school class for emotionally disturbed children. *Journal of Child Psychiatry,* January 1967, 6, 86–97.

UNESCO. *Statistics on Special Education.* Place de Fontanoy, Paris, 1960.

4

What Is Special about Special Education?

Blackman and Heintz (1966) state that placing mentally retarded children into special classes has not yet proven to be more effective than placing such children into regular classes. They further observe that "Special educators are still faced with the task of developing educational methodologies which, when applied to the mentally retarded, will prove superior to methods currently in use" (p. 12).

McCarthy and Scheerenberger (1966) state that "In the main, regular class retardates do as well, academically, as their special class counterparts; there seems to be some evidence that special class retardates are better adjusted than retardates maintained in regular classes. Considering the methodological problems which plague efficacy studies, it would seem the better part of wisdom to accept both of these general conclusions as tentative. Indeed, it appears to the present writers, that enough of this type of research has been done; there is probably more profit in further investigating factors which affect academic gain" (p. 485). Kirk (1964) and Quay (1963) have written more detailed reviews.

Simches and Bohn (1963) examined five volumes of the *American Journal on Mental Deficiency,* four volumes of *Exceptional Children,* and more than 250 curriculum guides to study "the present state of the curriculum for the mentally retarded" (p. 115). They state that "Over and over again, our research has shown that different curricula just do not exist for the educable mentally handicapped. What does exist is the rephrasing and reemphasizing of available courses of study used for normal children that do not even have the benefit of the form, structure, and sequence connected with standard curriculum development" (p. 115).

Billingsley (1966) comments, in discussing reviews of research on curriculum for the mentally retarded, "[these] have caused some of us to blink our eyes, but as yet, I see no extensive revision of teacher training curriculum that would remedy the situation" (p. 132).

Morse, Cutler, and Fink (1964) studied public-school classes for emotionally disturbed children. They observe that "in 1958, 47 of the 48 states reported programs, while in 1962, only 30 of the 50 claimed to have programs. Some sharp individual decreases are also included in this general decline" (p. 3).

In a paper titled "The Neurological Study of Children with Learning Disabilities," Cohn (1964) says, "Of the 45 children first studied as part of the Syracuse University project in the Montgomery County [Maryland] Schools in 1957, only three have achieved regular school. Most of these children (on repeated neurological examination studies) remain in special education. All have learned to read and write with some proficiency. Two children have learned to read well, but they have not learned to organize and utilize the information they have acquired. Nearly all are loners; they have few associates and appear isolated. . . . It will be most interesting to see how, and if these children integrate into society" (pp. 184-5).

Rubin, Simson, and Betwee (1966) published the results of their experimental special educational program for emotionally disturbed children conducted jointly by the Wyandotte Public Schools and the Lafayette Clinic in Michigan. Fifty-eight children were involved in the experiment, half of them placed into special classes and half placed into regular classes and serving as a control group. The authors point out that the program was patterned after residential programs (p. 215) and that seriously disturbed children were not included in either the experimental or the control groups (pages 53 and 216). In his critical review of this book, Birch (1966) points out that "At the conclusion of the study the vast majority of the differences [in measures obtained] were not significant at the five percent level of confidence" (p. 80). This book is interesting because of some comments made indicating that traditional medical labeling procedures were found to have limited utility in the program ("We have avoided the term 'emotionally disturbed child' because of its vagueness," p. 35).

Need for Reappraisal

These selected but fairly representative comments are cited in support of the view that some consideration should be given to an examination of current conceptions about what is special about special education. The impression is that present conceptions are quite shallow to begin with and when we do begin to probe in some depth the direction is not always appropriate. We tend to look for our missing article not where we might have lost it but where the light is the greatest.* The idea that we are approaching a "new era" because of the invention of another label, "learning disabilities," is indicative of the state of affairs. Perhaps we need a sober reappraisal of where we should be looking, and furthermore why we are looking and what we are looking for.

Johnson (1962) focused attention on the issue of "special class versus regular class" placements of retarded children. Blackman and Heintz (1966) and McCarthy and Scheerenberger (1966) shifted the focus by indicating this was not really the important issue, but rather what is done with retarded children.

PRESENT BASIS FOR SPECIAL EDUCATION

Special education usually is defined as an area within the framework of general education that provides (1) appropriate facilities, (2) specialized materials and methods, and (3) teachers with specialized training for children considered handicapped. The handicapped are those classified as mentally retarded, emotionally disturbed, brain injured, speech defective, blind and partially seeing, deaf and hard of hearing, orthopedically impaired, homebound, and special health problems. One common characteristic of all the classifications is that they are medical disability areas or they are directly derived from medical conceptions. Special education has been constructed around a series of medically defined problems.

One of the major criticisms that can be leveled at educators is that they appear too willing to allow others to define their problems for them. In so doing, schools often are faced with having to implement programming that was conceived by well-meaning but naive pressure groups who succeeded in obtaining legislative or other mandates for programming for certain "types" of children.

Too often, when special education programs are established, there

* Reference is made here to the story about the drunk found looking for his wristwatch under a streetlight one evening. When asked, the drunk indicated that he did not lose his watch there but the light was better for searching.

is a noticeable absence of any apparent depth to the planning involved. There may be quantity in planning but quality is buried in frenzied "team meetings," consultations with non-educational personnel, and leaderless scramblings for any patchwork of opinions.

Professional Understanding

After programs are established they are consistently poorly related to every other school program. Teachers in special classes often must rely for support on janitors, bus drivers, and a few individual colleagues who happen to become friendly. In some instances administrators are among those who become friendly toward the special class teachers. Quite often, however, administrators and other colleagues will plead ignorance about handicapped children, saying they prefer not to get involved because they do not possess the necessary credentials for understanding. And every time a special class teacher cries "You don't understand the mentally retarded child" whenever he does not get his way, he reinforces the wall between himself and others.

The frequency of the statement indicating a lack of understanding of the handicapped by building principals and other educators in responsible administrative positions is a serious indictment against educators. Too often, administrators are considered to be "understanding" to the extent they make concessions to the special education teacher.

A Hypothetical Program

Let us review briefly a hypothetical history of how a special education program for the emotionally disturbed might be created and implemented in a medium-size (e.g., 12,000 children) school district. In so doing, we will be looking critically for just what is special about the special educational provisions made.

Often the impetus for establishing a program for emotionally disturbed children is either a state legislative mandate or the availability of funds from the state to offset local costs.

A school district that intends to establish a program for emotionally disturbed children usually will already have a program— meaning special classes—for the mentally retarded. Thus, there is a director of special education, a coordinator of pupil personnel services, or some other administrator who can take responsibility for the new program.

The first step taken by the administrator will be to determine the precise requirements for certifying children as being eligible for the program. He also will review certification requirements for teachers, numbers of children allowed in each class, and similar regulatory matters.

The second step will be to make a survey of the numbers of children who might be eligible for placement into the program. Along with this will be a recognition that regardless of how many children might be eligible, the program will be small by comparison with anticipated needs. Thus, although there are estimates that 10 percent of the school-age population is emotionally disturbed (Pate, 1963), the administrator will typically plan for the creation of one or two special classes.

The third step will be finding classroom space and teachers and arranging for the services of various ancillary personnel. Classroom space will be sought in a building with one of the school district's better principals—that is, he is considered well-liked; understanding of children, staff, and parents; and above all else, cooperative. Preference for teachers will be for those who have been with the school district and who have taken a college course or two on "The Emotionally Disturbed Child."

The fourth step will be the formal selection of children. Frequently some thought will be given to including those children who have been exempted from school because of emotional disturbance. In many cases these children actually are included in the classes but they do not remain for long because they are considered "too disturbed." The reason is then given that only children who can profit from special class placement should be included. The seriously disturbed child ends up no better off than he was before.

Selecting children becomes a vexing problem. Parents must cooperate by having a psychiatrist or psychologist, or usually both, officially certify that their child is emotionally disturbed. Sometimes parents become emotionally disturbed about this. Thus, in spite of initial surveys and nationally derived figures published that show 10 percent of the school-age population should be eligible for the program there are relatively few takers. Of those children who could be placed, many obstacles are found: the special class teachers do not want serious problems in the classes; principals do not want children who would upset the serenity of their schools. The children the special class teachers would like to see placed, primarily because of the few problems they display, suddenly find people trying to "save" them from being placed into the special classes.

Many people are involved in deciding who should and should not be placed and there can be disagreements. Conflicts arise between school social workers and school psychologists, each group feeling emotional disturbance is its private "specialty." Subtle conflicts arise between community mental health agencies and school personnel, with the parents sometimes serving as carriers of missles from one group aimed at the other.

The fifth step is the opening of the school's doors on the first Wednesday after Labor Day. And in many instances, the fifth step is, for all practical purposes, the final step.

What is special about the program just described? In fact, no program has been described; only the administrative steps taken to bring about the physical existence of the program have been mentioned.

Absence of Program Content

"Special" programs such as the one almost described are typical. They consist of (1) finding and labeling children for placement; (2) finding classroom space; and (3) employing teachers and arranging for assistance from ancillary personnel. Conspicuously missing is the essence of the program.

Aside from being called "emotionally disturbed," which has little relevance for educational programming other than sanctioning placement, why are the children placed into the special classes? What are the special class teachers, principals, and others supposed to do with the children? Who has authority for making decisions—the psychologists, the social workers, the building principals, the special education administrator, the psychotherapist in the community mental health clinic? What can be expected of parents, and who should work with them? What kinds of curriculum materials should be used—those used by other children in the same school building or those especially designed for the emotionally disturbed? How long is the school day? Where do the children eat lunch? What should be done about foul language on the bus? How much physical abuse should the teacher tolerate? Should the teacher be concerned with "behavior" or just "academics"? Is the teacher doing remedial work or what should it be considered—rehabilitative or habilitative, re-learning or learning, therapy or education?

The progress of such so-called programs can be predicted. First, as previously mentioned, any really disturbed child will soon find himself out of the special classes, which means out of school. Second, the teachers will initially send out many distress signals. The pattern of "teachers seeking assistance" can be forecast, depending upon the school district and the surrounding community. It can be anticipated that the teachers will reach out to all available personnel and agencies. Interestingly enough, however, the more the teacher asks for help the less he depends upon his own abilities to handle his own problems. In turn, the less he depends upon himself the greater his problems become; frequent pleas will be made for removal of certain children, for shorter days, and for additional teacher aides. The teachers will eagerly request staff meetings but curiously will say very little at the meetings other than to answer questions when asked; the feeling seems to be on the part of the teachers that some-where in the group will be the answers to all their problems and so they listen very carefully.

Because the teachers no longer are thinking for themselves their problems will continue to increase and, correspondingly, others will become less and less interested in offering assistance. The feeling is aroused that the teachers do not really follow advice that is tendered. Advisors increasingly suspect that the teachers only listen and give lip service in agreeing to follow their sage prescriptions ("be firm but fair," and "he needs to know he is loved"), otherwise they would not have so much trouble.

At the end of the first year everybody concerned is fed up with the non-program. Unless there is a legal mandate, the chances for special class mortality are high (as illustrated by Morse, Cutler, and Fink, 1964). Whatever else might happen, there will be little simi-larity between the program at the beginning of the first year and at the end of the year. Where at first many experts are vying for the opportunity to pass along advice to the teachers, eventually the experts are back with their feet on their desks criticizing the teach-ers. The chances are high that the teachers will not be in the same position any longer than one year.

A group of children labeled as emotionally disturbed in a class-room with a teacher trained to work with such a group is not in itself "special" education. Placing a small number of children into a class does not necessarily constitute anything special; some teachers would do exactly the same things with two children as they would with thirty children. It is what the teacher does—and does with administrative and supervisory assistance and direction—that determines whether there is anything special about the special education program.

The School Psychologist and the Program

A comment should be made about the way school psychologists often find themselves involved in many new programs for problem children (Reger, 1965). Often psychologists in the schools seem to want to have a great deal of authority in special programs, but at the same time have a lack of interest in assuming a commensurate level of responsibility. This can be detected if a psychologist says he is "sort of" in charge of "the special class."

This kind of structure typically ends up as a sorry disappointment for everybody concerned, and in the end the psychologist is a primary loser. The psychologist thinks he really is "in charge" of the program as an administrator, but soon finds that he really has little or nothing to say about the actual administrative management of the program. The program director initially wanted the psychologist involved to serve as somebody to dash into the classrooms with instant solutions to any problems the teachers might be having. The psychologist, having little or no perspective on the general problems of administration, attempts to make some decisions but usually finds his way blocked. He then gets discouraged, feeling he somehow has been misled.

Knowing the psychologist was to be involved in a "sort of in charge" fashion, the teachers build up certain expectations based on their previous experience with psychologists. The teachers expect the psychologist to test the children whenever a problem arises; the psychologist is an expert who uses tests to find out why people behave as they do. Why, then, cannot the psychologist give little Jimmy a test to find out why he always hits Mary? In his turn, the psychologist has no objections to testing children in the classes occasionally, but he really feels his job is to come into the classrooms as a "consultant" on human relationship problems.

What actually happens, of course, is that the teachers find they obtain nothing of any usefulness from the psychologist because he does not seem interested in testing the children and his suggestion in September that Jimmy should be treated firm but fair has been repeated several times and has worn thin. The administrator finds it impossible to support the psychologist's requests, now being made primarily to establish a position as really being "in charge," and so in meetings the administrator braces himself to the necessity of tactfully using as many dodges as possible to avoid any kind of direct confrontation.

By January the psychologist is seldom near the classrooms and he often becomes an object of scorn because he has not delivered the goods as far as anybody is concerned.

It can be recommended that before psychologists take the kind of bait that often is offered to them in such instances, they work out a definite schedule of times, role expectations, and other matters with all concerned with the program. The psychologist may be disappointed at the small morsel he ends up with in such a meeting of the minds but he will be far better off knowing precisely where he stands from the beginning.

Individualized Programming

The essence of *special* education is the provision of individualized instruction for children. This is actually unattainable, even if there were one teacher for every child, but it is possible to obtain approximations of this essence. More will be said about individualized programming throughout the book.

 ✳ Failure to understand and provide individualized programming is probably a major reason for many of the problems faced by teachers in the field of special education. Teachers are trained to think in terms of the emotionally disturbed or mentally retarded child rather than in terms of a *child* who may have retarded learning abilities or emotional problems. The child is lost in a maze of stereotyping.

Even some who feel they are in the *avant-garde* will make such statements as, "It is ridiculous to think that the brain-injured child needs a completely different program from that provided for the emotionally disturbed child." This statement indicates little more than a higher level of ignorance because it suggests there are only two children involved: *the* brain-injured child and *the* emotionally disturbed child. Saying "Some children are *both* emotionally disturbed *and* brain injured" perhaps adds an aura of sophistication to the speaker, but once again the implication is that "the" child now is made up of composites of two children. Another problem is illustrated by the statement of Mitchell's (1966) indicating that behavioral disturbances observed in "children with minimal cerebral disorders" (p. 110) should not be attributed as "the direct consequences of damage to the brain" (p. 110); the existence of "minimal cerebral disorder" is predicated on observations of the behavioral disturbances.

REFERENCES

Billingsley, J. F. Apprising teacher appraisal of methods and materials. *Education and Training of the Mentally Retarded,* 1966, 1, 131–5.

Birch, J. W. A review: *Emotionally Handicapped Children and the Elementary School,* by Eli Z. Rubin, Clyde B. Simson, and Marcus C. Betwee. Detroit: Wayne State University Press, 1966 (286 pp.). *Journal of School Psychology,* Autumn 1966, 5, 80–81.

Blackman, L. S., & Heintz, P. The mentally retarded. *Review of Educational Research,* 1966, 36, 5–36.

Cohn, R. The neurological study of children with learning disabilities. *Exceptional Children,* December 1964, 31, 179–85.

Johnson, G. O. Special education for the mentally handicapped—a paradox. *Exceptional Children,* 1962, 29, 70–72.

Kirk, S. A. Research in education. In Stevens, H. A., & Heber, R. (Eds.) *Mental Retardation: A Review of Research.* Chicago: University of Chicago Press, 1964, pp. 57–9.

McCarthy, J. J., & Scheerenberger, R. C. A decade of research on the education of the mentally retarded. *Mental Retardation Abstracts,* October–December 1966, 3, 481–501.

Mitchell, R. G. Minimal disorders of cerebral function. *British Journal of Disorders of Communication,* October 1966, 1, 109–13.

Morse, W. C., Cutler, R. L., & Fink, A. H. *Public School Classes for the Emotionally Handicapped: A Research Analysis.* Washington, D.C.: NEA, Council for Exceptional Children, 1964.

Pate, J. E. Emotionally disturbed and socially maladjusted children. In Dunn, L. M. (Ed.) *Exceptional Children in the Schools,* New York: Holt, Rinehart & Winston, 1963, pp. 239–83.

Quay, L. C. Academic skills. In Ellis, N. R. (Ed.) *Handbook of Mental Deficiency.* New York: McGraw-Hill, 1963, pp. 664–90.

Reger, R. *School Psychology.* Springfield, Ill.: Charles C Thomas, 1965.

Rubin, E. Z., Simson, C. B., & Betwee, M. C. *Emotionally Handicapped Children and the Elementary School.* Detroit: Wayne State University Press, 1966.

Simches, G., & Bohn, R. J. Issues in curriculum: research and responsibility. *Mental Retardation,* 1963, 1, 84–7, 115–18.

5

What Is Handicap?

A personal disability considered "handicapping" is not an isolated event, separate from a surrounding context. Whatever is called a *handicap* depends upon demands made that cannot be met. Basically, the definition of handicap is a philosophical problem.

Educators have been told over and over that the reason we have so many mentally retarded children in the schools today, where there were only a few several years ago, is due to a combination of factors. Among these factors is the increasing complexity of society which has caused the so-called mentally retarded to stand out more today than previously. Many of us can recall a classmate who was considered "dumb" but who nonetheless was accepted as a fellow citizen, who today would probably be in a special class for the "educable" mentally retarded. Similarly, we can recall that this same individual a few years ago went to work on a farm or found a steady laborer's job around town as soon as he was legally able to leave school. Today, we would think of this individual as a dropout, as a potential troublemaker if special educational intervention is not provided before he leaves school.

There is little about this to argue with except that the analysis does not go deep enough. As society becomes more complex, that is, as fewer non-skilled jobs are available, there are fewer places for the deviant individual to fit and still survive without formal assistance. As our schools become more concerned about brighter, conforming students, the less tolerance there will be for deviant children. Dreeben (1967) points out that "There is no question but that schools are engaged in an instructional enterprise, but the preoccupation with instruction has been accompanied by the neglect of equally important problems" (p. 212). Dreeben questions whether the dissemination of knowledge really represents the particular contribution of the school.

DIMENSIONS OF HANDICAP

There are two major dimensions of handicap, most often found intertwined: the existence of some kind of condition that would be handicapping under any circumstances, and the existence of social contexts in which some conditions sometimes are handicapping and at other times are not. It is the latter that we most often deal with but the former should be considered as well.

Handicapping Under Any Circumstances

For the most part this includes conditions where the individual has no awareness of himself as a human being, or at least his awareness is grossly impaired. Individuals with severe mental retardation or severe behavioral deviation can be included in this group. But even here we find our own social standards necessarily imposed.

If an individual is severely mentally retarded and spends his time in a "crib," lying in an institution, he is handicapped by the way he compares with others on almost all counts. If this person is well cared for, receives the food and attention he desires (or it is thought that he desires), he may be relatively happy. When we observe such an individual our own standards dictate that the person is unfortunate, that we are better off than he is, and that we ought to do something not only to ensure that this person receives good care but to try to prevent the occurrence of such conditions in other persons.

Our thoughts about individuals with severe behavioral deviations are similar. If we visit a mental hospital where people sit and stare for hours or even days and months, moving only when told to eat and sleep, our desire is (aside from keeping them there as long as they behave in such a manner) to provide them with good care, to rehabilitate them, and to prevent such conditions from happening to others. We look upon the hospital as undesirable, a place we would not want to find ourselves.

We can note, incidentally, some similarities in our thinking about the severely impaired and "primitive" peoples. History—both ancient and modern—is studded with examples of how more "enlightened" societies feel the urge to impose their civilizations upon societies considered backward. In the past the primary justification for this was to introduce religious beliefs to the non-believing (or the "other-believing"), while today political beliefs appear to be behind most efforts to civilize the uninitiated. Perhaps the primary motive always has been economic.

The assumption seems to be that primitive peoples are lacking in self-awareness, that they do not know how miserable they are: they just *think* they are happy and content. Whatever the explicit and implicit rationalizations, outside judgments are imposed on backward countries. It is important to have good medical care, to have schools, to have wide participation in government, to have certain religious beliefs, and to refrain from killing women and children to satisfy what are considered by us pagan gods.

Sometimes the cure is worse than the disease. Linton (1957) observes that in early efforts to civilize primitive peoples, "It is interesting to note that the South African natives, who still live mainly on a mush and milk diet supplemented by beer, suffered from a dietary deficiency and consequent lowering of disease resistance when missionaries stepped in and stopped their brewing" (p. 95). Similar miscarriages have occurred in our own time, when excessive oxygen after birth produced blindness in many children and a drug (thalidomide) taken by pregnant women resulted in many deformed babies.

Residential institutions for the severely deviant, as well as primitive societies, have their own peculiar social environments where adjustment and handicap are evident. There are stratifications into various levels of prestige and social adjustment. The person institutionalized because of a handicap may find himself with high personal adjustment and social prestige within the institution. The arbitrariness of the definition of handicap becomes apparent: handicapped outside the institutionalized context, "well-adjusted" (or non-handicapped) within this context.

Some individuals may not be able to "adjust" to institutional life and are considered handicapped within that particular social environment. Such an individual might, for example, end up on a locked ward. But whenever there is a group of persons the same stratification process occurs, and the locked ward will have its own unique definitions of adjustment and handicap.

Physical conditions such as blindness, deafness, and cerebral palsy might be considered handicapping under any circumstances but this is true only to a degree. Disability is not necessarily the same as handicap. Blindness, deafness, cerebral palsy, poverty, "primitiveness," lack of saleable skills, missing limbs, obesity, cosmetic disfigurements, and other conditions definitely *are* handicaps from certain perspectives. But not being the brightest child in class or not being the star of the football team is handicapping from certain perspectives. Cerebral palsy is without question a physical disability; but whether it is a social, vocational, or educational handicap is another matter.

Handicap and the Social Context

The social context becomes an important aspect in defining handicap for school-age children. The following factors are important in determining whether a condition is considered handicapping: (1) *who* defines the condition as handicap, (2) *when* and *where* the condition is a handicap, and (3) *how* and *why* the condition is a handicap. While there is much overlap among these three factors they will be discussed separately to bring out their independent elements and to illustrate the point that there is much more to defining handicap than applying a medical diagnosis to a child.

1. *Who defines handicap.* A parent and a teacher may disagree that a certain condition exists at all, long before the question arises as to whether the condition is handicapping.

A teacher may say a child cannot do certain things in school while the parent has observed the child doing these very things at home. Both could be right, and here we immediately find overlap with other factors: the child could respond in a different manner under different conditions. On the one hand, what a teacher expects from the child could be far different from what the mother expects. The teacher might say the child does not know his numbers, meaning he cannot count to ten during a lesson in a group setting, even when she stops to offer help for brief periods of time. The mother might disagree, stating that the child does know his numbers, meaning that he can count to ten when he is alone with her and using a certain method that has been carefully reviewed a number of times.

When such a situation exists it is apparent that the primary need is for communication between parent and teacher. This does not mean having the parent come to the school to be told face to face that the child cannot count to ten. The mother and the teacher should review with each other just what they mean by "not knowing his numbers." Because it is the teacher who will define whether the child does or does not know his numbers she should not avoid letting this fact be known, but should explain that ability to count to ten within a group context in the school setting is *her* (or the school's) basis for evaluating the child's performance.

Even when a parent and a teacher agree that a certain condition exists they may disagree that it is handicapping. For example, a child might be overactive, a condition that helps him in competing with his older brothers and neighborhood friends. In turn, being successful in such competition might bring the child praise from his father. For the teacher, however, overactivity presents a serious management problem. Here again a need for communication between parent and teacher exists; the teacher is obligated to discover the parent's conception of the condition and then to explain the effects this condition has in the classroom. The teacher is, in effect, defining a behavioral condition as a handicap.

2. *When and where a condition is a handicap.* Looking at who defines handicap from a broader perspective we can see that the school as an institution makes demands on children that can be strikingly different from those made by the home or by other social institutions. When a demand is made that a child cannot meet, he is considered to be handicapped. A child in the fourth grade is expected to have achieved a certain level of proficiency in reading; if he is unable to read he is handicapped. This was never a problem before the child entered school and it is always possible that deficient reading skills will not be a serious problem in achieving successful employment after leaving school. But in school it is without question a problem.

Masland, Sarason, and Gladwin (1958) state: "Two facts force us immediately and constantly to be aware of the intellectual problems presented by the school. First is the fact that school is the principal, and often the only, context in which many children of borderline intelligence are labelled and treated as mentally retarded" (p. 212). In reviewing a study conducted in Onondaga County, New York, the authors observe that the prevalence of mental retardation rises with age until "with the years of compulsory schooling behind, from age 16 onward the age-specific rates drop off dramatically" (p. 213). They further observe that "Unless one wishes to make the preposterous assumption that the majority of retarded children do not live beyond 16 or 17, one is forced to conclude that retardation means different things to different people, and that the criterion changes at about 16 . . ." (p. 208).

It thus becomes obvious that age is an important element in knowing when a condition is considered to be a handicap. Many parents look with apprehension to the day their children enter school. They fear there might be something wrong with them, something that is not particularly handicapping while they are still at home but which will manifest itself upon school entrance.

Even within the school there are conditions that are handicapping at some times but not at other times. A blind child for instance may have initial difficulties in finding his way about and in becoming accepted by his teachers. As the school year progresses these circumstances may change favorably. Still, the blind child may be unable to participate in sports, music, and art because of the assumption that he cannot fulfill the demands made by these activities. This assumption, in itself, may be a great handicap for this child because if given a chance he possibly could meet the necessary demands. He is excluded not because he is unable to perform successfully, but because of stereotypes about blindness formed by the school, often strongly reinforced by the parents.

Again, still within the school setting, certain behavior ordinarily considered a reflection of a handicap could serve the individual successfully. For example, a child pegged as a loner who does not play with other children but who concentrates instead on his studies may be more effectively preparing himself for a career than the socially minded, sports-oriented child. There seems to be something frightening about the child who prefers to be alone, or who is alone not by choice but because he cannot "mix." Similar fears are not experienced in regard to children who would prefer to be alone but who feel forced to be with others at every opportunity.

Our stereotypes could stand in the way and lead the school to conclude that the child who is a "loner" is socially maladjusted. This view obtained strong impetus from a study published forty years ago by Wickman (1928) which has been widely quoted. Ashcroft (1963), for example, cites the study, saying that "regular classroom teachers by contrast with mental health clinicians were inclined to be more sensitive to aggressive behavior than to withdrawing behavior (considered more serious by mental health clinicians) and thus tended to fail to identify many cases of children with potentially serious emotional problems" (p. 529). Ashcroft goes on to state that a study reported in 1957 "indicates that teachers now may be very much like clinicians in their sensitivity to withdrawal behavior as well as aggressive behavior" (p. 529). Tolor, Scarpetti, and Lane (1967) report a replication of the Wickman study.

For years nobody seemed to bother finding out whether the teachers or the clinicians were more accurate in terms of some kind of outcome criterion. It was just assumed that since the two groups differed, the clinicians must be right and the teachers wrong. Lewis (1965) reviewed several followup studies and came to the conclusion that "it is the acting out, disturbing child who is likely to become seriously mentally ill as an adult, rather than the shy, withdrawn child. It is interesting to note in passing that in the much quoted Wickman study, comparing teachers' and clinicians' judgments about problem behavior in children, the teachers may have been better predictors of adult psychiatric status than clinicians" (p. 467).

3. *How and why a condition is a handicap.* In a review of various systems used for classifying individuals as mentally retarded, Gelof (1963) concluded that "Classification systems of mental retardation are based on cause, condition, functioning, prognosis or some combination of these factors. As a consequence, considerable confusion is generated by attempts to extend into general or comparative usage terms to which specific denotations had been assigned in various classificatory systems. . . . Classifications are formulated by authorities whose disciplinary orientations are medical, educational, psychological, social, legal or some combination of these . . . . Some terms have acquired different meanings and some meanings have acquired different terms" (p. 315).

Gelof's comments suggest two significant areas for closer examination. The first is that handicap is perceived in a different manner by members of various professions. The second is that each professional group, in defining handicap, has in mind causation, the condition itself, functioning, and predictions about what will happen in the future.

Since professional groups have different orientations, it is not likely that every group will define handicap in the same way. The medical specialist sees the emotionally disturbed child from the viewpoint of medical causation and medical treatment. To this specialist it is important that the child receive some form of drug treatment or psychotherapy. Educational programming is considered of secondary importance because, it is reasoned, education will be of little value if the child's mental disease or emotional disturbance is not first cured.

Educators who are not aware of this emphasis, but who use medical specialists as consultants or even ask them to make decisions about certain functions in the educational program, often find a developing state of confusion. Children are being provided with special programming for five hours each day but this is supposed to be of secondary value to weekly one-hour visits to a mental health clinic. Everything done in the school each day must be oriented toward the weekly clinic visit, yet nobody in the school has a clear idea of what happens at the clinic.

A kind of mystical aura develops about the clinic visits; nobody dares to ask—the child especially is not to be questioned about what transpires between him and his therapist—so guesses or superstitions develop. Another disturbing thing to the teacher is that for all she knows the child may "report" on her to the therapist, who may in turn relay the information to the medical consultant. When the therapist occasionally does send formal reports to the school, or participate in a team meeting, the teacher feels she is looking at the proceedings through the wrong end of a telescope and is being observed from the other end.

REFERENCES

Ashcroft, S. C. Exceptionality and adjustment. In Dunn, L. M. (Ed.) *Exceptional Children in the Schools.* New York: Holt, Rinehart & Winston, 1963, pp. 521–55.

Dreeben, R. The contributions of schooling to the learning of norms. *Harvard Educational Review,* Spring 1967, 37, 211–37.

Gelof, M. Comparison of systems of classification relating degree of retardation to measured intelligence. *American Journal of Mental Deficiency,* November 1963, 68, 297–317.

Lewis, W. W. Continuity and intervention in emotional disturbance: a review. *Exceptional Children,* May 1965, 31, 465–75.

Linton, R. *The Tree of Culture.* New York: Knopf, 1957.

Masland, R. L., Sarason, S. B., & Gladwin, T. *Mental Subnormality.* New York: Basic Books, 1958.

Tolor, A., Scarpetti, W. L., & Lane, P. A. Teachers' attitudes toward children's behavior revisited. *Journal of Educational Psychology,* June 1967, 58, 175–80.

Wickman, E. K. *Children's Behavior and Teachers' Attitudes.* New York: Commonwealth Fund, 1928.

6

Education and Handicap

Educators typically have been quite lax in not recognizing the differences in professional orientations to handicapping conditions. Most continue to assume that handicap just "is," that whatever definition is presented by an individual of high social and professional status must be the proper and the only definition.

Eventually educators will have to take the initiative in forging relevant definitions of handicap, recognizing that these often may not be identical with medical, psychological, legal, or other definitions. In a few areas of special education this is gradually happening. Where a child classified as medically or legally blind a few years ago was provided with Braille and other programming for the blind, it is becoming more common to find educational programs for the visually handicapped based on educational needs rather than medical or legal definitions. Many visually impaired children today are attending their community schools rather than residential schools, and whether they receive Braille instruction depends upon their inability to read either regular or enlarged print.

Definition and Placement

It was suggested earlier that the school today does rather surreptitiously define handicap when it comes to the actual placement of children into special education programs. That is, not all children who score below a certain level on an intelligence scale are called mentally retarded and placed into special classes, and not all children who could be classified as emotionally disturbed are so classified and provided with special programming.

The actions of the school are, for the most part, without self-awareness. That is, educators feel they really are placing children into special classes *because* they are mentally retarded, emotionally disturbed, or brain injured. There is little recognition that it is only after a "child versus curriculum" problem is seen fairly clearly that an appeal is made to the evaluation-diagnostic process.

The result is that once children are "identified" and placed, curriculum provisions are based on attempts to translate non-educational concepts into educational practices.

Condition Versus Disease

We find in many instances there is disagreement over whether a condition in fact is a disease or a symptomatic reflection of a disease. It is commonly recognized today that mental retardation is a condition, not a disease (but see Jastak, 1967). But this is not true of emotional disturbance, which is supposed to be a kind of psychodynamic disease or at least to be a symptomatic reflection of such a disease. Unfortunately, neither viewpoint provides any clarification for the educator. Calling mental retardation a condition suggests that nothing can be done about it; a child is mentally retarded and the school should try to help him adjust to his condition.

We see examples of differences in orientation when a child's problem is considered a *condition* or when it is considered a *symptom* of a condition. The speech correctionist (or speech *therapist;* Macbeth, 1967) either works with children under the assumption that their problems are directly remediable, or that they are only symptoms of an underlying problem. Stuttering may be approached with direct corrective efforts or this problem may be treated indirectly, depending upon whether the speech correctionist feels stuttering is a learned speech pattern or a symptomatic manifestation of an underlying "emotional pathology" that requires psychotherapy rather than direct treatment of the speech pattern itself. Still another way of viewing stuttering, similar to that held about mental retardation, is that it is a neurologically determined *condition* and will always exist, so the proper treatment is to train the stutterer to live with the condition.

EDUCATIONAL PERSPECTIVES ON HANDICAP

Educators should not decide whether a certain problem is a condition or a symptomatic expression of an underlying but unseen and unspecific disease or illness. The major reason for this is that the history of truly educational approaches to problems has been so brief that no reliable information is available upon which to base judgments. Even if we could predict at the first-grade level that certain children will drop out of school at age sixteen (and thus be labeled as having a *condition* of "potential dropout"), we would not want to adopt the fatalistic attitude that it is necessary to prepare these first-graders for lives as school dropouts. We want to remain optimistic that there will be some way of altering the predicted outcome.

We have educational programs for the mentally retarded but these have so faithfully adopted the rationale used by medicine that very little is known about how educational technologies might work with children in the program. Indeed, so faithful has been this adoption that when a retarded child is found who responds to the program to the extent that he can be returned to the general curriculum program the conclusion is drawn that there was a "misdiagnosis." The child was never retarded in the first place. The alternate conclusion is that mental retardation—which is not a disease—is curable.

It appears to be regarded as unthinkable that children once classified as mentally retarded should be responsive to specialized programming in the sense they become "average" in their intellectual abilities. This would be similar to saying a child "diagnosed" as a future dropout, who in fact completed his schooling, was "misdiagnosed." With this kind of thinking we leave ourselves no room for intervention, for the assumption that behavior can be changed. We bind ourselves to a commitment that certain expectations must come about when there is no need to do this.

It is not necessary for educators to concern themselves with whether a child is "really" mentally retarded or "really" emotionally disturbed or brain injured. Yet this concern consumes a great deal of professional time. An enormously popular title for any local school district conference is "Identification of the Emotionally Disturbed Child." A speaker at such a conference can satisfy everybody with a few jokes about psychiatrists, some pious remarks about how administrators fail to support special education programs for the emotionally disturbed, and listing about fifteen "symptoms," such as nailbiting and aggressiveness, taken from any one of a number of journal reports on factor-analytic studies on the topic. Unfortunately, the satisfaction everybody feels is impossible to translate into educational practice.

The Myth of Basic Causes

The history of the close association between medical concepts and special educational practices has led to the myth that if only one could find a basic cause of a child's problems everything from that point on would be easy. In medicine, the cause of a disease is usually directly related to its treatment and cure; obviously, it is assumed by analogy, the same process must be true in education. But in most instances it is not true, and in such instances, as well as in those instances where it is true, there is nothing that can be done that is relevant to knowledge of the basic cause. For example, the school may find that failure in reading is directly related to poor home conditions and negative attitudes. It is highly commendable to begin work toward eliminating the poor home conditions and negative attitudes, but what about Johnny who can't read? While the school is chasing down basic causes, the child is no better off than he was. Along with long-range programs for eliminating problems there must be attention to the immediate effects seen here and now.

The school must take a position in recognizing its responsibilities for defining handicap in terms that are meaningful and relevant to the educational processes, both here and now and in the immediate and distant future. Members of the professions must admit that there are many ways of looking at and defining handicapping conditions and that the school is one of the major defining institutions in society. Whenever a specialist from another profession, whether the legal, medical, or psychological profession says, "This child has such-and-such a condition," the school always must ask itself what this means when translated into the educational context.

Defining special educational problems is on the one hand amazingly simple and on the other hand astonishingly complex. The process is simple because the schools can observe problems and are in the unique position of having the responsibility and the authority to do something about them. But the process is complex because the schools seemingly refuse to take the responsibility for defining problems and implementing total programs based on the definitions.

Changing the General Curriculum

Schools are not going to change their curriculums just because handicapped children are present; this is dictated by experience. A more appropriate strategy seems to be one that shows how special-ized programming under the "special education" category can be applied in the general curriculum. Hopefully, conceptions about special education, and specialized approaches to programming, can lead toward changes in the general curriculum. Much of what is done in a special education program also can be done in a general education program. If there were a method of teaching reading that was successful with certain types of handicapped children, there is no reason to believe that the same method would not be just as suc-cessful with non-handicapped children.

No teacher should say, "I can't work with Johnny because he's mentally retarded and I have never taken a course on mental re-tardation." The teacher's judgment about whether he can work with Johnny should not be based on his lack of knowledge about how children learn. As a professional educator the teacher should assume he is more than a tradesman qualified to work only with certain types of children; he is a specialist in the processes basic to formal educa-tion: learning and directed behavioral change. If a teacher cannot work with a child the basis should be on realistic factors that have a direct bearing on the educational process and structure. It is realistic for a first-grade teacher with thirty children in her class to say that a hyperactive, destructive child who consumes all her time and energy should receive consideration for specialized programming. It is realistic for a school principal with a fifteen-year-old child, who cannot read, who cannot easily find his way about, and who is the butt of taunts from other children, to say the child needs specialized programming.

In every case, the form of the specialized programming should depend upon the observable needs of each child. Classes with smaller numbers of children, with the assistance of teacher aides, may be required for some children. For other children specialized assistance from itinerant teachers or counselors may be required. And for still other children a curriculum that is completely different in every way from the general curriculum (and from most special education programs) should be provided.

"Clinical Teaching"

Frequently excellence in individualization of instruction is referred to as "clinical teaching." For some reason, strangely enough, the best of the profession is stripped of its rightful status and classified as something belonging outside of education as a field of professional endeavor. Educators need not apologize for the best of their work. Good teaching can be called *good teaching* without appending another term to suggest that superior performance under ideal conditions is so uncommon or so atypical, or so foreign to teaching, that in fact it is not really teaching (Reger, 1967).

REFERENCES

Jastak, J. F. Mental retardation (letter). *Science*, August 4, 1967, 157, 577–8.

Macbeth, R. Speech therapy as a paramedical subject. *British Journal of Disorders of Communication*, April 1967, 2, 69–72.

Reger, R. Teachers in special education. Paper presented at the University of Kansas, Lawrence, May 13, 1967.

7

Teacher Preparation and Certification

Teachers have for some time lamented some of the unusual aspects of certification. Popular magazines often highlight instances where professional writers, scientists, or others who have demonstrated competency in their fields, and who may have taught college courses, are unable to teach in elementary and secondary schools because they lack the requirements for becoming certified as teachers at those levels. Teachers have complained about the difficulties involved in moving from one state to another and finding that what was considered adequate preparation for certification in one state is not considered adequate in the other state. Some persons with advanced degrees find they cannot teach in elementary or secondary public schools, but can teach courses to others in college that are required by the state for obtaining certification.

There is much about the teacher certification process that is arbitrary and that often leads to seemingly ridiculous contradictions. But this is not unique to the teaching profession. It is not paradoxical that a college professor who teaches courses required for obtaining teacher certification is not himself able to teach in the public schools. A professor of physiology or chemistry may teach medical students but would not assume that, therefore, he should be qualified to practice medicine.

When general rules are made for the benefit of the whole, often the individual with unique talents or background suffers. Undoubtedly there are many individuals who have never been to college who could be excellent teachers. Some persons without medical training perhaps could be effective practitioners of medicine. But lines must be drawn; how would it be possible to determine which individuals without college preparation would be excellent teachers? Once an exception is made for one on the basis of subjective judgments, then other persons may claim they, too, have the special talents to be excellent teachers without going through the channels of formal preparation, and there would be no basis for refutation.

CERTIFICATION IN SPECIAL EDUCATION

In special education, as in general education, teachers obtain certification in various specified areas from state departments of education, and universities typically attempt to provide the courses needed by teachers to obtain their certificates. Often, particularly in new areas, universities play a large role in determining what is necessary to achieve competence, and state certifying agencies co-operatively base their criteria upon these determinants.

Special education has grown from a field concerned with just a few areas of exceptionality to many areas. As newer areas are appended, new certification requirements are established. Because almost all areas of special education to date have been derived from medical-personal disability areas, certification requirements usually are built around these conceptions. The medical model—that is, considering *children* to be disabled (rather than assigning any responsibility for the problem to the curriculum)—is being extended even to areas where medical classifications are not particularly relevant. Thus, there is some possibility that certification requirements will be built around an increasing array of "diagnostic" characteristics of children.

Today there are different certificates for teachers of the blind, the partially seeing, the deaf, the hard of hearing, the mentally retarded, the speech defective, the emotionally disturbed, the homebound, the orthopedically disabled, and so on. When such areas as the minimally brain injured, the culturally disadvantaged, the multiply handicapped, and others emerge and gain respectability it is not unlikely that separate requirements for each "area" will be created.

If the current trend continues, with each diagnostic category having its unique certification requirements, eventually it will be necessary to distribute to each school administrator and to each parent a dictionary that defines the terms used for classifying teachers around the United States.

The administrator in Texas will not understand what the teacher from Michigan, who is certified as a "learning disabilities specialist," is qualified to teach in his school. Or the administrator in Michigan will not understand what the teacher trained in Texas in the area of "bilingual cultural disadvantage" is qualified to teach in his school.

The Administrator and an Impractical Joke

Earlier we mentioned the teacher of the mentally retarded who arrived in the administrator's office to announce, "I have an emotionally disturbed child in my class; I'm not qualified to teach the emotionally disturbed, so therefore that child does not belong in my class!"

When besieged by such a proclamation, the administrator may experience a feeling of guilt. Is he, after all, in spite of his conscientious attempts to properly place children, just "dumping problems" into a teacher's class? According to the latest thinking, if the child really is emotionally disturbed he should be in a different kind of program, not with a teacher of the mentally retarded.

Mental retardation and emotional disturbance, of course, *can* occur in the same child, and this becomes a perplexing problem. If the child were placed in a class for the emotionally disturbed, the teacher there undoubtedly would protest that as a teacher of the emotionally disturbed he clearly is not qualified to teach such a child.

Now, if the administrator tried to please both teachers and at the same time achieve a high level of sophisticated special educational programming in his school, the solution, obviously, would be to establish a class for the "mentally retarded emotionally disturbed" or the "emotionally disturbed mentally retarded." If he is near a college that has a well-developed special education program for training teachers he might be fortunate enough to employ a teacher who acquired sufficient credits and student teaching experience to obtain "dual" certification in both mental retardation and emotional disturbance. More than likely, however, he would have to offer inducements to a teacher already on his staff certified in one area to go back to the university to obtain the requirements necessary to become certified—or at least knowledgeable—in the other area as well.

The administrator, now having established a special class for the mentally retarded emotionally disturbed (which would probably be called "an MRED class," and the children called "MREDs") can rest assured that he is providing the ultimate in specialized educational programming needed by each handicapped child in his school. That is, until the teacher of deaf children on his staff finds out about the new development and announces that she has a child who, besides being deaf, also is mentally retarded and emotionally disturbed. The administrator, perhaps sensing that he had started something, but not quite able to put his finger on it, finds he can resolve this latest dilemma by placing this newly discovered child into the class for the mentally retarded emotionally disturbed and providing an itinerant teacher of the deaf to assist the classroom teacher in matters pertaining to the child's deafness. The teacher of the mentally retarded emotionally disturbed perhaps would be unhappy since the new child, in a strict sense, differed markedly from the other children in the class (and thus, as far as the teacher is concerned, was "dumped" into her class because nobody else wanted him).

This flexible and agreeable administrator's problems, however, have only begun. He soon finds at his door a teacher who says she has a child misplaced in her class. This child, besides being (1) mentally retarded, is (2) hyperactive and thus brain injured, (3) perceptually handicapped, (4) emotionally disturbed, (5) hard of hearing, (6) speech defective, (7) partially sighted, (8) culturally deprived, (9) epileptic, and (10) displays delinquent tendencies.

By this time the administrator has had to buy a new edition of his now well-worn dictionary of certification terms. He is unable to determine how he can accommodate the last teacher who confronted him with the guilt-provoking issue of whether he is a professional educator interested in *really* providing for the needs of handicapped children or one who consistently "dumps" children into classes where unqualified teachers have to "babysit," due to his lack of foresight, interest, and professionalism.

The Concept of "Primary Disability"

As a last resort the administrator consults with the nearby university department of special education. There he finds that special class placements should be based on "primary disability" rather than on various permutations. It is obvious, he is told, that if a child is mentally retarded this condition can *cause* a variety of other problems such as speech defects and emotional disturbance. In addition, mental retardation often is "associated with" cultural deprivation and visual and auditory defects. Furthermore, brain injury can cause mental retardation but still not be considered the primary disability. It is too gross to suggest that mental retardation causes brain injury.

Determination of what is to be considered the primary disability is usually based on tradition and available programs rather than on presumed basic causes of a condition. Programs for brain-injured children are not for brain-injured children; they are for certain children who demonstrate certain kinds of problems and who fit into the program that might be available. The concept of primary disability is an administrative convenience, not to be confused with the putative primary reasons why a child is handicapped.

Even when primary disability is admitted to be an administrative convenience the conceptual and practical problems associated with special educational programming do not cease. Arguments over what is primary and what is secondary can rage on as endlessly as arguments over the chicken and egg problem. The teacher of the mentally retarded who has an emotionally disturbed child in her class will remain convinced that the child is not "really" mentally retarded but that his emotional disturbance is "depressing" his intellectual functioning.

Teacher Preparation

It is, of course, grossly unfair to attribute to certification procedures all the problems suggested in the illustration above. Through these illustrations we wish to emphasize that certification for teachers in the field of special education should be reviewed and some changes should be made. In turn, the preparation required of teachers during their training should be revised.

Departments of special education in almost all colleges and universities in the United States have established a pattern of categorization that would undoubtedly be a major hindrance to any changes that might be deemed desirable. One exception has been proposed by Schwartz (1967), who reports a teacher-training program that moves away from the medically defined, discrete-handicap specialization approach. The attempt, apparently, is to train "generalists" in special education.

Usually, however, there are professors in programs for the mentally retarded, the emotionally disturbed, and other categories, and strong elements of control, status, and power have become institutionalized. The professor specializing in emotional disturbance has worked hard to obtain federal grants to train teachers of the emotionally disturbed (and the more grants he gets the higher his personal stock goes on the academic job market). He provides an intensive curriculum around what he believes to be relevant for teaching emotionally disturbed children. He sees his candidates graduate and wants to see them placed into the best possible positions, and especially into positions as teachers of the emotionally disturbed. When his former students have had some field experience he wants to place student teachers with them because he knows there will be a certain consistency between his own efforts and the initial experiences provided by his former students. He likes to maintain contact with his former students; he wants continuity and he wants positive feedback to know his work has been meaningful.

Secondary-Level Certification

One of the major drawbacks in preparing teachers in the area of special education is that almost no preparation is provided for secondary-level teachers. Teacher-training institutions typically make no distinctions between elementary and secondary levels. A teacher certified in mental retardation in many states can teach a class of five-year-old "trainable" retarded children or a class of nineteen-year-old "educable" retarded youth. A certified teacher of the blind can work with kindergarteners or high school seniors even if she has never been any closer to a high school curriculum than when she was herself a high school student.

The special education teacher should be expected to be a specialist in the sense of being able to provide an individualized educational program for any child—handicapped or not handicapped. (The implication is that every teacher in the schools should similarly be trained, but one problem at a time.) Teachers in special education should be well versed in all concepts and descriptions of disability and handicap. The important goal for teacher-training institutions should be to provide a program based around principles of individualized instruction for children. The teacher should be "special" because of training in curriculum content, method, and purpose for helping individual children meet their educational needs.

Principles Rather than Child-Types

Teachers would be better trained if they knew how to provide an arts and crafts program for any child; certainly, there must be basic principles about instruction in arts and crafts that would be useful to any teacher working with any child. Similarly, teachers should be offered training on when and how to provide instruction in reading. The curriculum aspects of reading as a skill in itself should be emphasized, with an awareness instilled that not all children are ready to read at a certain predetermined age, that some children will never achieve high levels of reading proficiency, that some children will have been able to read before they entered school, and so on. Instruction should be offered on the many viewpoints on how reading can be taught and on the many materials that are available and what principles are behind their use.

Thus, instead of building stereotypes about children as handicapped and then attempting to provide narrow orientations around what and how to provide for the children who fit these stereotypes, the process should be reversed.

Teacher-training institutions would do a service to their students by developing first an orientation as to if, why, how, what, and when certain curriculum areas are important for children. Following this should be more specific orientations about how the general areas can be applied for individual children—dull, average, bright, deaf, blind, emotionally disturbed, brain injured, delinquent, bilingual, culturally disadvantaged, Negro, white, urban, and lower class. A teacher should be equally prepared for work with retarded lower-class children as with suburban middle-class "average" children.

Perhaps it is necessary to turn the light for a moment on the teacher trained to work not with handicapped children but with so-called normal children. Implicit always is the assumption that it is more difficult to work with handicapped children than with nonhandicapped children. This undoubtedly is often true—as we ourselves have found—but the reasons why sometimes suggest deficits in the work of teachers of non-handicapped children.

Teachers in regular classes can easily spend days doing nothing more than performing rituals that require little thought. The instructional map is drawn, the course gets under way and proceeds at a predetermined pace, and the destination is always reached at the end of the school year. That the children profited from the journey is assumed on the basis of superficial responses. We may be sure that some children did not profit. The fact that some did not follow the course, however, calls for an investigation of what is wrong with the children, never whether the course taken or the means were appropriate.

Because handicapped children, by the way the school defines

handicap, are those who fall by the wayside on this kind of journey, it *is* more difficult to work with them. The serenity of the "regular" classroom is a goal often sought by special education teachers when they ask that only children who "fit" their specialty be placed with them. But because the regular classroom teacher can use "a" reading method and singular course and pace and perhaps get by with it, is no reason to claim this as a model for special education teachers.

Some special education teachers will require training that is not essential to other teachers. For example, every teacher does not need to know Braille or the specifics of mobility training for blind children. The numbers of such specialized requirements are relatively small and are not justifications for continuing the practice of providing narrow curriculum experiences for all special education teachers.

Teachers in training do need practical experiences with existing programs for handicapped children. There should be as much contact with handicapped children as is possible during the short period of time spent in college. The major purpose of this is to acquaint the teachers-to-be with the children, to familiarize them with the conditions, the situations, the characteristics of the school environment.

Certification

Two basic certificates should be issued to special education teachers: elementary and secondary. A great deal of leeway should be given in what is required to obtain either certificate, making it possible in many instances for teachers to obtain both certificates or to concentrate heavily in certain areas within the requirements for either certificate.

The student teaching required to obtain either certificate should include a wider variety of experiences than currently exists. A model that could be examined for possible examples is that provided by nurses during their training. Student nurses must obtain experience in a variety of situations, both in general nursing and in various specialty areas. This model cannot be followed completely because it is based on "types-of-people" areas, but the pattern of rotation in general appears to hold some promise.

The First Year

Most of the critical experience obtained by teachers comes during their first year of paid employment, when they are considered professionally competent and thus without need of supervision beyond that provided by the local building administrator. Thus the student teaching experiences seem especially important and should provide variety in settings as well as sufficient time in each setting to become familiar with the children.

The assumption that a young person with a college degree will be a competent, well-trained professional teacher is questionable, as most persons forced to live with the assumption admit. College training programs can only do so much.

Because the teacher's first year of employment is usually a training experience, this year should explicitly be designed for this purpose. Certification should be withheld until the first year has been successfully completed.

REFERENCES

Schwartz, Louis. An integrated teacher education program for special education—a new approach. *Exceptional Children,* February 1967, 33, 411–16.

8

The Selection of Teachers

Selecting teachers to work with children who have special learning and/or behavioral problems is done primarily by sophisticated guesswork. To date there are no known characteristics that can be spelled out to identify teachers who probably will be successful. Teacher selection is briefly discussed to portray one set of opinions about what is an effective and what is an ineffective teacher.

It should be borne in mind that the positive and negative qualities sketched here are those considered important within the kind of educational context described in the first chapter. In another kind of context it is possible that a different set of evaluative criteria would be considered appropriate.

Characteristics: The Interview

Many of the qualities considered desirable in teachers are not discernible during an interview and thus there is little point in attempting to go beyond a certain limit in looking for them. For example, ability to control children effectively, to manage a classroom with maximum efficiency with regard to the learning process, is considered to be of basic importance. Yet it is extremely difficult to determine during an interview whether a teacher has this ability. Even more important is a recognition that children should be provided with an individualized curriculum program. Here the interview language is completely meaningless because most teachers believe their training and their work have been focused entirely on the individual child. It is only after a period of observation of actual performance that it can be ascertained whether a teacher is capable of working toward the provision of individualized instruction. Further, in many if not most instances, a teacher initially will not be providing this kind of instruction and the critical factor is whether he is capable of learning to do so.

Positive Characteristics

At the interview stage one should look for teachers with the following general characteristics: (1) the ability to mobilize and sustain a high level of energy; (2) alertness and responsiveness; (3) personal stability and self-control; and (4) an orientation toward being a teacher (rather than, say, a psychotherapist or an administrator).

Energy level is considered important because to provide an individualized program for six to ten children is an extremely difficult, physically tiring, enterprise. When a teacher is working with children exhibiting a variety of learning and/or behavioral problems the task is even more difficult. Classroom management in itself can exhaust the teacher with a low energy level.

Alertness and responsiveness are considered important because, tied with energy level, teachers must continuously be aware of each event in the classroom and be able to respond appropriately. Actions on the part of the children that will lead to disruptive behaviors must be managed immediately. A teacher who misses the nuances of disturbance in the initial stages will be forced to expend considerably more effort to correct the disturbance as it grows in magnitude. In the end, it is more economical to stop disturbances as soon as possible. (No teacher, however, is going to be able to curtail all disturbances in their initial stages because sometimes these begin at home or on the bus on the way to school.) Stopping the disturbances when they do become apparent, which may be after they are fairly well established, requires an ability to mobilize a high level of energy and sensitively manage the difficulty.

Personal stability and self-control are characteristics that are not uniquely desirable for any one educational program. They are mentioned only because in some instances there may be a naive assumption that a teacher who is "a little bit crazy," or who appears to enjoy wallowing in emotional turmoil, would be ideal for such work.

Again, an orientation toward being a teacher is nothing unique except there is today a great emphasis on "psychoeducation," "educational therapy," and other such conceptions for teachers of problem children. Our interest is not in psychoeducation or educational therapy; we are interested in individualized instruction in a framework consistent with sound educational philosophy and principle. When terms such as "educational therapy" are pared to their essentials, at best they stand for nothing more than techniques and at worst they cover a lack of knowledge of the educational process. One difficulty with employing teachers trained where such terms are the mainstay of the preparatory program is that educational and behavioral change are split into separate entities. Behavioral change is fundamental to the entire educational process, an especially critical area where problem children are concerned; our interest is in having teachers see their role, *as teachers,* as agents for assisting in behavioral change. Teachers trained to believe either that behavioral change is not their primary concern or that it is somehow separate from the educational process are incompletely prepared.

Negative Characteristics

Some of the negative characteristics, as we see them, would be the opposites of what were mentioned above as positive characteristics. However, in addition to these the following characteristics are considered unfavorable: (1) an expression of a sentimental attitude toward children—an apparent overzealous desire to "help" problem children; (2) an avowed or probable belief in permissiveness—that problem children should be free to continue expressing their problems with a minimum of interference; (3) an expressed desire to call frequently upon psychologists, psychiatrists, social workers, and others for assistance in daily programming; and (4) such attributes as an inability to follow the interview conversation, expressions of anger over trivia, unusual timidity, and an obvious lack of understanding of children and of curriculum.

An expression during an interview of a strong desire to "help" children in itself is not a negative attribute. However, if the interviewer probes the prospective teacher he will often find that zealousness is a kind of mask for ignorance. Sometimes the interviewer gets an impression similar to what a high school counselor might find in a teenager who indicates a fervent desire to be an airline pilot but whose grades, aptitudes, and general interests are such that it is obvious the youngster knows superficially only the glamour of being an airline pilot and has no interest in the hard work necessary to achieve such a goal. Such persons want to be at the top of the ladder while remaining standing on the ground. Some teacher candidates think of working with problem children as a glamorous opportunity to sacrifice themselves to society.

A few persons want to work with problem children because they feel they have "so much to offer." The difficulty with this is that what they have to offer may not be what the children need and the "offering" becomes an infliction upon the children.

Permissiveness, again, in itself is not undesirable—as will be shown in the next chapter. If permissiveness is defined as maximizing opportunities for children to develop self control, it would be considered desirable. At the interview stage it is difficult to discover whether a teacher really is permissive. Ordinarily, if a teacher admits to being permissive he usually will be a rather sophisticated individual and can explain his belief very well.

If a prospective teacher indicates a desire to seek the frequent assistance of psychologists, psychiatrists, social workers, and similar personnel to help with his daily programming, this may have several implications. It may reveal that the teacher anticipates difficulties in managing his classroom. Or that the teacher does not want to take responsibility for effective classroom management; thus, he anticipates difficulties and sees as a solution having experts advise him with formulas on how to resolve his difficulties since he probably does not relish the task of working them out on his own. It indicates that the teacher does not feel he has an understanding of children, that he feels instead there is some kind of mystery about behavior and the only persons with the keys to this mystery are non-educational specialists. In effect, then, he sees behavior as separate from education and his definition of education is likely to be quite narrow.

The other characteristics of teachers considered unfavorable—unusual timidness, expressions of anger over trivia, inability to follow the interview conversation—are rather gross and perhaps too obvious. A person who appears timid in an interview setting may, in the classroom, be an unusually sensitive individual intensely aware of the needs of children and may have a quiet but objective and effective way of managing the group. But a person who is downright fearful, or one who becomes openly enraged over trivia and who might be expected to have a series of temper tantrums throughout the school year is not a good choice to work with children.

One of the most significant of these gross unfavorable characteristics is an inability to follow the thread of the interview conversation. If, in the conversational exchange that occurs during the interview, it becomes apparent that the prospective teacher does not "get the message" about the program as it is explained this is usually—but not always—considered an unfavorable sign. Often it indicates that the person already has a set of preconceived ideas about what he intends to do in a classroom. In well-established programs where teacher-training institutions have prepared teachers for precisely what they will be doing in the classroom this perhaps is no major problem. In new programs, where a course different from that taken by most other programs is followed, and where teacher-training institutions have not prepared teachers for the new program, this can be a decided problem.

Characteristics: On the Job

Once a teacher is on the job a selection process should still be taking place. As much supervision as possible should be provided during the first year of employment to sensitize new teachers to their responsibilities.

The first expectation is that the favorable characteristics noted in the interview will be observable in practice. At the risk of being overly repetitious, once again a basic concern with teachers is that they be effective classroom managers and be able to learn to provide individualized instructional programs. Classroom management is the first requirement because without an efficient learning framework there can be no individualized programming.

Following are brief notations about previously unmentioned favorable and unfavorable characteristics of teachers who are in the type of setting described in Chapter 1.

Positive Characteristics

On the job, teachers should demonstrate (1) a real understanding of children, (2) a grasp of the relationship between children's needs and the curriculum, (3) an ability to talk with parents about children in descriptive, basically informative language, and (4) a willingness to continue professional growth with experience or an ability to outline reasonably why change is unnecessary.

A "real" understanding of children can be observed only when a person is in a working relationship with children. The language of the interview and the behavior in the situation often are completely unrelated. An ability to describe children verbally is important, but these descriptions may be maps of territory that really does not exist

—that is, the understanding on an action level is missing. Some experienced teachers apparently have been successful for a long period of time because they have been able to manage classrooms effectively, but without putting into the curriculum anything of substance.

Closely associated with an understanding of children is an understanding of children's needs and how they ought to mesh with the curriculum. Many experienced teachers have used *a* reading series, or *a* reading method. The first day of classes these persons will select a reading series and attempt to begin immediately where they left off in their last teaching job. It is necessary for these teachers—and for the inexperienced teachers as well—to gain a basic grasp of the principles of individualized instruction: that each child in the class may need a different reading series, a different reading method, or indeed may not be ready for reading at all and may first require language development training or other fundamentals. The teacher must be able to ascertain a child's needs and then search for materials or techniques to meet them. The materials and techniques must be closely matched with the child. Typically, materials and techniques are adopted and then children are expected to fit them, and a teacher's success in sticking to this pattern is considered a positive characteristic.

Teachers should be able to talk with parents in language parents can understand. The rationale for this is that teachers are in the best position to induce behavioral change in parents if such change is considered of benefit to the child. Teachers should stay close to topics directly related to the child when talking with parents; these topics should be discussed in "plain English," with an awareness of the need for tact. If a child is not performing as well as the parent might like, it would be inappropriate for the teacher to resort to jargon and point out to the parent that the child's IQ is low, that he has brain damage, or that he seems to have weak ego strength. It simply is not incumbent upon teachers to pretend to offer "explanations" intended to pacify parents who are not satisfied with their children. If a nine-year-old child is unable to read, the teacher need not manufacture reasons to try to explain why; his job is to explain to the parent what he is doing to try to help the child with his reading. If the parent insists on knowing why, and is not satisfied to hear the teacher admit that he does not know the answer, the parent should be referred to supervisory personnel. The ability of teachers to talk in direct, understandable language with parents and meaning-fully discuss children is a complicated but necessary asset.

A willingness to continue professional growth is a culmination of all the positive characteristics discussed. If a teacher does not have these positive characteristics he should be capable of acquiring them.

Negative Characteristics

Again, many of the negative characteristics of teachers on the job for the first time are the opposite of positive characteristics men-tioned above. In addition, we have found it is very difficult to change the following characteristics of a teacher on the job: (1) an inability to manage children, (2) a continued use of labels and jargon as explanatory devices and thus as substitutes for real understanding, (3) a continued dependence on gadgets and materials for their novelty effect rather than as appropriate to meet relevant needs, and (4) an unwillingness to participate in inservice training activities or to take supervisory assistance seriously.

It seems that a teacher who is unable to manage children with special learning and/or behavioral problems after a trial period of several months seldom shows any basic improvement. However, it has been difficult to determine whether an ineffective classroom manager eventually can learn to manage this kind of group because usually the effects are so disastrous that nobody is willing to wait to find out.

A teacher who continues to refer to children by labels that have been applied to them, or by ones he has invented, typically will see any problems he is having as being "inside" the children, with the labels explaining the problems. Thus the teacher having difficulty with a particular child will speak of the child as "psychotic" or "severely brain damaged," and all references to problems will focus on these labels. The teacher might say "Astro's brain damage is so severe that he simply will not respond," or "Freddy's psychosis ap-pears to be getting worse because his behavior is deteriorating." It is always interesting to note that when a child's behavior improves or when a child responds to the teacher's efforts, these labels are never used to help explain the change. The teacher will not say, "Freddy's psychosis appears to be getting better because he is learning to read now." Improvement is due to the teacher's efforts but failure is the

child's responsibility. Teachers who display this negative characteristic can be effective with some, but seldom all, of the children placed
with them because they frequently are pointing out that some of the
children in their class "don't belong" because they are "not responding"—the reasons lying in various forms of "pathology" within the
child.

Teachers who continue to use gadgets and materials for their
novelty effect rather than as means to meet individual needs usually
have one thing in common: no mater how short the days are, they
always say they are too long. The contrast sometimes is quite noticeable between the teacher who usually notes with dismay that the bus
has arrived signaling the end of the school day, and the teacher who
almost always sees the bus with a sigh of relief. Certainly for some
children any school day is too long and in many instances the day for
individual children or for whole classes is too long, but fewer than
5 percent of this group of children need a school day shorter than
from, say, 8:30 in the morning to 2:00 in the afternoon. Generally,
gadget-oriented teachers, those who use available resources as time-
fillers, will always find children catching on to them and responding
by becoming bored, tired, and unmanageable. Observing this behavior, the teacher then says the children should have a shorter day
because of their brain damage, emotional disturbance, or immaturity.

Teachers who display signs of unwillingness to participate in inservice training or accept other assistance of a supervisory nature
often are those who need such assistance the most. If a supervisor
knew nothing about how a teacher new to the program was doing on
his job, but did know the teacher seldom if ever participated in inservice training activities, it would be a safe bet that the teacher was
having difficulty. The teacher may not be aware of the difficulty—
or at least almost never admits such—but usually it is there and after
a period of time it presents itself. As might be expected, the reverse
condition usually holds true: those teachers doing the best work are
the most eager to be involved, even if silently, in group meetings,
and they usually look forward to talks with supervisory personnel.
The non-participants sometimes complain that it does no good to
attend inservice activities because "nothing goes on, it's just talk,"
although they would be no more interested in attending even if each
session opened with a steak dinner and closed with a variety show, as
long as there would be a discussion that in any way would show the
difficulties they are having in their work.

GENERAL IMPRESSIONS

There is a feeling among some persons that good teachers of children with special learning and/or behavioral problems should somehow be different from other good teachers. This is highly doubtful. That teachers of problem children should be more patient, or more indoctrinated with psychological jargon or psychoanalytic theory, or that they have had some experience in a psychiatric hospital or similar setting, are questionable assumptions.

If forced to select all of our teachers from one group having the same academic background and experience, and could make no exceptions, we would "choose" a group of speech correctionists who had either a student teaching experience in a regular classroom or one year of experience as a speech correctionist. The major reason for this is that these persons usually are trained in basic areas of communication and language, fundamental areas as far as we are concerned. Another reason is that the training of speech correctionists usually focuses more on the individual child than on stereotypes of groups of children.

Interestingly enough, staying with our hypothetical situation, perhaps one of the last groups that would be chosen would be those trained as teachers of the emotionally disturbed or brain injured. Even though there would be many exceptions, our impression is that more members of this group would be unprepared to work with problem children than would members of many other groups of teachers.

Because this statement has implications for teacher-training institutions the following reasons are given. First, teachers from training programs for the emotionally disturbed or brain injured typically are trained, as are teachers of the mentally retarded, around stereotypes of children. But unlike training programs for the mentally retarded, many training programs for the emotionally disturbed or brain injured have clinical psychologists as major professors for students. Many if not most of these professors have had no experience teaching children. Or, if they have had such experience it usually has been in a medical setting, such as a state mental hospital or a psychiatric clinic, where education probably was viewed as a kind of "adjunct therapy" or non-essential activity. ("In the traditional therapy model, the relationship established between the patient and the therapist and how it is utilized is the essential element in therapy.

Similarly, all of the work by adjunctive therapists—occupational therapists, special education teachers . . . " p. 98 in Rubin, Simson, and Betwee, 1966). Kaufman (1965) observes that in one teacher-training program for the emotionally disturbed, the structure of the program in 1965 was similar to the program for the mentally retarded ten years earlier.

Second, the training of teachers of the emotionally disturbed typically consists of becoming sophisticated in using psychiatric jargon and in learning the diagnostic classification system of clinical psychiatry. Labels and jargon are instilled and serve as substitutes for understanding children, an experience familiar to many clinical psychologists.

Third, many programs for teachers of the emotionally disturbed are heavily oriented toward a permissive, pseudo-psychoanalytic doctrine that encourages an engrossment in "emotional pathology." This sometimes becomes almost maudlin, with trainees encouraged to wallow in emotion-laden relationships with children that are based not on observable behaviors and educational goals, but upon "diagnostic clues," "interpretative hypotheses," and "clinical hunches." The trainees are impressed with the idea that it is far more important to "understand the pathology" than it is to worry about "education." "Anxiety" and "ego strength" are far more important than paying attention, developing acceptable manners, obeying commands (a terrible thing to be concerned about in a child laden with emotional pathology), and generally being as much as possible like other children. For these trainees, the pathology must first be cured, then education can take place; in the meantime, "education" is a time-filler, something for the children to occupy themselves with so they will not feel too different from normal children. The splitting of behavior and education makes it extremely difficult for these persons, once in a classroom, to understand what to do because in fact behavioral change is the primary function of the formal educational system.

REFERENCES

Kaufman, M. E. A teacher training program for socially and emotionally disturbed children. *The Winnower*, December 1965, 2, 2–4.

Rubin, E. Z., Simson, C. B., & Betwee, M. C. *Emotionally Handicapped Children and the Elementary School*. Detroit: Wayne State University Press, 1966.

9

Classroom Management and Behavioral Control

Classroom management and provision of an individualized curriculum are so closely related that their separate elements should be examined briefly. It was stated in a previous chapter that it is impossible to provide an individualized curriculum unless there is effective control in the classroom. Yet, effective management in the best sense is the maximizing of individualization within a group context.

Control of children in and of itself is neither good nor bad; it can be either, depending on the reasons why control is maintained and the techniques used.

These two elements should be combined: the basic reasons for maintaining classroom control should be tied to an effective technology that leads toward the achievement of specified goals. This, then, provides a connection between management and individualized programming.

Control and Choices

Some educators and others associated with the helping professions, indoctrinated with what Cremin (1961) believes to be a misinterpretation of both Dewey's and Freud's writings about children, appear to become upset with the suggestion that children should be "controlled." Encouraging a child to "behave himself" seems to conjure images of the instillation of servility and robotism, of stamping out creativity and ingraining habits rather than the ability to think. Indeed, Heckelman (1966) offers some support for this criticism when he says "The learning situation," in a program he describes for emotionally handicapped children, "was structured from the beginning to use conditioning processes. Creativity and extreme permissiveness were not encouraged" (p. 18). The implication is that creativity is associated with permissiveness but is incompatible with a non-permissive setting. (Crabtree, 1967, reports an experiment on this question, revealing that the matter is not a simple one.)

Children who display unusual behavior, such that they are considered significantly deviant from most other children, probably are helped by learning how to behave as other children. When these deviant children reach the point, usually as they approach adulthood, where they can decide whether they prefer being "normal" or "deviant," at least they are capable of making the choice. Thus, our goal is to assist children to secure control over themselves so they can decide what kind of persons they want to be.

It need not be assumed that a nine-year-old child is capable of deciding completely his life's career or how he intends to go about achieving his career goals. Such a child is typically not ready to fix the course for the remainder of his life. There are, of course, Mozarts whose life patterns and future careers are set long before the age of nine. But there also are Einsteins who fail mathematics in elementary school and are declared at an early age to be destined to a life of failure. We cannot take either of these extremes and use them profitably as a basis for determining a program for most deviant children.

Our desire is not to fix the kind of pattern in life that the children for whom we have responsibility will follow; rather it is to bring children to the point where they eventually can make rational choices for themselves. As educators we have completely failed the child who has a desire, and the basic capability, to become an engineer if we do not do whatever we can to help create within and around him the conditions to achieve his goal. If this child is obnoxious, unable to tolerate those who disagree with him, unable to concentrate on subject matter and, in short, at the whim of whatever stimulus confronts him at the moment, then he does not possess self-control.

How to Achieve Self-Control?

An interesting philosophical question is raised here. As Morris (1961) states the issue: "Discipline consists fundamentally in answering two questions: How should the child be controlled? and, How should the child be taught to control himself?" (p. 424). In discussing the ways various schools of philosophy might answer these two questions, Morris says, "To put the matter a bit too bluntly, and certainly too simply, we may say that the traditional educational outlooks (Essentialism and Perennialism) hold that the child is taught how to control himself by being controlled by the teacher, that self-discipline comes from being disciplined. The contemporary educational doctrines (Progressivism and Existentialism) hold that the child is taught to control himself by controlling himself, that self-discipline comes from practice in disciplining oneself" (p. 424).

Morris goes on to note that traditional philosophies have a far too sentimental outlook on deviant behavior; "Children have to be restrained; they are little animals, many of them. And by constant restraint they eventually learn to restrain themselves.

"Progressives understandably tend to reject this. It is precisely because boys and girls *are* restrained and controlled by adults that they feel no need to learn self-restraint. They are conditioned to expect somebody else to oversee their behavior. Hence the sure way *not* to develop self-discipline in a child is to make the teacher, rather than the child himself, the chief moral supervisor of the child's conduct" (p. 424).

We can agree that Morris has "put the matter . . . too simply," because our own view is somewhere between the two extremes illustrated. Neither Freud nor Dewey ever suggested that a child should be completely free from planned external restraints, in spite of what their misinformed followers often have indicated. Nor, incidentally, does A. S. Neill (1960) advocate the absence of external restraints although he feels children are equal with adults in imposing sanctions.

Children will be restrained in their behavior, whether it is planned by other children, by parents and teachers, or by direct experience with burning matches, exposed live electrical wiring, or the police. Nobody has ever seriously suggested that two-year-olds learn that playing in the street is dangerous by allowing them to experience the consequences of such actions. Nor has anybody promoted the belief that direct intervention by the police is the best way to allow teenagers to learn that joyriding in any handy car is an effective way of learning about society's rules of behavior.

Control and Rules

Society does have rules; in every peer group, every neighborhood, every school, and on every occasion where two or more persons interact with each other there will be rules. A complicating factor is that every group has different rules, and furthermore the rules continually change. Each generation of parents is faced with this, sometimes overwhelmingly, as they discover dress styles, tastes in music and dance, and sexual mores that were appropriate in "their day" no longer are relevant.

Even so, it seems advantageous for parents and teachers to outline rules so children, particularly younger children, know where they stand. You do not play in the street; you do not play with matches; you never assume guns are not loaded; you do not torment younger children; you do use certain table manners; you do respect the property of others; you do wear warm clothing in cold weather.

Many of the children about whom we are particularly concerned in this book have not learned appropriate rules of behavior. The "oddball" who wants to be liked by other children continually misinterprets what is going on around him. He does not know the rules, or if he does know them he does not have the necessary self-control to allow him to act accordingly. Cohen (1966) observes that "Pursuing a goal is largely a matter of doing what one must in order to insure that other people will produce the acts that we require of them" (p. 86).

In short, it appears that whenever feasible it is economical and efficient for children to be informed as much as possible about existing rules. Children will always test the rules to see if they really exist and to encourage the discarding of outmoded rules. Many parents and teachers will issue rule-statements but when these are violated no action is taken, or different forms of action are taken at each violation. If rule-statements that are ambiguously enforced involve significant behavior, the result is likely to be disruption or disorganization of behavioral patterns. Children will, ultimately, behave according to what the *consequences* are of their actions. And, ultimately, they will have to discover for themselves, individually, what kinds of consequences result from changes in their specific actions.

The Teacher and Rules

It is here that the philosophical question of how the child should be taught to control himself takes on great significance. The teacher with a group of children who have demonstrated an inability to follow rules must concentrate on providing consequences designed to change inappropriate—"rule-breaking"—behavior. Morris (1961) points out that, according to Progressive philosophers, "All that force does is to duplicate police action in the classroom. But one thing which police action does *not* do is to invite the culprit to consider the consequences of his behavior" (p. 427). This statement is not quite true; "police action" certainly *is* a form of consequence and if it is applied it may or may not lead to discussion with the culprit to consider why his behavior led to the particular kind of reaction. The problem is to change behavior before "police action" is necessary.

Talking as a Consequence

Teachers who work with problem children frequently are under the impression that talking with a child about his misconduct is the best way to help him. And, sometimes, these teachers do a great deal of talking with little noticeable change in the behavior of children.

What does the teacher discuss with the misbehaving child? Usually, the conversation centers around two concerns: (1) finding out why the child misbehaved, and (2) trying to tell him that misbehavior leads to negative consequences. The first of these concerns often is a legitimate one because many times a child's behavior is directed by forces beyond his control and he actually is inviting punishment; however, it is not very often that children can verbalize reasons for misconduct. Talking with a child about probable consequences, however, rather than actually invoking the consequences, is nonsense as far as the child is concerned. He sees clearly that misbehavior does not lead to negative consequences; it leads to a pleasant chat with the teacher.

REFERENCES

Cohen, A. K. *Deviance and Control.* Englewood Cliffs, N.J.: Prentice-Hall, 1966.

Crabtree, C. Effects of structuring on the productiveness of children's thinking. *Journal of Experimental Education,* Fall 1967, 36, 1–13.

Cremin, L. A. *The Transformation of the School.* New York: Knopf, 1961.

Heckelman, R. G. A lesson plan for educationally handicapped children in learning disability groups. *Academic Therapy Quarterly,* Fall 1966, 2, 18–22.

Morris, V. C. *Philosophy and the American School.* Boston: Houghton Mifflin, 1961.

Neill, A. S. *Summerhill: A Radical Approach to Child Rearing.* New York: Hart, 1960.

10

Permissiveness or Structure?

Those associated with programs for problem children frequently are asked if they adhere to a "permissive approach" or a "structured approach." It is somewhat difficult today to find many in special education who will admit to a permissive orientation. This is not so true in general education, perhaps in part due to the recent influence of Neill (1960), who has stimulated a renewal of interest in permissiveness. On the other hand, not many in either special or general education will admit to adhering to a structured orientation without adding a string of qualifications and definitions. For some reason it seems necessary first to point out that one is not a believer in military regimentation, physical abuse, or the production of thoughtless robots before admitting having a warm feeling for "structure in the classroom."

Our own preference is for a structured orientation. This should manifest itself in the administrative organization, in the teachers' behavior, and in the behavior of the children. Now for the qualifications and definitions.

General Objective

The single most important objective in work with children who manifest significant learning and/or behavioral problems is somehow to bring these children to the point where they can make *rational* decisions *for* themselves and *about* themselves and their relationships with their environments. Undoubtedly, this same objective can be cited as being very important for all children.

The question is: How do educators provide the conditions necessary for children to learn to make rational decisions? As mentioned by Morris, cited in the last chapter, some persons believe that the only way to accomplish this objective is to have adults stand back and allow the children complete freedom to find out for themselves what is appropriate and what is inappropriate behavior. Only in this way, through what is questionably titled "trial and error" behavior, are children going to gain the experience necessary to become competent decision-makers. Others—the adherents of "structure"—believe that children only learn to make decisions from being shown by adults what is appropriate and what is inappropriate behavior. Why, this argument runs, should adults permit children to repeat all the mistakes of mankind when by the imposition of adult direction most of these mistakes could be eliminated? It is considered to be grossly inefficient, after all, to suppose that everybody must rediscover the wheel.

It appears that both arguments appeal to the extremes. There is some question about whether "permissiveness" should be equated with Progressive education and "structure" with the Perennial or Essentialist schools of educational philosophy. Because one parent does not allow his two-year-old child to run into the street to learn by "trial and error" about getting hit by cars does not make him an adherent of the structured approach to behavioral management. Nor does the practice of another in inviting his eight-year-old son to decide for himself when to go to bed classify this parent as an adherent of the permissive approach to child behavioral management.

Every teacher would like to be able to leave his room and come back fifteen minutes later to find all the children as busy as they were when he left. Few teachers are overjoyed when they return to their classrooms after a brief absence to find a minor riot in process. But in either case it is not possible to "classify" a teacher as permissive or as structured on the basis of what happens after a brief absence from the classroom. Ordered behavior, as such, is the goal of both those who adhere to a permissive and to a structured approach to behavioral management. No sincere advocate of a permissive approach believes that chaos is a desirable end—although some may see it as a necessary means to an end. No permissively oriented teachers believe that abusive children have a right to inflict their terrors on smaller children, that physical destruction of one child by another is ideal. The issue is whether ordered behavior is achieved *through* being permissive or through maintaining a structured behavioral environment.

There is some self-deception practised by professional personnel who claim to be either permissive or structured in their work with children. Some so-called permissive settings are in fact nearly pure examples of minor autocracies, with a few gimmicks (such as having children ordered to call staff by their first names) thrown in that are supposed to qualify the setting as being permissively (or "democratically") oriented.

More frequently seen in the public schools are persons who claim to be adherents of a (qualified) structured approach when cursory observations reveal a rampant permissiveness. Children come and go as they please; teachers command no attention when they speak; and children can be seen running about the room chasing each other and climbing on desks and window sills. The teacher may point to several "cubicles" in the room and suggest that their presence makes the classroom "structured."

Value Judgments

It appears necessary to admit that value judgments enter into determinations of whether a permissive or a structured orientation is desirable. These value judgments stem from precise definitions of educational objectives and then additional precision in definitions of means to attain these objectives. It is for this reason that objective research on the merits of either approach would not have much meaning unless outcomes were measured by very narrow criteria. Further, because there is little self-awareness of practices used in many special classrooms it would be very difficult to determine whether, in fact, a so-called permissive or so-called structured approach was actually being employed.

There is "bad" permissiveness and "good" permissiveness, just as there is bad and good in a structured orientation. What makes either approach good or bad is the degree of consistency in achieving specified goals that have been established.

If there are no goals, if an individual simply believes that it is a "good idea" to "be permissive," with no conception of what purpose is behind such behavior, we may suspect that any labeling done by the individual is nothing more than an afterthought to justify an uncontrollable situation. For example, if a teacher finds himself unable to maintain effective control of a group and observes a condition of chaos, it is easy to then state a belief in being "permissive." Similarly, a teacher who finds it difficult to allow children any freedom of expression will find it convenient to claim a belief in a structured approach after observing his own behavior.

An unusually "bad" permissive approach exists when a teacher claims to be "structured" when this is not the case at all and the teacher is not aware of the discrepancy. Perhaps for this reason permissiveness as a technology of behavioral management has gotten much bad publicity. Those persons who truly are permissive, and know what the concept means and are striving for specific goals, probably are a rare minority. On the other hand, those who are permissive by default are more numerous, and tend to make the concept itself negative to many school personnel. It is unjustified for a teacher who lacks skills to claim that he is being permissive, a label applied more as an excuse than as a professional rationale for work with children.

Structure in Life

Life itself is structured—not necessarily the way we would like it to be, and not always consistently from one moment to the next. But structure is there, whether it is allowed to develop naturally or is imposed by one onto another. Children do learn from their successes and their failures as they encounter their environments each day. Why teachers and classrooms should be omitted from the environment, as suggested by some advocates of permissiveness, is not clear. That is, if a child should be allowed to make mistakes in order to find out for himself what the consequences are of his errors, it is difficult to see why the behavior of teachers should be excluded as a part of the environment that provides the consequences.

If a child kicks his mother's grocer in the shins he may find that the consequences of such an action are negative, but if he kicks his teacher in the shins he finds that his teacher does not consider this as "real behavior" and not worth providing consequences for; the teacher will talk about the consequences.

LaMancusa (1966) says "The very real task of helping children to understand their social limitations relative to classroom behavior is often set aside in lieu of psychological *tinkering*. Through misguided feelings of pity and compassion, initial errors in judgment are made by stepping between the act and the consequences for the act" (pp. 2–3).

Rational Behavior

Almost all human beings go through life, as the saying goes, getting smarter too late and older too soon. There perhaps is no person who could be considered truly rational in all his decisions and actions. "Being rational" is thus a relative matter. Rational decisions and actions are defined as those that (1) are consistent with an age group in a particular society or subsociety, (2) are consistent with assisting the individual in achieving maximal effectiveness toward a productive existence, (3) at a higher level are morally right in that they do not violate the rights of others, and (4) at a still higher level are such that they are beneficial to mankind.

By definition, almost all children with learning and/or behavioral problems by and large do not make rational decisions. They do things that are not consistent with their peers' actions, and their behavior typically works against rather than for their own effectiveness. Some of these children may frequently throw temper tantrums because such behavior formerly was successful in obtaining benefits from parents, but this kind of behavior eventually becomes self-defeating. Other children are unable to learn the mechanics of reading; this in itself is usually a technical problem, but the effects on children of not being able to learn to read often lead to irrational behavior—usually not without the large-scale assistance of parents and educators.

Structure is introduced—is imposed—from outside just as long as it is felt necessary, and no longer. If children could learn without the assistance of teachers perhaps this would be better. However, we discover that even in graduate school, doctoral candidates must account for themselves to various professors who are, in a sense, providing structure. Almost all persons employed on jobs, whether working in small independent businesses or for large corporations, find their activities are structured. It would seem almost bizarre to assume that children with a history of inability to control themselves effectively should be provided with less structure than is imposed on most adults, to say nothing of most children.

STRATEGIES

A teacher working with a child who typically displays inappropriate behavior must regard one of his objectives as "teaching" the child how to behave more appropriately. This goal is not accomplished by verbal monologues from the teacher; for young children, issues of right or wrong are meaningless and teachers cannot effectively change behavior by appeals to moral principles. Such appeals similarly are ineffective for older children (and adults) whose whole life orientations are toward rule-breaking behavior.

The teacher initially will begin the year using the time when the children are getting to know him and other unfamiliar aspects of the environment to establish a set of norms for the group. At the same time, the teacher will attempt to place himself in the position as dispenser of reinforcers (negative and positive) with the group. Reinforcers will be used to maintain behavior around the norms that have been established. As far as the children are concerned, they will attempt to find ways of getting the teacher to do what they want—what they have been used to obtaining from adults in the past.

The first weeks in a classroom are the critical ones, although if mistakes are made they can be gradually corrected later. It is very important for the teacher to be sensitive to the situational facts in the classroom. These facts are not always readily apparent because in the interpersonal game between teacher and children, and among the children themselves, many masks are worn to conceal feelings and hide intentions.

Many beginning teachers take surface appearances for facts; in addition, some teachers' own idealistic conceptions about children often lead them into vulnerable positions with children who will quickly take advantage of this superficial idealism. For example, a teacher may have an idea that all children are basically good; this idea, taken in its most shallow sense, may lead the teacher to act as if children can do no wrong. The philosophical issue over whether men are basically good or evil cannot be translated into simple formulas for easy relationships in the classroom.

The teacher frequently must deal with children on the basis of *predictions;* in fact, much of the teacher's most sophisticated responsibility is being able to guess what kinds of behaviors to expect from children before these behaviors actually manifest themselves. He cannot wait until Billy and Joe are rolling on the floor in a fight before he steps in to stop the action. This fight should be stopped long before it starts. It is not necessary for the teacher to assume he must operate like a criminal trial judge, collecting evidence and issuing opinions only on the basis of actions that have already taken place.

A common error made by many new teachers is thinking that respect is the same as being liked as a "good guy," or as a "pal," for passing out positive reinforcers to children no matter what they do. This is an exaggeration of the notion that a good relationship between adult and child is desirable and that this relationship will be built completely on positive reactions on the part of the adult with a total absence of any negative reinforcers.

The teacher must establish norms and then must see to it that children adhere to these norms. Children must find that the rules they have lived by, that others have found obnoxious, also are now obnoxious for them. They must see that jumping out of their seats at any time produces negative consequences rather than the positive reactions they have been used to receiving. The teacher is the major source of the child's "trial and error" consequences.

It is important that norms established are flexible and somewhat broad, at the same time having avenues of expression that are quite specific. The teacher wants the child to learn behavior appropriate for a particular classroom but he also wants the child to learn to follow—or at least be able to decide whether or not to follow—normative rules in a general sense, in or out of the classroom. For example, the teacher may establish a general norm that children must employ basic manners in their dealings with each other and then establish a specific rule that turns must be taken in the use of a certain toy in the classroom.

It seems to be generally assumed that there is an association between permissiveness and creativity, and that almost by definition, if a situation is structured it cannot be "creative," or cannot allow for the growth of expression of creativity. This is questionable. An individual may very well exhibit a higher frequency of manifest activity in a permissive situation, much of it rare and "different," but whether this has anything to do with creativity is open to question.

Van Patten (1967) writes that men are continuously plagued with forces of conformity, with pressures that would make them faceless; he then observes there is a difference between obeying laws and being creative, that it is not necessary to run a red light to assert one's individuality.

An individual who has the most self-control is likely to be the most creative; an individual who lacks control of himself may display rare and unusual behavior but is not likely to be creative in the sense that he can do something useful. To assume otherwise is to suggest that the "weaker" members of society should be the most creative— the drunks, prostitutes, drug addicts. This also carries the assumption that creativity is a product of some kind of effortless "growth" rather than of hard work. The fact that some highly creative persons display periods when they lack self-control attests to the difficulty and stress of creative behavior rather than that such behavior produces creativity.

REFERENCES

LaMancusa, K. C. *We Do Not Throw Rocks at the Teacher!* Scranton, Pa.: International Textbook, 1966.

Neill, A. S. *Summerhill: A Radical Approach to Child Rearing.* New York: Hart, 1960.

Van Patten, J. Individualism: the case for individual man in the educational environment. *School & Society,* April 1, 1967, 95, 231–2.

Part II

THE CURRICULUM

The remaining chapters are devoted to practical matters. How does one furnish a classroom for the children described? Are "cubicles" necessary, and why? What kinds of materials should a teacher buy? How many children should be placed into each special class? Should teachers prepare daily lesson plans or should they "shoot from the hip" when they walk into their classrooms each morning?

A major focus is on language: what it is, how it develops, and what kinds of things can go wrong with a child's language. Language is essential to communication, and communication is fundamental to the learning process. When language is defective in some way, there are likely to be problems in learning.

The major areas of language are discussed individually. Informal methods are described for evaluating a child's visual perceptual skills, his auditory perceptual skills, and other skills necessary for communication and, thus, for learning.

The final chapter looks briefly at three children: Andy, Betty, and Charles (names invented to fit alphabetically). Their histories are reviewed, their problems are evaluated, and a suggested program is presented on *what to do* about the problems.

11

The Classroom

There are many opinions about the ideal special education classroom. Most schools will find they cannot work with ideal arrangements but must make use of space that is available. Classrooms with special lighting, special cubicles built with strong material that cannot be moved or marred by children, and similar characteristics might be desirable. But most schools will make classrooms available that have been used for "regular" classes of children. If a school district cannot afford "ideal" classroom spaces for most of its children, then special education classrooms furnished in outstanding design with expensive materials probably will be out of place in such a district. Educational personnel need not feel they are cheating children placed into special classes if the physical provisions made are similar to those made for other children.

The space provided should be located next to space provided for other children in regular elementary and secondary buildings. A second-rate space in a regular elementary building is better than a first-rate space in a building isolated from children in the general curriculum program. "Second-rate" space does not include boiler rooms or other basement facilities decorated with plumbing designs and other undesirable features, although desirable space may include the janitor's suite, the board room, or the art room.

Unfortunately, there frequently is much interest in having special education children placed in what are sentimentally referred to as "new buildings" that are constructed away from other children, where personnel could be employed who "really understand" handicapped children. This sentimental expression is really an attempt to get rid of problem children because "new" buildings do not stay new very long and many countries have had years of experience with institutional settings where people are employed who "really understand" the inmates.

Those who feel that problem children would be better off "somewhere else" than in regular school buildings along with non-handicapped children do not think through the implications of such a move. The major implication of removing problem children is that it would not be too long before 20 to 30 percent of the school-age population would be attending classes "somewhere else," a move that would, in effect, make public schools into private schools with eligibility requirements. The educational definition of handicap should not be perverted into use as a device to screen children to deny them their right to attend the same schools as their neighborhood friends.

Removing handicapped children from the regular educational setting has merit only if the general curriculum program offered in that setting is defined in such a way that only some children are seen as "qualified" to attend school. A school that is for all children does not have to remove some children because they do not "fit." Kolburne (1965) in a book titled *Effective Education for the Mentally Retarded* concludes that "We must abolish mass education for these children. Mass education may be feasible for the normal population, but it is hopeless when applied to the subnormal because of the very nature of their disability" (p. 262). Kolburne undoubtedly was making an appeal for *special* education in his criticism of "mass" education but the strong implication is that he has accepted the conclusion that many children do not "qualify" for (mass) education.

The argument is frequently used that a major reason for including handicapped children in schools along with non-handicapped children is the opportunity provided for social "integration" with peers. This argument is too narrow because it puts the problem much too simply. A principal who might want to demonstrate that handicapped children are not "accepted" in his school can exert enough subtle influence to show that "integration doesn't work." The problem is not one that easily lends itself to research analysis because it is a philosophical issue: Are the schools for all children or only for some? Can "school" be defined in such a way that "separate but equal" facilities for handicapped children can be justified?

Cubicles

Many classrooms for children with learning and/or behavioral problems are found with individual "cubicles" or study areas installed. Whether these are provided and whether they are permanent or temporary fixtures will depend largely on the available facilities. Teachers will find cubicles to be of use for children easily distracted, who often enjoy having a place to work undisturbed, and for other children when periods of concentrated individual study are desired.

Cubicles about four feet square in size can be built with sheets of three-fourths-inch-thick plywood and fastened to the wall and to the floor. They should be low enough to allow room light to enter. If the cubicles are placed on opposite sides of the room the teacher can see all the children from the center of the room, while the children cannot easily see those next to them but can see children across the room.

More elaborate and expensive cubicles can be constructed, using metal rather than wood for additional sturdiness, although this is not necessary. Desks or shelves can be built into the cubicles with individual lights in each space but again this is not essential. If the space is large enough, children can move their desks in and out with ease.

Cubicles that are too elaborate suggest that too much dependence is placed on them, when in fact they are in themselves only aids for the teacher. For example, in a recent conversation a psychologist claimed that a child's "whole year" had been "wasted" because the teacher did not have a cubicle available for him in the classroom. Such exaggeration is not uncommon.

If permanent spaces cannot be constructed small dividers can be used, although these frequently get moved around excessively. These dividers can have corkboard material on one side and chalkboard on the other, although again this is not necessary.

Stimulus Control

There is some controversy over whether classrooms should be relatively free of external stimuli by having them painted all one (drab) color, having all windows covered, and generally having the rooms free of everything except what is being used at the moment.

It is a mistake to assume that "stimulus-free" classrooms will solve management problems, or that hyperactive children will be more or less active depending upon what is in the classroom. A teacher who lacks the ability to manage children effectively will have problems in any kind of classroom—one free of everything but four walls and chairs or one that contains a variety of equipment and materials. A hyperactive child—or any child—responds primarily to his teacher rather than to the facilities in the classroom, and the makeup of the classroom is primarily for the benefit of the teacher—not the condition of hyperactivity. Cubicles, chalkboards, and color designs in the classrooms are secondary matters.

Other Space Utilization

Small-group work areas should be included, with a table for a tape recorder and headphones. This arrangement allows teachers to tape material for individual children or groups of children. Record players with auditory training material can be used in the small-group work areas.

Another small table conveniently near the teacher's desk allows her to observe other children while at the same time working with individuals or small groups.

Bulletin boards should be used because children like to see their work displayed. Some teachers keep their bulletin boards outside the general visual fields of the children while others keep them openly displayed.

Movable desks are recommended and should be without storage areas. Children's material can be stored in an area of the classroom away from the desks.

When it is possible to have easy access to a gymnasium it is not necessary to equip the classroom with special equipment for use in development of gross and fine motor coordination skills. However, it is advantageous to have some equipment available because it can be used during periods when the gymnasium may not be available or for a brief activity. Such equipment might include a balance board, a small ladder, roller boards that move from side to side as weight is shifted, and activity dollies that resemble scooters that children can sit, kneel, or lie on.

In the gymnasium such equipment as a rope ladder, a climbing rope, pogo sticks, and wooden stilts are useful.

An interesting device was observed in one classroom in the suburban Chicago area, developed by Mrs. Jan Miller, the teacher. It was called a "light table," consisting of a regular table about two feet by four feet in top dimensions but with a sheet of translucent plexiglass placed at a twenty degree angle. If one were sitting at the side of the table the plexiglass top would be slanting upward and away from that position. Under the plexiglass are fluorescent lights so if any paper is placed on the top the light shines through the paper but is not glaring. This device is useful for tracing activities that can be rather extensively developed.

REFERENCES

Kolburne, L. L. *Effective Education for the Mentally Retarded.* New York: Vantage Press, 1965.

12

Introduction to the Curriculum
and Sample Lesson Plans

A child who may not be able to discriminate fine sounds may learn from a lesson presented in a traditional fashion. However, what he learns may be quite different from what another child learns whose auditory discrimination ability is adequate and who can begin to make a sound-symbol relationship for the sight presentation of the lesson. Thus, when a lesson is presented, portions of it are likely to be learned by children in ways that are more different than they are alike. Children appear to have rather good ability to compensate for areas of difficulty, so in a class instructed with a single approach to reading, each child may take something quite different from that taken by everyone else.

We often find ourselves still looking for an approach that fits a whole class, rather than for a number of methods designed to meet the needs of individual children. If a child needs some remedial training in auditory perception and discrimination before he can hear differences between sounds and profit from a phonics approach to reading, it may be advisable to see that he learns a basic sight vocabulary first and hold off on the sounds approach. On the other hand, there are children who are unable to see differences in letter and other visual forms. These children cannot profit from either a sight or phonics approach because the forming of an association between a sound and a symbol is required.

It is necessary to move from a teaching-oriented program of instruction to a learning-oriented program, from teaching to learning, from teacher to child, from approach and technique to approaches and techniques, from groups to individuals, and from searches for an answer to searches for answers.

Let us assume that a child is having reading difficulties because he cannot learn with a phonics approach. The child's sight vocabulary and comprehension of the material he reads appears adequate and even at grade level. This tells us that he can make associations with the printed symbol, that he understands what he reads. But it also tells us that he cannot use phonics, which involves something quite different from what is needed for the development of a sight vocabulary. The fact that he cannot put together an association of a sound and a written symbol does not in itself pinpoint the difficulty; it indicates only the *effect* on the acquisition of a skill. The solution would not be to teach phonics in a different way, with different materials in a different class. It becomes necessary to find if the problem is at the auditory level. If it is, there are still a number of factors that must be evaluated to determine the difficulty more precisely. It is possible the child is not able to hear differences between sounds and therefore has a sound discrimination deficit. However, if that area is tested and found to be within normal limits it is necessary to look further and determine if the child can hear differences between sounds but cannot remember them in proper sequence. Or, it is possible that he can do this but cannot synthesize the sounds into a word or combination of words.

Knowing a child has difficulty with phonics only tells us what he cannot do at that level of functioning but does not provide us with enough information to help him learn phonics.

Developing an Individual Program

Aspects of learning and variety of frustration levels in different activities should be considered when the teacher first begins to develop a program for a child. If we know a child has had a gross failure experience with reading before coming to a special class we then know that whenever reading instruction is provided there are likely to be difficulties. If we also know the child likes arithmetic, this information can be useful in scheduling his work. Everything introduced to him in the first few weeks of school is carefully structured to insure success. Alternating enjoyable activities with less enjoyable ones begins to build tolerance while at the same time helps him to feel immediate "relief" when the more undesirable task is completed.

Since many children placed into special education programs have had experiences with failure in almost every social and academic endeavor it is essential to build up their self-confidence and their belief that school is worthwhile. It is easy to criticize and discuss the inadequacies of children but it may take some effort to praise and create confidence. Children gain few positive feelings from a situation when negative responses are consistently applied to them. It becomes necessary to develop within the child the ability to take failure and to show him that he can change his behavior toward self-control.

False praise should be avoided. If a paper is not completed properly and the teacher knows without a doubt the child is capable of working through the tasks presented, the paper should be returned to be correctly completed before any other activity can be undertaken by the child.

Usually when a child is not ready for a task and completes it incorrectly it is better to tell him this and indicate that something else will be provided for him to work on. Marking the paper with Ds and Fs does not add anything to the child's understanding of what he did wrong or why and how to do better next time. On the other hand, a positive report will be greatly relished by the child and will long be remembered. Positive reactions to a child's work and actions in the classroom provide incentive for him to continue trying to obtain further positive consequences, while negative reactions that dwell on a child's inadequacies leave him no place to turn.

Children are shown and told immediately after coming into the classroom what is expected of them under various circumstances. Nothing is assumed and constant reminding and reinforcing of what is accepted and what is not accepted is important. For example, children are not allowed to get out of their seats without permission, they must ask to leave the room for the lavatory, they walk rather than run in the halls, they do not shout for help from the teacher. Generally, the children in the special classes have the same limits as other children and must comply with the same standards and rules.

A perceptive teacher is constantly watching for signs of irritation and distractibility. She moves in every direction to observe what children are doing, when they need her help and support, when she can push into an area of possible minor frustration, when she can criticize effectively, where she must restructure and reprogram, when to go ahead and when to go back. She needs to admit when things do not go well that changes have to be made.

Type of Activity

Because the time a child can concentrate and work at a particular task will vary it is necessary for the teacher to know what the child's attention or "learning bit" span is for each activity presented. If she knows, for example, that a child can work at arithmetic for ten minutes and can work independently on writing for twenty minutes this will influence the time allotted these activities. She cannot schedule an arithmetic lesson for a thirty-minute period for all the children in the group and expect this child to look forward to this each day; she must prepare a ten-minute lesson for the child.

Consistency in Daily Scheduling

It is important to control the activities that precede and follow each other. If a child has a particular dislike for a certain task, following this task with something he enjoys and looks forward to may add incentive to complete the less desirable one. The teacher will have to be constantly observing work periods to determine whether a lesson is long enough but not too long, difficult enough to be challenging but not too difficult, easy enough to ensure success but not too easy so there is no feeling of achievement. The goal is to work below the child's frustration level with gradual increases anticipated as success experiences are obtained and competency is established.

It is necessary that a child know what is expected of him in situations because the choice then can be made by the child for taking one or another course of action, and then accepting the consequences. Ultimately, it is the child who must make changes in his own behavior. Children are given a limited range of choices; they can be asked which of several activities they want to do at a certain predetermined time. In the beginning a child is not asked if and when he wishes to work. Later his choices are broadened to include various materials that become available as a school year unfolds.

Group or Individual?

Often at the beginning of a school year children have considerable difficulty working in groups so most work is provided on an individual basis. It should be noted that providing individual attention for children is not necessarily providing individualized instruction and the two terms should not be interchanged. Early attempts should be made to have children work in small groups. Perhaps two children who can work together can make a basic group and another child added.

Varying of Activity

The material a child needs to use in completing an activity can vary with the place and kind of activity. For example, if he has just used pencil and paper for a fine motor activity the next task might be one where pencils and paper are not used. If the child has been required to pay close attention, such as in reading, the next activity might involve the use of earphones with a taped lesson where only limited visual attention is required.

If the environment the child is working in can be changed when the activity is changed, generally this can have a positive influence on his attention span. When a child is participating in a group activity it may be desirable to move his desk to another location when he goes on to another task.

Organization of Materials

One effective way of leading toward the building of independence for the child and freeing some of the teacher's time is to provide each child with a daily schedule of activities and a place for organizing them. One way to do this is to have wire baskets in which to keep children's work for the day. Folders having other special work can be kept so that when children have finished one activity and it has been corrected and again completed, the children can go on to other activities without the teacher's immediate attention. Consistency in the use of this procedure is important or more time will be spent in the procedure itself than is gained in return time saved.

Integration into Regular Classes

As soon as children are ready to conduct themselves adequately in group activities they can begin to "integrate" into regular classes. Everybody concerned with this should be involved; it should not be assumed that the principal approves without first finding out, and it should not be left to the child to tell the parents about the undertaking. If proper preparations are not made, any minor problems that may arise will often be blown up out of proportion and attributed to the child's handicap rather than to the newness of the situation, the teacher's attitudes, or other real causes.

SAMPLE LESSON PLANS

Following is a series of daily group lesson plans that were prepared by teachers* to illustrate the kinds of activities their classes might be involved in during September, January, and June of the school year. A sample lesson plan is taken for a primary-level class (ages six to nine), an intermediate-level class (ages nine to fourteen), and a junior high-level class (ages twelve to sixteen).

These lesson plans, being for group activities, do not include plans made for individual children. It is interesting to note that earlier in the school year teachers are likely to have to prepare lesson plans that are more detailed for group activities, while at the same time the children typically can tolerate few group activities. Later in the school year group lesson plans become more sketchy and less detailed, and yet the children are capable of more group work. The difference lies in the teacher's greater differentiation of tasks and the greater assortment of activities available to the children as there is increasing refinement in the meshing of children's needs, techniques, and materials.

These lesson plans were taken, with a few changes, from actual plans that were prepared by teachers. They are considered illustrative rather than ideal.

PRIMARY

Primary Level (September)

9:00——Pledge to flag, discuss date, weather.

9:15——Pre-writing exercises at the board.

9:45——Arithmetic; group work with Stern materials; ten-minute followup worksheet.

10:15——Visual perception activities for each child (pegboards, block designs, visual memory).

10:45——Readiness or reading activities (programmed readers, phonics).

* Thanks to Mr. Edward Dale and Mr. Timothy Rochford.

11:15——Language and auditory perceptual training (auditory memory, sequencing, classification of objects, discussion of pictures).

11:45——Lunch.

12:30——Quiet period: books, records, painting.

1:00——Motor work in gym (hand-foot dominance, left-right, balance beam, walking tape).

2:00——Dismissal.

Primary Level (January)

9:00——Flag salute, discuss weather, date.

9:15——Cursive writing (crayons and 2-inch lined paper).

9:45——Arithmetic (individual work).

10:30——Perceptual activities (Frostig program).

11:00——Reading activities (programmed readers, phonics work, SRA, *Reader's Digest*).

11:45——Lunch.

12:30——Motor program in gym (team games, relays, motor patterning).

1:15——Social studies or science work.

2:00——Dismissal.

Primary Level (June)

9:00——Flag salute, date, weather (discussion of seasons, temperature).

9:15——Individual work from folders.

10:15——Break for lavatory, stretch.

10:30——Individualized work in small groups with ongoing activities.

11:45——Lunch.

12:30——Motor activities in gym (balance beam, mat, ladders, shooting baskets, team games).

1:30——Science or social studies.

2:00——Dismissal.

INTERMEDIATE

Intermediate Level (September)

8:30——Ditto review of right and left hands.

9:15——Tracing and coloring with templates.

9:45——Exercises for balance and body image.

10:00——Individual reading.

10:45——Group game of visual memory; recognizing missing objects.

11:15——Individual spelling.

12:00——Lunch.

12:30——Story and discussion of main events.

1:00——Visual perceptual training.

1:30——Gym; recreation, exercises and relay races to practice skills.

2:00——Dismissal.

Intermediate Level (January)

8:30——Individual spelling.

9:15——Areas of need (visual discrimination, English, arithmetic, phonics).

9:45——Individual motor program.

10:00——Individual English or discrimination practice.

10:45——Individual arithmetic or reading, or group social studies.

11:30——Classroom game of spelling password, hangman.

12:00——Lunch.

12:30——Story and quiz on main events.

1:00——Writing program.

1:30——Organized game in gym.

2:00——Dismissal.

Intermediate Level (June)

8:30——Spelling and work in individual areas of need (visual discrimination, writing, social studies, balance).

9:45——Individual motor program.

10:00——Reading, arithmetic.

11:30——Gym, perceptual-motor patterns (kickball, three lives dodgeball, rhythm patterns, guitar rhythms).

12:00——Lunch.

12:30——Story and detailed quiz.

1:00——Auditory perceptual training.

1:30——Classroom games, gym games, or outdoor games, possibly combined with another class.

2:00——Dismissal.

JUNIOR HIGH

Junior High Level (September)

9:00——Individual reading programs.

10:00——Free expression (topic: Ways to Know Yourself).

10:45——Lunch.

11:22——Movie: *The Dropout* (16 min.).

11:40——Outside. Motor program (balance, physical fitness exercises):
    1. Exercises
    2. Walking a line
    3. Standing on one foot
    4. Running
    5. Bouncing a basketball.

12:30——Rest period:
    1. Lights out
    2. Heads down
    3. Get drinks
    4. Musical appreciation
        a. One class choice
        b. One my choice.

12:55——Oral reading: *Treasure Under the Sea,* Berres, Coleman, pp. 12–16.

1:30——Work on game project (art: twister).

2:00——Clean-up; free time.

2:15——Talk about possible courses of study in the junior high; physical layout of new school building and locations of office, gym, etc.

2:45——Dismissal.

Junior High Level (January)

9:00——SRA Reading Laboratory, individual work levels.

9:45——Spelling Unit #17; drill; crossword puzzle.

10:10——Science, art projects:
    a. Work on human body unit
    b. Paint internal organs and label.

10:40——Clean-up.

10:45——Lunch.

11:22——Movie: *Learning From Disappointments* (20 min.).

11:45——Gym.
>   1. Exercises
>   2. Basketball teams
>   3. Foul shooting championship.

12:30——Free time, rest period.

12:45——Arithmetic work groups (subtracting dollars and cents).

1:20——Silent reading, projects for book reports; two students have library passes.

1:40——Oral reading, social studies: *Exploring New York State,* pp. 181–4; matching quiz.

2:20——Free time:
>   1. Hot rod magazines
>   2. Drawing
>   3. Clean lockers or organize notebooks.

2:45——Dismissal.

Junior High Level (June)

9:00——Movie: *Smoking and You* (29 min.).

9:30——Free expression (topic: Occupations. Use government pamphlets).

10:00——English lesson (finish ditto on parts of speech).

10:25——Art: Modern art (free), tempera paint on cardboard.

10:40——Clean-up.

10:45——Lunch.

11:22——Gym: trampoline.

12:00——Rest period, free time. Musical appreciation:
>   1. Dixieland
>   2. Monkees
>   3. Classical.

12:20——Spelling test: Unit #33 (dictated).

12:55——Oral reports on plans for the summer.

1:30——Social studies quiz, matching (ditto).

2:00——Free time:
>   1. Clean-up
>   2. Clean lockers, organize notebooks
>   3. Plans for next week
>   4. Hot rod magazines
>   5. Free drawing, card games.

2:45——Dismissal.

13

Language

To plan a curriculum program for children in special education programs it is necessary to take a look at the mechanisms a child needs to acquire the skills of speaking, reading, and writing. Since these skills make up the over-all picture of *language*, these different but interrelated aspects of communication all involve the use of symbols of language. Many children seem to develop an early facility for these symbols with seemingly no specific training. We know, however, that much of what children are exposed to in their early years does help or hinder them in their language development.

What is Language?

Language, as defined by Carroll (1963), is

a structured system of arbitrary vocal sounds and sequences of sounds which is used, or can be used, in interpersonal communication by an aggregation of human beings, and which rather exhaustively catalogs the things, events, and processes in the human environment. (p. 16)

Carroll indicates further that

Reading, and writing, at any rate, happen to be of fundamental importance in our culture, and the mastery of these skills, even at a relatively simple level, multiplies the potentialities of the child for further learning and for increased self reliance. The academic phases of school life are wholly dependent on these skills, perhaps too much dependent on them. Hence the teaching of reading and writing comes to be thought of as the principal task of the elementary school—whatever else is to be taught; the training of other linguistic competence is apt to fall by the wayside. At least, this would be a fair comment on the orientation of much of American elementary education—an orientation which, incidentally, insidiously carries over even the teaching of foreign languages at the secondary and college levels. Only in rare instances is it realized that the child needs training in speaking and listening as well—that the experience and training the child gets in the family and in his general social environment do not necessarily suffice in this respect. Not only this. The conception of reading and writing as ends in themselves sometimes leads to an overwhelming concentration on driving the child onward and remedying his deficiencies by frontal attack, to such an extent that the precious first three or four years of schooling can be too little used for teaching art, music, science, social studies, and responsible citizenship, to say nothing of the danger of creating emotional difficulties in the child. (p. 144)

Later Carroll says

progress in reading depends upon progress in speech, and particularly upon vocabulary development. Oral-language development should be allowed to run ahead of reading development at all stages . . . . The influence of the home can undoubtedly be highly beneficial when parents take pains to expose the child to a suitable range of verbal experiences in meaningful contexts . . . (p. 149)

According to Cruickshank *et al.* (1961) language is the "ability to comprehend and use symbols (words, pictures, numbers, letters) as the accepted means of communication in society" (p. 142). They go on to explain that oral speech is "merely the uttering of the articulate sound, the mechanism or tool used to serve a function of language, whereas total language includes such functions as reading and writing" (p. 142).

Artley (1948) states that "speaking and reading comprise two sides of a square known as communication or language, the other two sides being writing and listening. Being inextricably associated, any limitation or facility in one is reflected to some degree in the others" (p. 351).

Kottmeyer (1947) states, "attention has often been called to the fact that although reading is one facet of language, its close relationship to other language areas must always be borne in mind . . . . An oral account of an actual happening becomes in a sense a series of sound symbols for that happening and is one language step away from reality. A written or printed account of the happening becomes a symbol or series of symbols for its oral counterpart and further removed from that experience. Reading then becomes an interpreting of the written symbols of the oral symbols of an actual event" (p. 41).

Goldstein (1948) says that one must build receptive and expressive language to the point where one normally expects language to be when a youngster is handed his first book. Oral language must develop before reading can be taught, and writing develops last in the sequence of total language formulation.

Three Main Areas of Language

Let us take a look at the three main areas of language development that we find ourselves most concerned with in academic programs and try to determine why the areas are interrelated and how this is important for programming.

First of all, we can determine that much of what we ask a child to do in the early years of school requires him to use language. We make the assumption that the first parts of language have already developed sufficiently to allow for the next areas to be developed.

These first areas of language involve the child's ability to use the spoken word or what is referred to as the verbal symbol of language. Speech begins when a child is able to utter a sound or combination of sounds that resemble the person, place, or object named by that sound. The first words, then, are usually nouns and the things in the child's environment that hold some emotional meaning for him. In the beginning speech may have occurred merely by accident when a child uttered a sound or groups of sounds similar to a "real" word such as *Da*. If Daddy happens to be listening at the time he may react with a smile or some other favorable reaction which the child finds pleasant. If the child then makes the same sound again and the response he gets is similar he quickly associates his utterance of a sound with certain responses.

When the child finds he can get his mother or father by vocalizing and begins to use the vocalizations to obtain a desired response, he is talking and now using the first avenue of speech. To place a verbal symbol with an object is to make the association that they are the same object under consideration. When this association takes place, then either the spoken word or seeing the concrete object that the word stands for may evoke a similar response. Later we will see how other symbols and their associations are necessary for further language development, particularly in the areas of reading and writing.

As the child matures he finds various avenues for communication with his environment, all of which require an abstraction of the initial concrete associations with objects, ideas, etc. These different ways the child finds to express himself and make known his desires and ideas to others in his environment make up his communication with the world around him.

To progress from verbal language into the next area, the child must enter into a more abstract relationship, that of relating the spoken word to the written word. When this can successfully be accomplished a child has learned to read. The child, then, must begin to read by first having established a verbal symbol for the word which is dependent upon his having had an experience with the object itself or a picture of it. He is taken from seeing a "cat" to saying *cat*. To read the word the child must know that whenever he sees the written symbols c-a-t together it refers to the furry creature we know as a cat. Provided a similar association is made when he hears *cat*, says *cat*, and now reads *cat*, we assume the heard and spoken symbols have established associations with the written symbol.

The next step in the ongoing development of language is the ability to put letters down on paper to convey ideas to others. Not only is motor coordination needed to write the letters, but the differences in copying versus "creative" writing must be noted. Among other things, to copy a word, the child must see the letters that make up the word; he then needs the eye-hand coordination necessary to form the letters on paper, and he must put them in the proper order. On the other hand, if he wishes to write something that cannot be copied, then in addition to needing the coordination to form the letters he has to have gone through the early developmental steps in learning language. These include the association between the spoken symbol and the read symbol. In addition, the child must now remember and be able to re-visualize the word (the sequence of letters) if he is to write it correctly. This particular aspect of language is better known as *spelling*.

It is important to note that the spoken, read, and written forms of words that make up our system of language for communication have both a reciprocal and hierarchical relationship manifested in the fact that they appear in a logical and sequential order. If difficulties in any one of these language areas occur it is possible that difficulty may appear in areas that have not yet developed, unless sufficient help is given to correct the difficulty before the next level is attempted. Similarly, if a writing problem exists it is possible that it may be influenced by a disturbance in either of the other two areas which normally precedes its acquisition.

Myklebust (1965) asserts that achieving the read and written forms of language assumes greater complexity and maturity of the psychoneurosensory processes. He goes on to say, "From research and experiences with normal children as well as with mentally deficient children, it is apparent that additional maturation both psychologically and neurologically are required for reading and writing in comparison with the spoken word. Not only is more intelligence required, but a higher degree of intersensory perception and facilitation are essential" (p. 4).

A study of the mode or modes through which language can develop in a child is necessary. The avenues for collecting and getting data ready for a proper response are actually channels for receiving stimuli and for sending responses. Stimuli may be received visually, aurally, tactually, and kinesthetically. Visual stimuli are received through the eye and the reception mechanism of the eye must be fairly normal in order to receive the correct image. However, even with a normal receptive mechanism, difficulty can be found in the visual area but at a perceptual rather than a sensory level. Perception of visual objects and material involves the ability on the part of the child to interpret, make associations, and discriminate between one piece of information and another.

Similarly, stimuli may be received by a normal ear so that the child may hear sounds in the environment such as words, phrases, and sentences, but again if the proper interpretations, associations, and discriminations cannot be made the reception of the stimuli alone will not be sufficient for the learning of language. Similar situations may take place with the perception of incoming data from the other sensory areas such as tactile and kinesthetic. Associations and interpretations of data must take place if correct responses are to be coded for release. These coded responses are said to be *expressive* language in that they express a response to stimuli. Expressive language may be verbal or written.

The stimuli coming into the brain may be referred to as *receptive* language. The interconnections made between the various receptive and expressive language functions are necessary for associations and interpretations to be made adequately. *Decoding* is another term sometimes used to describe the receiving of stimuli and *encoding* a term to describe the expression of the stimuli.

Skills for Speaking, Reading, Writing

In order to *speak,* a child must hear sounds, be able to produce them, and combine or synthesize them into words.

In order to *read,* a child must have made a previous association with the auditory word, can probably speak it, and now must be able to see the visual configuration of the word, distinguish it from other symbols, and associate it with the concrete objects these new abstractions stand for on the printed page. If he cannot see differences in alphabet letters, he cannot possibly see differences between words. Also, if he has trouble associating sound and letter and thereby making an auditory-visual association, phonics will be difficult.

In order to *write,* the child must have developed, according to Myklebust (1965): (1) position in space; (2) spatial relationships; (3) figure-ground perception; (4) form constancy; (5) visual-motor coordination; (6) right-left orientation.

Myklebust's discussion of the visual processes involved psychoneurologically in producing the written word include the following. Suppose a child is to write, "I see the girl." First he looks at the situation in general. He sees the paper and pencil. He then must make a judgment as to: (1) how he should grasp the pencil; (2) where the paper is to be placed; (3) where to begin writing; (4) in what direction to write.

Writing turns out to be not only copying a word (the motor act), but also visualizing the word if it is to be written as a spontaneous expression of ideas. The child will have to establish an association with the read word, and prior to that an association with the spoken word. We can see the progression and orderly development necessary in the acquisition of language skills if a child is to be able to use these skills for further learning.

In summary, Orton (1964) points out that "communication is always a two-way process: sending and receiving" (p. 9). She also observes that in reading, the printed word is a visual stimulus that arouses the auditory memory of the sound pattern of the spoken word with recognition of its meaning. The process is primarily language-receptive. "In writing, the physical circuit may start with the spoken or remembered sound of the word—an auditory stimulus —which arouses the associated visual memory of a particular group of letter symbols and the kinesthetic memory of their writing patterns, and leads to the motor act of writing. It is a language-expressive process."

It is Orton's belief that writing patterns should be developed along with the beginning of the learning of the "alphabet code." Some believe that writing is the natural way for children to learn to read but usually the linkage must be taught in both ways: letters-to-sounds for word recognition (reading, decoding); sounds-to-letters is the basis for writing and spelling (encoding) (p. 9).

REFERENCES

Artley, S. A. A study of certain factors presumed to be associated with reading and speech difficulties. *Journal of Speech and Hearing Disorders*, 1948, 13, 351–60.

Carroll, J. B. *The Study of Language*. Cambridge, Mass.: Harvard University Press, 1963.

Cruickshank, W. M., *et al*. *A Teaching Method for Brain-injured and Hyperactive Children*. Syracuse, N.Y.: Syracuse University Press, 1961.

Goldstein, K. *Language and Language Disturbances*. New York: Grune & Stratton, 1948.

Kottmeyer, W. *Handbook for Remedial Reading*. St. Louis: Webster Publishing Company, 1947.

Myklebust, H. R. *Development and Disorders of Written Language*, Volume 1. New York: Grune & Stratton, 1965.

Orton, J. *A Guide to Teaching Phonics*. Cambridge, Mass.: Educators Publishing Service, 1964.

14

Curriculum Materials

One of the most important aspects of programming for the child with learning problems is flexibility. This is possible only when the teacher has flexibility in materials available for use. It should not be necessary to use the same reading books that other children of similar age are using because it "looks better."

A detailed curriculum guide probably is not useful to the special class teacher. However, it is advisable to have outlines in the various subject areas so the teacher can cover with the class some of the same areas covered by other children in the general curriculum program.

By being acquainted with the subject material covered in the regular seventh-grade social studies curriculum, for example, the special class teacher can present information that the children in regular classes are learning. This information may have to be presented in group discussion, with lessons taped rather than read from a textbook, and through such supplementary materials as film strips and movies.

If the child's behavior is under reasonable control he may be able to attend a regular social studies class for the oral presentations and discussions. The special class teacher would then be responsible for any supplementary work the child needed. If the child could handle the lecture and discussion aspects of the regular class but was unable to handle the reading material, the teacher could arrange for the material to be read aloud and perhaps even tape-recorded so the child could listen to it either in school or at home. Parents can become involved at this time if both child and parent have worked with the teacher to establish a program for the home that helps the child prepare for each day's presentation.

On the other hand, if a child is able to read the material but has difficulty writing, the special class teacher may provide him with a typewriter, or if need be give him questions on a test orally.

It is necessary to acquaint the rest of the children in the special and regular classes with the idea that children all learn differently and have various ways of receiving and responding to information. It is often rather amazing to see how flexible children are in responding to individual differences among themselves.

Materials should be something children can use. It is of no value to present a child with a book he cannot read and which otherwise does not suit him even though it may be the best possible textbook available in a particular subject area. For example, a textbook may have to be chosen for the visual presentations rather than the written material. It may be chosen for size of type and the amount of printing on each page. It may be chosen because the reading level is such that the child can handle it on an independent level. Other supplementary books from the library may take the place of a textbook. Books the child has not used before may be more advisable because in some instances books previously used may serve as reminders of past failure experiences.

Another important aspect of programming and selecting materials for use is that of variety. It is advisable to vary the kinds of materials presented from day to day in the subject areas. This does not imply inconsistency, but does indicate that programming is established for a group of children who generally have difficulty staying with a task to completion and whose attention is difficult to hold for long periods of time.

Programmed material that allows for immediate correction of a wrong response and immediate approval for correct responses is useful for some purposes. Again, it cannot be used for all areas or for the same subject each day. Capobianco (1966), in commenting on programmed instruction, observes that "it has been suggested that the purpose of instruction is to change behavior. But apparently, the major change thus far accomplished by programmed instruction has been predominately in the researchers and graduate students who deal with programming; schools and pupils remain relatively unaffected" (p. 1).

Materials initially published in special large type for children with visual handicaps are often useful. Catalogues of these materials can be obtained from the American Printing House for the Blind, 1839

Frankfort Avenue, Louisville, Kentucky.* Large-type books for the partially seeing are available in most of the standard curriculum areas in reading, arithmetic, science, and social studies. Workbooks are also enlarged, mostly without color, and are effective with some children. It should be observed that these materials will not necessarily be effective for developing basic visual perceptual skills.

Following is a section devoted to a discussion of each of several subject areas. These are expected to serve only as an initial presentation and possible way of providing teacher and child with information on materials, methods and guides. It will require considerable planning on the part of a teacher to choose those things most appropriate to a particular situation and group. Individualized programs of instruction may be developed in part through the use of several of the materials mentioned.

VISUAL PERCEPTION MATERIALS

Many teachers feel that even though a particular area of weakness may be brought up to the developmental level assumed to be necessary for a specific skill to be learned, the integration of that skill and associations with other skills still are vital to many language-learning experiences. For example, a child who is shown to have definite visual perceptual problems may be taken through a developmental program in this area. However, if a child still is unable to use the visual perceptual skills along with certain auditory skills it may be difficult to learn phonics, since phonics requires not only visual discrimination and perception but also auditory. Similarly, a child may be able to make an auditory-visual association of a sound and a symbol, but may not be able to remember more than one or two symbols together. Further difficulty may be found in recalling the stimulus after it has been removed, or if the material used in the learning situation changes, such as from a word on the blackboard to a word on paper or in a book. While training for further growth and development of sensory modalities may be effective when carried on to the exclusion of all other sensory modalities, most language-learning experiences need the total integration and association of all the modalities.

* A list of resources with names and addresses of publishers will be found at the end of this chapter, following the references.

One of the programs designed to be used with children who have visual perceptual problems is the *Frostig Program for the Development of Visual Perception,* by Marianne Frostig and David Horne. The program consists of a diagnostic test, a *Teacher's Guide* (1964), a set of training dittos for each of the five areas identified in the program, and a series of worksheets bound in a workbook-type program at beginning, intermediate, and advanced levels. The five areas of visual perception included are: eye-hand coordination, figure-ground perception, form constancy, position in space, and spatial relationships.

The Frostig program has become quite popular in the past few years. Many schools seem to be impressed with the idea that if the material works for some children it must be a good thing to use it with all children. Dr. Frostig refers to this as "one hundred percentism."

Frostig defines perception as the ability to recognize stimuli. She suggests that this ability includes not only the reception of sensory impressions from the outside world and from one's own body but also the capacity to interpret and identify the sensory impressions by correlating them with previous experiences. She says this recognition and integration of stimuli is a process that occurs in the brain, not in a receiving organ such as the ear or the eye. In perceiving these four lines □, for instance, the sensory perception of them occurs in the eye but the recognition of them as a square occurs in the brain. Frostig says the maximum visual perceptual development of the child normally occurs between the ages of three and one-half and seven and one-half.

The Fitzhugh Plus Program by Kathleen and Loren Fitzhugh (1966) consists of materials for two main areas: spatial orientation and language-number study. It is a useful program for older children, those who are placed in intermediate-level or junior high-level classes.

Another area of the visual process to develop is visual discrimination. The Frostig program does not deal with letters, words, or numbers. This program can be supplemented with the materials published by the J. B. Lippincott Company, a workbook called *Readiness for Learning.* A program published by Teaching Resources, Inc., written by Ruth Cheves, called *Visual-Motor Percep-*

tion Teaching Materials is valuable in training visual perceptual skills.

Other materials for use with training in the visual area are listed in the book *Teaching Devices for Children with Impaired Learning* by Helen Epps, Gertrude McCammon, and Queen Simmons. It is printed by the Parents' Volunteer Association, 1601 W. Broad Street, Columbus, Ohio.

The Continental Press, Inc., publishes a variety of materials in the form of pre-printed master units for liquid duplicators and also individual workbooks. Those found to be most useful are on visual-motor skills, visual discrimination, independent activities, thinking skills, and the various readiness and beginning reading materials.

Filmstrips and other material for use with overhead projectors can be employed for training in visual perceptual skills. *Look About You,* published by Guidance Associates, Pleasantville, New York, consists of a two-part filmstrip program that takes children on an excursion "into the variety of colors, shapes, sizes and patterns that make up their world." It describes and helps to make the children aware of what we can see if we look carefully. Part Two of the program explores the sizes and concepts of groups of animals and plants. Records, teacher's guide, and script are included in the set of materials. Its counterpart for use with auditory perception will be discussed in the next section.

There are a number of materials available for use by the Montessori *Learning Aids for Young Children,* published by Teaching Aids of Chicago. The materials included for developing spatial concepts are sets of cylinder blocks. Block towers of varying sizes are included for teaching the concept of size. Geometric form cards, geometric insets, shapes, insets for design, and other such visual aids are included.

Building Stories with Julie and Jack, by Sister Mary Walter, O.S.F., published by St. John's School for the Deaf, Milwaukee, Wisconsin, consists of material for visual sequencing. It comes in three parts, one for teaching the sequence of a story, one for sentence sequence, and one for word sequence. *Writing Stories with Julie and Jack,* also by Sister Mary Walter, has twenty complete stories to be used for group story-telling, sequence, making inferences, and drawing conclusions. While these materials can be used very effectively with visual-process production they are also valuable for use with oral language production.

Many materials usually seen in early primary-level classrooms can be used in special programs although they may need to be cut up, used with special colors, mounted on colored paper, made larger, or separated so that there are fewer items on the page.

Alphy's Show-and-Tell by James F. Brown (Visual Products Division, 3M, 2501 Hudson Road, St. Paul, Minnesota 55119) is a combination of visual-centered materials for teaching "the visual act of reading." It comes in a kit that includes a teacher's guide, materials for making transparencies, and a text for use by the student. There is further discussion on this in a later section on reading.

Manipulative materials that can be used to develop visual perceptual skills in the classroom include page and pegboard designs, colored blocks, beads, and parquetry blocks. Designs can be made for children to copy. These items lend themselves to many uses. The teacher can provide a number of different children with lessons using the parquetry blocks because of the number of different designs and degrees of complexity they allow. The teacher should start a child with something to insure success, perhaps giving the child only those blocks required to complete a simple design. The child may be asked to copy the design by placing the proper size, shape, and color block on top of the one in the picture. Covering the paper with clear plastic gives it durability and thus makes it something that can be used over and over.

After the child completes various parquetry designs of increasing difficulty the teacher may give the child many blocks to see if he can still pick out only those needed for the particular design. The next step might be to ask the child to make his copy of the design next to the one drawn on the paper. Again, this may have to start with the correct number given to the child. Later the entire box can be given. Visual memory can be introduced into the lesson by having him look at the design and turn it over to see if he can reproduce it. Oral language experiences can further be introduced, by asking the child to tell what color blocks were in the design, what shape they were, how many were used, and so on. Many children then like to make their own designs; this presents an opportunity for two children to work together.

Similar activities can be done with pegs, beads, counting cubes, and square counting blocks. An effective way of arranging this in a classroom where many children need this kind of experience is to rotate the activities, or the children, so they have experiences with different kinds of material. This procedure helps with short attention spans and also allows for individual differences.

Language Development Experiences for Young Children by Rose Engel, William Reid, and Donald Rucher (Department of Exceptional Children, School of Education, University of Southern California, Los Angeles 90007) provides a section on activities for developing visual processes as well as fun and game-like experiences. Each activity is described and includes material needed, things to do, and several suggestions for varying activities. Sections also are included for other sensory modalities.

Programs to Accelerate School Success (P.A.S.S.), written by educators and optometrists (Programs to Accelerate School Success, Inc., Box 1004, Minneapolis, Minnesota 55440) consists of materials for use with visual perception. The program contains *The Physiology of Readiness Manual* and includes the following areas: general coordination; balance; eye-hand coordination; eye movement; form perception; visual memory. The visual memory kit includes seventy-nine slides that can be rotated and turned to produce a total of 348 experiences.

While this is by no means a complete description of materials available for use in developing visual perceptual skills, we feel that they provide a beginning and that teachers will be able to make many of their own materials and find unique uses for those described here.

AUDITORY-VERBAL LANGUAGE MATERIALS

This is an area not as well supplied with commercial materials as the area of visual perception. Many of the things the teacher uses will require her own resourcefulness. Materials that are available commercially still require adaptive use; for example, a tape recorder is one of the most effective training devices available. Headphones for tape recorders can be purchased in sets of six, eight, or ten with outlets in a carrying case. Each set of headphones can be plugged into a jack where volume can be controlled individually.

It becomes necessary for the teacher using such materials to be clearly aware of her objectives. For example, we think of phonics work as involving a child's learning to hear sounds, yet much phonics work in the classroom is done quietly with the phonics written on paper. If the teacher is using the auditory materials for developing skill in that area she must be careful to use the task at hand only for developing the child's listening or auditory sense modality. However, if she is interested in developing an auditory-visual association skill, then she will need to present the visual stimuli as well as the auditory.

Another effective machine for use with auditory-visual association training is the *Language Master,* by Bell and Howell. While there are many programs available for purchase with the machine, blank cards also can be purchased, which enables the teacher to program such symbols as circles, squares, diamonds, or letters and their sounds or words, and sentences. Headphones also can be used with the *Language Master.*

Record players can be equipped with headphones. There are records that come with various reading and reading readiness materials, such as the *Listen and Do* program published by the Houghton Mifflin Company (53 West 43rd Street, New York, N. Y. 10036). This is a series of thirty-two recorded lessons in establishing an auditory-visual association pattern for pre-reading experiences. The program consists of sixteen records, thirty-two duplicating masters, and a teacher's guide.

Educational Developmental Laboratories of McGraw-Hill has published a program called *Listen and Think.* This is a "developmental program designed to improve listening comprehension and to develop the specific thinking skills necessary for good listening . . . and for good reading, too." Each lesson opens with an attention-getting situation that demonstrates the specific thinking skill to be learned. Stories are presented in segments with questions at various stages in the presentation. The materials are available at the third-, fourth-, fifth-, and sixth-grade levels. There also are materials for grades seven through twelve, adult basic education listening programs, and college-level materials.

Other uses of the record player as a training tool for auditory perceptual training would be with the use of short stories recorded for listening by the child. The teacher might have the child listen to a short story on a record instead of listening to her read it for the entire class. By using headphones the child can listen to it when the teacher is busy with another child.

Harr Wagner Publishing Company (609 Mission Street, San Francisco, California 94105) publishes a set of high interest, low reading level books, some of which have the stories not only in written form but also on records. These materials could be effective in creating interest in books, where past failures with reading may have built negative feelings in the child. The series is called *The Time Machine Series* and has reading levels of pre-primer, primer, 1.6, 2.0, 2.2, 2.3, 2.5, and 3.0. The interest level is kindergarten through third grade. The story on the record gives added cues to the child who may not be able to handle the reading material, or who may need to hear the story before he wants to see it. Using the book to look at and to follow the story as it is read may be of value in helping the child gain comprehension and in building auditory-visual associations. Other activities in the teacher's manual add to the combinations of sensory experiences available to the child.

Language Development Experiences for Young Children by Engel, Reid, and Rucher (mentioned in the last section) has a part devoted to providing listening experiences for young children. Each activity is described fully with lists of materials needed, a variety of things to do with the materials, and variations to keep the activity interesting for children.

Listening Aids Through the Grades by David and Elizabeth Russell (Teachers College Press, Columbia University, New York, N.Y.) provides many listening and auditory perceptual activities for use individually or in group learning situations. Listening is the term they use to describe simple perception of sounds and words, whereas *auding* refers to "listening with comprehension to spoken language." The publication is divided into one section for kindergarten and grades one through three, and another for intermediate grades (four, five, and six).

The *Echorder*, built by RIL Electronics Company of South-ampton, Pennsylvania, is a machine designed to be used for auditory training experiences. *A Manual of Speech and Language Training: Methods Using the Echorder,* by Ronald K. Sommers and Dorothy Brady (1964) is helpful in planning special auditory and auditory-visual association and language experiences. The *Echorder* provides for delayed feedback so a child can make a response into the machine and get an instant playback or a response delayed two, four, eight, or twelve seconds.

Listen—These Are Sounds Around You, published by Guidance Associates, is a sound and filmstrip program designed to introduce children to many of the sounds around them. It includes sounds from "the beach, the woods, a train, city traffic, and two musical instruments." Children can listen to many different sounds and then a group of sounds from one location such as a playground. Such sounds are produced as happy sounds, sad sounds, and angry sounds. Part II begins with the "imaginative re-creation of the sounds of various weather conditions." Also introduced are sounds of people working and playing, farm and wild animals, and differences between noise and music. Many musical instruments are introduced. A review section at the end helps children assimilate what they have seen and heard. This program not only encourages listening skills and sound discrimination activities, but also helps children with the organization and classification of sounds.

Other material used for the growth of discrimination and listening skills are the records published for use by speech correctionists. Several of these are:

Maico Company
Maico Building
Minneapolis, Minnesota
    Auditory Training Album for *What's Its Name?*

Educational Record Sales
157 Chambers Street
New York, New York 10007
    1. *Fun with Speech,* Volumes I and II
    2. *First Listening Experiences*
    3. *Listen and Learn Speech Improvement,* Volumes I and II
    4. *Listening Time*
    5. *Listening Skills for Pre-readers,* Volumes I and II
    6. *Ear Training for Middle Grades* (Grades two through five).

It is necessary to program not only for the continued development of the auditory sense modality but also other sense modalities, to provide children with a *multi-sensory* approach to learning. However, the teacher should know whether she is trying to increase a child's use of a single modality or a combination of modalities. The objective of a particular lesson becomes the criterion in establishing the sensory modality or modalities to be used, and these undoubtedly will be different for each child.

PERCEPTUAL-MOTOR ACTIVITIES

When children are evaluated for placement into special education programs many of them come with descriptions of having exhibited gross and fine muscle coordination problems. Teachers comment about difficulties in tying shoes, drawing, cutting, and pasting. Written work appears to be "messy," with letters poorly formed. Generally, children are called clumsy, disorganized, and seemingly disoriented. Many older children have developed negative attitudes about physical education and art classes.

The special education teacher must identify the specific areas of disability in perceptual-motor development that are related to reading, writing, and spelling.

Children who are poor in motor skills and who dislike physical education classes and do not play games in their neighborhoods often are also lacking in physical fitness. Many of these children are avid television watchers and because they get little exercise often are overweight.

Perceptual-motor activities should not be thought of as isolated programs but as integral parts of auditory, visual, and associational programs. Kephart (1960) says "we cannot speak of, or think of, input and output as two separate entities; we must think of the hyphenated term input-output. In like manner, we cannot think of perceptual activities and motor activities as two different items; we must think of the hyphenated term perceptual-motor" (p. 63).

Our interest is not in developing isolated skills but rather in developing a generalized motor pattern. For example, a child must first establish balance, then be able to coordinate his arms and legs, then be able to run, and finally be able to play soccer or basketball.

Further information about perceptual-motor activities can be found in:

1. Hellmuth, J. (Ed.) *Educational Therapy,* Volume I. Seattle, Wash.: Special Child Publications, 1966.

2. Hellmuth, J. (Ed.) *Learning Disorders,* Volume I. Seattle, Wash.: Special Child Publications, 1965.

3. Hellmuth, J. (Ed.) *Learning Disorders,* Volume II. Seattle, Wash.: Special Child Publications, 1966.

4. Kephart, N. C. *The Slow Learner in the Classroom.* Columbus, Ohio: Merrill, 1960.

5. Getman, G. N., & Kane, E. R. *The Psychology of Readiness.* Minneapolis, Minn.: P.A.S.S. Publishers, 1964.

Perceptual-motor equipment for classroom use can include a balance beam, balance board, ladder, balls of various sizes, shapes, and weight; a mirror, barrel rack and board, and climbing equipment. Many activities for use in perceptual-motor training do not require specific pieces of equipment. Also, by shopping in the toy sections of department stores teachers can find many appropriate items, such as a game called "Twister" by the Milton Bradley Company of Springfield, Mass.

Further information about general physical fitness can be found in:

1. Dauer, V. P. *Fitness for Elementary School Children.* Minneapolis, Minn.: Burgess Publishing Company.

2. Clarke, H. H. *Application of Measurement to Health and Physical Education.* Third Edition. New York: Prentice-Hall, 1959.

3. McClay, C. H. & Young, N. *Tests and Measurements in Health and Physical Education.* Third Edition. New York: Appleton-Century-Crofts, 1954.

4. Richardson, H. A. *Games for the Elementary School Grades.* Minneapolis, Minn.: Burgess Publishing Company.

5. Richardson, H. A. *Games for Junior and Senior High Schools.* Minneapolis, Minn.: Burgess Publishing Company.

6. Stuart, F. R. & Ludlam, J. *Rhythmic Activities,* Series 1 and 2. Minneapolis, Minn.: Burgess Publishing Company.

7. Stuart, F. R. & Gibson, V. *Rhythmic Activities,* Series 3. Minneapolis, Minn.: Burgess Publishing Company.

Records for use with physical activities can be obtained from:

1. Educational Record Sales
   157 Chambers Street
   New York, New York 10007

2. Concept Records
   North Bellmore
   Long Island, New York

REFERENCES

Capobianco, R. J. Role of programmed instruction in special education. *The Winnower*, March 1966, 2, 1–8.

Fitzhugh, K., & Fitzhugh, L. *The Fitzhugh PLUS Program*. Allied Education Council, Distribution Center, Galien, Michigan 49113.

Frostig, M., & Horne, D. *Frostig Program for the Development of Visual Perception, Teacher's Guide*. Chicago, Ill.: Follett Publishing Co., 1964.

Kephart, N. C. *The Slow Learner in the Classroom*. Columbus, Ohio: Charles E. Merrill Books, 1960.

Sommers, R., & Brady, D. *A Manual of Speech and Language Training: Methods Using the Echorder*. RIL Electronics, Southampton, Pennsylvania.

RESOURCES

American Printing House for the Blind
1839 Frankfort Avenue
Louisville, Kentucky

Bell and Howell Corporation
6800 McCormick Road
Chicago, Illinois 60645
   Language Master Machine

The Continental Press, Inc.
Elizabethtown, Pennsylvania 17022

Department of Exceptional Children
School of Education
University of Southern California
Los Angeles, California 90007
   Engel, R., Reid, W., & Rucher, D. *Language Development Experiences for Young Children*, 1966.

Educational Developmental Laboratories, Inc.
Division of McGraw-Hill Book Co.
284 Pulaski Road
Huntington, New York 11744
   Listen and Think

Educational Record Sales
157 Chambers Street
New York, New York 10007

Educators Progress Service
Randolph, Wisconsin 53956
> *Elementary Teachers Guide to Free Curriculum Materials.* 24th Edition, 1967.

Guidance Associates
Pleasantville, New York 10570
> *Look About You*
> *Listen—These Are Sounds Around You*

Harr Wagner Publishing Company
609 Mission Street
San Francisco, California 94105
> *The Time Machine Series*
> Also: (not mentioned in text)
> *The Jim Forest Readers*
> *Americans All*
> *The Wildlife Adventure Series*
> *The Deep-sea Adventure Series*
> *The Morgan Bay Mystery Series*
> *The Reading Motivated Series*
> *The Checkered-flag Series*

Houghton Mifflin Company
53 West 43rd Street
New York, New York 10036
> *Listen and Do*

J. B. Lippincott Company
East Washington Square
Philadelphia, Pennsylvania 19105
> *Readiness for Learning*

Maico Company
Maico Building
Minneapolis, Minnesota

Milton Bradley Company
Springfield, Massachusetts

Parents' Volunteer Association
1601 W. Broad Street
Columbus, Ohio
> Epps, R., McCammon, G., & Simmons, Q. *Teaching Devices for Children with Impaired Learning,* 1958.

Programs to Accelerate School Success, Inc.
Box 1004
Minneapolis, Minnesota 55440

RIL Electronics Company
Southampton, Pennsylvania
The Echorder

St. John's School for the Deaf
3680 S. Kinnickinnic
Milwaukee, Wisconsin 53207
Sister Mary Walter, O.S.F. *Building Stories with Julie and Jack, Writing Stories with Julie and Jack.*

Special Child Publications
Seattle Sequin Schools, Inc.
71 Columbia Street
Seattle, Washington 98104

Teachers College Press
Columbia University
New York, New York
Russell, D. & E. *Listening Aids Through the Grades,* 1959.

Teaching Aids
Division of A. Daigger & Co.
159 West Kinzie Street
Chicago, Illinois 60610
Learning Aids for Young Children (in accordance with Montessori methods).

Teaching Resources, Inc.
334 Boylston Street
Boston, Massachusetts 02116
Cheves, R. *Visual-Motor Perception Teaching Materials*
Erie Program #1, *Perceptual-Motor Teaching Materials*
Fairbanks-Robinson Program #1, *Perceptual-Motor Development*

Visual Products Division
3M Company
2501 Hudson Road
St. Paul, Minnesota 55119
Brown, J. F. *Alphy's Show-and-Tell.*

15

Curriculum Materials: Reading (Continued)

There is much interest at the present time in trying to predict which children probably will have significant difficulties with reading and other language areas such as spelling and writing. The hope is that in the future reading and writing problems can be prevented by identifying the areas of difficulty before children are placed in a reading or writing program and have an opportunity to fail.

While our general concern so far in these pages has been with finding ways of helping children who already have failed in the regular curriculum program, this is not the limit of our concern. The methods and materials are suitable not only for a special class. The name of the classroom and the labels applied to the children do not identify the curriculum or limit its usefulness with children.

REVIEW

Before a child can read there are many phases of growth and development that must be recognized and identified. In *Children Discover Reading* by Stern and Gould (1965) reading readiness is described as a prerequisite to the actual teaching of reading. "Learning to read requires both maturation and certain well-defined abilities which do not spring forth of themselves on a child's sixth birthday, but must be developed by proper instruction, which, without strain and without drill, will lead naturally to the first steps in reading" (p. 41).

Stern and Gould go on to describe the following abilities as essential for the development of reading readiness: (1) adequate language development; (2) a capacity for visual and auditory discrimination; (3) interest in learning to read. An oral language arts program is emphasized when the child is encouraged to express his ideas

118

and his experiences are broadened so his command of language may be strengthened. A description of activities they feel are of much greater scope than the usual readiness programs emphasize the "systematic study of sounds heard when words are pronounced, as well as the correspondence between those sounds and the letters that stand for them . . . " (p. 42).

Further emphasis on the development of oral language before reading is begun is found in *Predicting Reading Failure* by Katrina de Hirsch, Jeanette Jansky, and William S. Langford (1966). "Children seen in clinical practice may show a variety of verbal-symbolic disturbances. There are some with adequate intelligence and essentially intact hearing who at the expected age or much later fail partially or entirely to interpret or use the language of their culture" (p. xii). They go on to attribute this failure to children's difficulties with the decoding and encoding of verbal symbols. "Their intake is diffuse and undifferentiated. To them, both the configuration of the word and its meaning are highly unstable, and this instability seems to be related to their inability to assign consistent symbolic significance to input events" (p. xii). The authors indicate that many children suffering from spoken language disorders often present difficulties with the decoding and encoding of printed and written language—reading and writing.

In the de Hirsch *et al.* study thirty-seven tests were administered to determine whether the tests could predict reading and spelling difficulties in a group of children referred because of oral-language deficits. It was found that the tests had little predictive utility.

Ilg and Ames (1965) in *School Readiness* state that "what we really need to know in determining readiness for school entrance is a child's developmental level. We need to know at what age he is behaving as a total organism" (p. 17). A description of the developmental tests administered includes an initial interview consisting of questions about age, birthday, and similar information. Then pencil and paper tests were given, including writing name and address, numbers from one to twenty, copying six basic forms and two three-dimensional forms, and completing an incomplete man figure and giving it facial expression. Other test items include Right and Left form tests (adapted from Jacobson's Right and Left Tests), naming of animals for sixty seconds, a concluding interview, and examination of the teeth.

In the *Physiology of Readiness Manual* (Getman & Kane, 1964) six specific programs designed to aid readiness are presented, including programs for general coordination; balance; eye-hand coordination; form perception; visual memory; eye movements. Templates for desk and chalkboard assist in developing form recognition and those visual-motor coordinations said to underlie the basic performance areas related to reading.

Durrell (1956) indicates that being able to hear sounds is one prerequisite to beginning reading, noting that the ability to use phonics rests upon ear training. Durrell feels no attempt should be made to teach either the sounds of letters or the use of phonics until the child can identify separate sounds in spoken words. The most common difficulty found among children who have been given phonics before ear training is thought by Durrell to be lack of ability to use phonics.

Bryant (1965) suggests that the ability to associate sounds with letters and perceive word parts is a basic element of all reading. He notes that until basic symbol-sound associations are established, learning new words and increasing reading level are likely to provide only limited gains.

June Orton (1964) in *A Guide to Teaching Phonics* describes readiness training for phonics as including the development of good speech patterns and oral vocabulary, visual differentiation of letter shapes, auditory discrimination of speech sounds, motor control of pencil and paper, awareness of laterality and left to right directionality, and general perceptual-motor skills. "It is a continuing program to strengthen all areas of language development throughout the entire course in phonics. Enriching experiences and the development of verbal concepts are also most important in preparing the child for reading" (p. 13).

Anna Gillingham and Bessie Stillman (1965) in *Remedial Training for Children with Specific Disability in Reading, Spelling, and Penmanship* propose that contrary to many current practices in teaching phonics, in which a "dash . . . serves as a sort of garnish or embellishment of the sight-word procedure . . . " (p. 40), their technique is to teach the sounds of the letters and then build these letter sounds into words, like bricks into a wall. They feel that this method of word-building cannot be used as a supplement to that of learning words as sight units. The two concepts are mutually exclusive. They further observe that there are three methods of teaching remedial reading: the "sight-word" method, the "tracing" method which stresses the kinesthetic impression, and the "phonetic" method which is also often mistakenly said to be the essence of their technique. "On the contrary, our technique is based upon the class association of visual, auditory, and kinesthetic elements forming what is sometimes called the 'language triangle'" (p. 40).

Gillingham and Stillman go on to say that "This association consists of two parts—associations of the visual symbol with the name of the letter, and association of the visual symbol with the sound of the letter" (p. 40). In the second association, the teacher makes the sound represented by the letter and asks the child to name the letter that has a particular sound. Association three comes after the teacher carefully makes the letter and explains it to the child. The child then traces the letter over the one made by the teacher, then copies it, writes it from memory, and finally writes it again with eyes averted and teacher watching. The teacher next makes the sound of the letter and asks the child to write the letter that makes the particular sound.

In *They Were Not Born Equal!*, McDonald (1966) indicates that "possibly, through the systematic teaching of auditory and visual attention and discrimination, reinforced by kinesthetic awareness, the child can learn the basic skills upon which the majority of his scholastic performance depends. And, may I add, this training is needed early, long before the child develops the habit of failure, before he is categorized by the school and society, and before he is so far behind that 'catching up' is virtually impossible" (p. 67). McDonald goes on to discuss the importance of giving sensory and remedial training in the early grades where the child displays the first signs of learning deficiencies.

Training of the various sense modalities would appear to be of prime importance and the added development of building associations among them of no less importance. Many of the readiness programs and programs for developing various perceptual skills are not sufficient for all children and may leave off before letters, words, and sentences can be used. We must be careful to relate the perceptual skills taught to the kinds of symbols needed in reading, and to integrate the modalities so that stronger sensory areas may be used to compensate for weaker sensory areas.

MATERIALS

By the time most children enter special education programs they have already been through many failure experiences with reading. It is critical for special education staff to identify language characteristics as soon as possible to avoid treading on sensitive, well-worn failure areas.

Our experience has suggested that information contained in most "clinical" reports of evaluations on children is not of much use. The reports typically are either descriptions of tests or test results, or are "interpretations" of "causes" of problems, but the problems are not defined in relevant terms. For example, it may be true that a child scores ninety on an intelligence scale, is passive-aggressive and deficient in ego skills, and hates his father, but how does the teacher translate this information into something useful? Our own preference is for information obtained by a person trained in language skills, whom we call a language consultant.

The language evaluation usually includes descriptions of the various auditory, visual, perceptual-motor, and association skills needed for learning reading, writing, and spelling. This evaluation would constitute the basis for the beginning readiness work done with each child. The usual materials accompanying the basal series to be used for reading readiness may be adequate for most children in the regular curriculum program but generally do not give those children with special learning problems enough experiences to be sufficient.

The following lists the materials and other curriculum supplies for use with the reading program, including phonics materials, basic reading texts, and supplementary readers for use at primary, intermediate, and junior high school levels. The list is meant to be used for instructional purposes after the various language and perceptual areas of readiness have been evaluated. The teacher should be sufficiently informed to be able to choose the best materials available.

Phonics

The Houghton Mifflin *Listen and Do Phonics Program* for establishing the sound-symbol associations of reading was mentioned earlier under materials for auditory-visual perceptual training. It is a program consisting of records, ditto masters for student work-sheets, and a teacher's guide. Materials that can be used with it are *Getting Ready to Read,* a special phonics workbook *Learning Letter Sounds,* and a series of filmstrips for use with the phonics program called Learning Letter Sounds Filmstrips.

Durrell and Murphy (1964) have a phonic series called *Speech to Print Phonics.* The teacher's manual indicates that "These lessons are designed to assure success in beginning reading. They combine established linguistic principles with techniques of high efficiency in learning, to increase both quality and amount of learning in each class period." The program consists of a manual containing fifty-five lessons in helping the child learn the relationship between phonemes in words and the printed form. There are ten lessons devoted to letter names and forms. Materials in the kit include 233 cards to use for practice on the newly learned phonic elements in words. There are sets of letters, blends, yes-no cards, and number cards in the kit.

Another approach to phonics is presented in Stern and Gould's (1965) *Children Discover Reading.* The authors feel that while they emphasize teaching sounds they do not start with the study of disparate, meaningless letters and the piecemeal blending of the sounds they represent. "Structural reading follows a new course. Our children start by sounding out each word—analyzing each spoken and printed word into its component parts; since the children know what they are doing, they can proceed confidently, each at his own rate, to the recognition of the studied words 'at sight' " (p. viii).

The Stern program is one where structural analysis forms the center of every lesson. This method was used for the writing of the following series of five combination workbook readers.

BOOK	TITLE	LEVEL
A (readiness)	*We Learn to Listen*	Kindergarten
B	*We Discover Reading*	1a
C	*We Read and Write*	1b
D	*We Read More and More*	2a
E	*Now We Read Everything*	2b

These books are designed to constitute a complete program for teaching reading, writing, spelling, and even elementary grammar.

The Makar Company (4 Balla Road, Carmel, New York 10512) produces a series of materials for young children called *Primary Phonics*. Included in the set is a workbook of seventy-two pages and three storybooks: *Mac and Tab, Ted,* and *The Wig.* The materials are done in black and white and the printing is large and well spaced, making short and easily read first books for many children. The vowels introduced and practised in varying consonant combinations make the set easily used with other materials discussed in this section.

A Guide to Teaching Phonics by June Orton (1964) provides much information. Orton defines phonics as that system of associating letter-symbols with speech sounds. A discussion of the various vowel and consonant sounds is presented with information about voiced and unvoiced speech sounds and various language skills. Part II is concerned with the actual teaching procedure and describes readiness, teaching materials, and beginning lessons in phonics, reading, spelling, and writing. The book also includes a section on planning a lesson and a "teacher's check list of units taught." Part III consists of the phonics lessons themselves.

Educators Publishing Service (Cambridge, Mass. 02139) offers materials for all age and class levels. These include the book *Remedial Training for Children with Specific Disability in Reading, Spelling, and Penmanship* and additional materials for use with this book. These include a set of *Phonetic Drill Cards, Phonetic Word Cards,* and a packet of materials called *Dictionary Technique* which is appropriate only for use later in the reading program. Additional material for the teacher to use with the program includes *Syllable Concept, Little Stories,* and *Introduction of Diphthongs.*

Educators Publishing Service has also, for use with remedial as well as developmental reading programs, a set of six booklets called *Learning the Letters: A First Course in Phonic Reading,* plus *A Second Course in Phonic Reading,* Books I and II. These are available in a student's edition and with a teacher's manual. *Sound Phonics* is a teacher's manual with a set of records that can be used with headphones much the same as the program described, *Listen and Do.*

Phonovisual

The phonovisual method (Phonovisual Products, Inc., Box 5625, Washington, D.C. 20016) has been found useful in developing a readiness-for-reading program, for teaching sound-symbol associations, for beginning reading experiences, and for children with spelling problems. For visual and auditory training at a readiness level or kindergarten level the following materials are available:

1. Phonovisual unit for kindergarten use

2. Phonovisual readiness book

3. Phonovisual transition book

4. Phonovisual game book

5. Phonovisual consonant filmstrips

6. Phonovisual skill builders

7. Phonovisual consonant picture-pack.

Other materials for use at the readiness and primary level might include:

1. Phonovisual consonant chart (wall and desk)

2. Phonovisual vowel chart (wall and desk)

3. The phonovisual method book

4. Phonovisual record of sounds

5. Phonovisual magnetic boards

6. Vowel filmstrips

7. Phonic rummy games.

At the primary reading level consonant and vowel workbooks are available.

Additional Filmstrips

A group of filmstrips available from Educational Record Sales (157 Chambers Street, New York, N.Y. 10007) is useful in readiness programs. It stresses visual discrimination activities and classifications. The following is a list of titles:

1. Going Places

2. Going Shopping

3. Going to the Country

4. Going Downtown

5. Playing Community Helpers

6. All Kinds of Houses

7. Roy's Toys

8. What's Wrong?

Primary, Intermediate, and Junior High Reading Materials

Solving Language Difficulties: Remedial Routines, by Amey Steere, Caroline Peck, and Linda Kahn (1966), published by Educators Publishing Service, is for use by teachers who want to know about the structure of our language. It is divided into four sections and includes discussions about syllables, syllable division, accents, prefixes, suffixes, accent patterns, tenses, spelling rules, diphthongs, and other topics of value for teachers who work with language disabilities. The authors' work has been based on an alphabetic-phonetic approach, combining visual, kinesthetic, and auditory clues for solving the riddle of identifying the printed word.

One of the reading series that has been used successfully with a number of children is *Programmed Reading,* by Sullivan Associates, published by the Webster Division, McGraw-Hill Book Company. As described in the catalogue, the program is based on an analysis of language in which all sound-symbol groups have been classified and organized for an effective learning sequence. Because it is programmed, a child can work alone and correct his work as he goes. The progress of the materials is slow and repetitious enough to give many children the feeling of success and independence. The books can be used with plastic overlays and grease pencils so they can be used over again and also to make corrections easier.

The pages of the programmed readers are well planned and are easily divided to give the child with spatial orientation and discrimination problems the opportunity of using a book that he can adequately handle. The readiness program has a strong auditory-visual approach for establishing basic sound-symbol relationships. The primer activities are usually done with the teacher and child working together. Independent work in the remaining programmed work-

books, one through twenty-one, is done along with the lessons outlined in the teacher's guide. A teacher's guide is necessary for the
pre-reading program. Series I is for pupil's programmed workbooks
one through seven, Series II for the next seven workbooks, and
Series III for workbooks fifteen through twenty-one. Supplementary
materials include storybooks, hardbound and carefully correlated
with the corresponding programmed workbooks, filmstrips to be used
with Series I, books one through seven, and duplicator master units
to be used with the storybooks. Pre-reading materials for use with
the program include pupil alphabet card, alphabet strips, teacher's
alphabet cards, and sound-symbol cards. Test booklets for each of
the three series are available.

A program found to be helpful for use with the McGraw-Hill programmed readers is one published by Charles E. Merrill (1300 Alum
Creek Drive, Columbus, Ohio 43216) called the *Merrill Linguistic
Readers*. It is a reading series designed for use in the primary grades,
but has been used at all age levels through the junior high level. The
program is helpful because it gives flexibility in providing a variety
of materials children can work with while the materials still maintain consistency. Many children need to move slowly, with much
review and repetition, so having a number of materials is helpful in
holding interest.

To help with some of the readiness activities of the Merrill series a
special book called *My Alphabet Book* may be used for helping children identify letters of the alphabet. Other areas discussed are the
broadening of oral language skills, the relating of written language to
oral language, and motor development skills. *Visual Experiences* is a
set of six large photographs to be used by the teacher to encourage
language development. The materials for reading include six readers,
six skill books, and an annotated teacher's edition of each reader.
Spelling and writing activities are also correlated with the reading
materials.

The Bank Street Readers, published by Macmillan (866 Third
Avenue, New York, N.Y. 10023), are used particularly for children
who have completed several years in other programs. They add
variety and maintain interest in reading. The program begins at a
readiness level, has a readiness extension area, and goes up through
the second half of the third grade. The workbooks have large print
and adequate spacing.

The basal reading series published by Houghton Mifflin Company (53 West 43rd Street, New York, N.Y. 10036) has served as a text for those children who have completed the developmental or remedial reading program used with many of the previously discussed materials, particularly children who have completed the first three grade levels of material.

Many students also are using *Reading in High Gear;* this, along with the *New Rochester Occupational Reading Series* is of interest to junior high school students. These materials are available through Science Research Associates, Inc. Some teachers of younger children have used these readers as supplementary material while some have used them in their social studies programs.

Educators Publishing Service has recently published a program called *Language Training for Adolescents: Curriculum Outline* compiled by Dorothy Bywaters. Additional information can be found in *Language Training for Adolescents: Guide to Supplementary Materials.* A student workbook is also available for use with these outlines.

The Macmillan Company publishes an entire program called *The Spectrum of Skills* for use in grades four and up. The specific areas for skill-building include word analysis, vocabulary development, and reading comprehension. These three sets of skill booklets come with four copies of the booklet, a teacher's guide, and a student record book. The booklets in each area progress from easy to difficult and offer a wide range of levels and challenges. Each child has an opportunity to work in his own area of weakness.

The materials presented in this section do not cover all of those that are available. The intention has been to describe some that have been found useful in practice. Every classroom need not be equipped with all the materials described but teachers should be acquainted with what is available.

Classroom libraries are of particular importance for children with reading difficulties. This is partly because without assistance all children who want to read at home may not choose a book that is at the proper reading level.

Harr Wagner (609 Mission Street, San Francisco, Calif.) publishes a number of books with many topics that can supplement science and social studies programs as well as reading programs, adding to a classroom library. It is called *The Harr Wagner Reading*

Tree and provides low levels of reading difficulty. *The Time Machine Series* has an interest range from kindergarten through third grade and each book in the series has a record to accompany the story. A teacher's manual includes ideas for art projects and specific suggestions for using the books in various ways. *The Jim Forest Readers* have an interest level of about grades one through six and include a teacher's manual and practice books. *Americans All* has an interest range from grades three through eight and each book has as its main character a member of some ethnic group in North America. Other series include *Wildlife Adventure Series, The Deep-sea Adventure Series, Morgan Bay Mystery Series, The Reading Motivated Series,* and *Checkered-flag Series.*

Additional supplementary readers at all levels can be obtained from Benefic Press (1900 North Narragansett Avenue, Chicago, Ill.). The Dolch books are published by the Garrard Company (Champaign, Ill.). *The Refresher Program* of the *Merrill Linguistic Readers* provides additional material for use by older students in the junior and senior high school age ranges.

REFERENCES

Bryant, N. D. Some principles of remedial instruction for dyslexia. *The Reading Teacher*, 1965, 18, 567–72.

deHirsch, K., Jansky, J., & Langford, W. *Predicting Reading Failure.* New York: Harper and Row, 1966.

Durrell, D. *Improving Reading Instruction.* New York: World, 1956.

Durrell, D., & Murphy, H. A. *Speech to Print Phonics.* New York: Harcourt, Brace & World, 1964.

Getman, G. N., & Kane, E. R. *The Physiology of Readiness.* Minneapolis, Minn.: P.A.S.S. Publishers, 1964.

Gillingham, A., & Stillman, B. *Remedial Training for Children with Specific Disability in Reading, Spelling, and Penmanship.* Cambridge, Mass.: Educators Publishing Service, 1965.

Ilg, F., & Ames, L. B. *School Readiness.* New York: Harper and Row, 1965.

MacDonald, R. L. *They Were Not Born Equal!* Van Nuys, Calif.: Remediation Associates, Inc., 1966.

Orton, J. L. *A Guide to Teaching Phonics.* Cambridge, Mass.: Educators Publishing Service, 1964.

Steere, A., Peck, C. Z., & Kahn, L. *Solving Language Difficulties: Remedial Routines.* Cambridge, Mass.: Educators Publishing Service, 1966.

Stern, C., & Gould, T. *Children Discover Reading.* Syracuse, N.Y.: The L. W. Singer Co., 1965.

RESOURCES

Benefic Press Publishers
1900 N. Narragansett Avenue
Chicago, Illinois 60639

Educational Record Sales
157 Chambers Street
New York, New York 10007

Educators Publishing Service
Cambridge, Massachusetts 02139

> Gillingham, A., & Stillman, B. *Remedial Training for Children with Specific Disability in Reading, Spelling, and Penmanship,* 1965.
> *Phonetic Drill Cards*
> *Phonetic Word Cards*
> *Dictionary Technique*
> *Syllable Concept*
> *Little Stories*
> *Introduction to Diphthongs*
> *Learning the Letters: A First Course in Phonic Reading*
> *A Second Course in Phonic Reading*
> *Sound Phonics*
>
> Bywaters, D. *Language Training for Adolescents: Curriculum Outline*
> *Student's Workbook*

Garrard Printing Company
Champaign, Illinois
(The Dolch Books)

Harr Wagner Publishing Company
609 Mission Street
San Francisco, California 94105

> *The Time Machine Series*
> *The Jim Forest Readers*
> *Americans All*
> *Wildlife Adventure Series*
> *The Deep-sea Adventure Series*
> *Morgan Bay Mystery Series*
> *The Reading Motivated Series*
> *Checkered-flag Series*

Houghton Mifflin Company
53 West 43rd Street
New York, New York 10036

> *Listen and Do Phonics Program*
> *Learning Letter Sounds*
> Learning Letter Sounds Filmstrips

The Macmillan Company
866 Third Avenue
New York, New York 10022
   The Bank Street Readers
   The Spectrum of Skills

The Makar Company
4 Balla Road
Carmel, New York 10512
   Primary Phonics
   Mac and Tab, Ted, The Wig

Charles E. Merrill Books, Inc.
1300 Alum Creek Drive
Columbus, Ohio 43216
   Merrill Linguistic Readers

Phonovisual Products, Inc.
Box 5625
Washington, D.C. 20016

Science Research Associates, Inc.
259 East Erie Street
Chicago, Illinois 60611
   Reading in High Gear
   New Rochester Occupational Reading Series

Webster Division
McGraw-Hill Book Company
330 W. 42nd Street
New York, New York 10036
   Sullivan Associates. *Programmed Reading.*

16

Curriculum Materials: Spelling, Writing, Science, Social Studies, and Numbers (Continued)

SPELLING

The majority of children placed in special education programs come with spelling abilities from two to three years below their reading level. This is not surprising because written language develops last in the sequence of total language formulation. According to Orton (1964) "a direct association of the pattern of language sounds in a spoken word with their letter symbols (sounds to letters) is the basis of writing and spelling" (p. 10).

Spelling problems can be identified by examining the types of spelling errors made on tests and other forms of written work. The majority of problems we have observed are related to:

1. poor visual memory
2. difficulty in re-visualizing words
3. difficulty in visual sequencing
4. difficulty in symbol-sound associations
5. inability to use auditory clues for spelling
6. lack of training in how to use auditory clues for spelling
7. auditory perceptual problems
8. problems in the motor act of writing
9. inability to use spelling rules.

When we have identified the specific language, perceptual, motor, and/or other problem areas, a training program is planned. The spelling program is integrated with reading and writing programs.

The following materials have been found useful for spelling activities:

Primary

1. *A Guide to Teaching Phonics,* by June Orton (1964).

2. *Let's Start Phonics: Graded and Classified Spelling Lists for Teachers*, by Celeste T. Forbes (1956).
3. Parts of *Spelling Workbook for Early Primary Corrective Work*, Book I, Grade 2, by Mildred Plunkett and Caroline Z. Peck (1960).

Intermediate and Junior High

1. *A Guide to Teaching Phonics*, by Orton.
2. *Sound Spelling*, by Sally B. and Ralph de S. Childs (1963).
3. *Spelling Rules*, by Childs and Childs (1965).
4. *Spelling Lists*, Forbes (1956).
5. *Spelling Workbook for Corrective Drill*, by Plunkett (1961).
6. *A First Course in Phonic Reading*, by L. G. Helson (1965).
7. *A Second Course in Phonic Reading*, Books I and II, by L. G. Helson (1965).
8. *Spelling and Writing Patterns*, by Morton Botel (1963).

In training children to use auditory clues for spelling we have found the use of nonsense syllables useful. These also may be used for diagnostic purposes.

WRITING

This section will serve only as a listing of some materials teachers would need and as reference for where these may be obtained.

Many of the first activities in writing call for work on the chalkboard. We have used an oversized chalk for this; it can be purchased at stationary stores or other school supply outlets; it sometimes is referred to as railroad chalk, number 888.

Materials needed for use with pre-readiness writing programs include chalkboard and oversized chalk, finger painting materials, large newsprint, and various colored magic markers for drawing lines on paper and for children's use. Templates may be used and can be purchased from Montessori Materials, Teaching Aids, 159 West Kinzie Street, Chicago, Illinois. Plastic templates can be purchased from P.A.S.S., Inc., P. O. Box 1884, Minneapolis, Minnesota. Teachers may wish to make individual sets for use on bulletin boards or on the child's desk; tagboard or heavy cardboard can be used for construction.

Other materials easily obtainable from school supply houses include: clay, pipe cleaners, colored duplicating master units, and sandpaper letters and numbers. Sandpaper letters in cursive writing probably will have to be made by the teacher from sandpaper mounted on cardboard or heavy tagboard. Letters and numbers for tactile-kinesthetic practice can be made by writing a letter or number on a card and covering it with pieces of yarn or pipe cleaners. Some children can make their own sets, which provides them with fine motor coordination activity as well as a useful end product.

We have found sand or salt trays useful for writing and other motor development activities. An easy way to make a tray is lining a cafeteria tray with a sheet of brightly colored paper; the visual image becomes more clearly visable. Mistakes are easily corrected, the device is new and interesting for many children, and the visual-tactile-kinesthetic combination is helpful as a training experience. The salt tray provides freedom of movement and appears to be a good medium for writing after chalkboard work but before paper and pencil work.

There are some materials made by the American Printing House for the Blind that have been found useful with some children. These consist of a sheet of heavy white paper with the letters of the alphabet in raised cursive writing. A heavy sheet of black material also is available and has the cursive letters depressed so they can be traced.

For much of the initial writing program on paper, magic markers, felt marking pencils, primary writing pencils, and a special pencil made by Zaner-Bloser have been used.

Overhead projectors can be used in writing and in readiness activities for teaching letter names and sounds. Visual discrimination lessons can be given with use of this machine and transparencies. An attachment can be made for the projector to introduce the effect of movement with the writing symbols and to help children with left to right progression. The materials used are known as technamation and consist of a polaroid filter mounted on a clear plastic wheel that is motorized. These materials are placed over the transparencies and can be used with letters and numbers.

SCIENCE

Not all the children in special education programs are able to handle a science program that is dependent on a textbook series. By obtaining information from local and state curriculum guides, the special class teacher can present science programs similar to those in regular classes.

Two books published by the University of the State of New York are *Science for Children: K-3* and *Science for Children: 4-6*. The units covered and areas designated for study are the same for all grade levels; however, the material in each level varies with respect to difficulty, amount, and concepts to learn. The main units are:

1. Living things
2. Our growing bodies
3. Air, water, and weather
4. The earth and its composition
5. The solar system and beyond
6. Matter and energy.

Each unit follows a sequential teaching pattern organized as follows:

1. Purpose of the unit
2. Introduction of the unit
3. Experiences relating to the unit
4. Enrichment
5. Organization and use of information gained
6. Basic understandings to be gained
7. Vocabulary.

It is suggested in the guides that they may be used with varying basal science textbooks.

The science program may include discussions, films and filmstrips, and actual experiences with subjects.

A textbook series that begins with an emphasis on visual presentations is published by the Silver Burdett Company. It consists of a beginning readiness program called *Pictures that Teach* with thirty-six charts or pictures. The Science I program includes *Pictures that Teach* and a teacher's manual. These two programs provide an entire unit of material based on the pictures, with a theme, picture explanation, concepts to be developed, suggested study questions, related topics, and activities. There are hardbound textbooks for science levels for grades one through six for children able to handle the reading material. Teachers are encouraged to supplement the units with field trips.

The Webster Beginner Science Series is by Harold Tannenbaum and Nathan Stillman (1960). *The Webster Classroom Science Li-*

brary consists of twenty-four books on more than 700 topics and can be used by intermediate and junior high school groups. Additional library materials by Webster are *It's Fun to Know Why, The Wonderful World of Science,* and *Exploring Science.*

Continental Press publishes science materials available at all levels in the form of duplicator master units.

Social Studies and Geography

The University of the State of New York has published a social studies experimental outline for grades kindergarten through three. It gives an overview of the program for these grades and includes sections on social, economic, and political organization, geography, and building patriotic citizenship. At the end of the book there is a tentative flow chart of the social studies program for grades kindergarten through twelve, to inform the teacher about what concepts are being presented at regular grade levels.

Benefic Press (1900 North Narragansett Avenue, Chicago, Ill.) has developed an *Experimental Developmental Program* designed for use as an initial school experience for young children in the areas of language arts and social studies. It consists of three teacher's "big books" and an accompanying pupil's independent activity book.

Silver Burdett publishes a social studies program similar to their science program, consisting of pictures and discussion. The *Primary Social Studies Picture Packets* introduce children to the world in which they live. There is a series of twelve different pictures in the packet for kindergarten and grades one and two. There also is a grade-one readiness packet with a total of thirty learning situations. The subject areas covered are families around the world; holidays and special occasions; and the earth, home of people. Hardbound textbooks are available for grades one through six and again these emphasize the visual and discussion approach.

A book called SPARK (Educational Service, Inc., P.O. Box 112, Benton Harbor, Michigan) contains many ideas for the teaching of elementary school social studies, and is suitable for all levels through grade eight.

The material published by Continental Press includes duplicator masters in social studies areas.

NUMBERS

In our experience there has been little variation in arithmetic materials available commercially and teachers have had to make many of their own materials. One of the basic difficulties with many commercial materials is that frequently there is too much on each page. If a math series has a great deal of language and material that must be read to understand or find directions, many children immediately experience difficulty.

A child with a receptive language problem may be able to do mathematical computations but may be unable to do word problems that involve the same type of computational skill. Another area of difficulty is going from the concrete to the abstract, so much number work has an initial emphasis on concrete materials.

At the primary and intermediate levels the basic arithmetic series has been the *Structural Arithmetic Program* by Catherine Stern, Margaret Stern, and Toni Gould (1965), published by Houghton Mifflin Company. It is a program designed for use with kindergarten through grade three. *Structural Arithmetic* presents a complete program of building number concepts in the primary grades. The organization is clear and logically developed with a definite step-by-step plan of trial, practice, and review, leading pupils from simple number concepts to mastery of arithmetical computations and problem-solving. The materials can be purchased in the form of kits and accompanying workbooks designed for use at various levels.

The Hayes School Publishing Company (321 Pennwood Avenue, Wilkinsburg, Penn. 15221) has a number of liquid duplicator lessons for use in the elementary grades. Continental Press also has materials for developing number skills.

A series of mathematics programs published by Science Research Associates (259 East Erie Street, Chicago, Ill. 60611) has been used with some children in intermediate and junior high classes. It is called the *Greater Cleveland Mathematics Program*, prepared by the staff of the Educational Research Council of Greater Cleveland under the direction of George S. Cunningham (1964).

Cuisenaire rods (9 Elm Avenue, Mt. Vernon, N.Y. 10550) also are used with some children, particularly older children. The younger members of the class find the size difficult to handle.

Addison-Wesley Publishing Company has a junior high school series found to be appropriate with some older children. It is a special low-track series by Robert Eicholz and Phares O'Daffer (1966). There are three books in the series. They provide the slow learner with a reduced reading level and amount of reading material necessary for working through word problems and directions. Teachers' editions are available as are special workbooks and testing materials. Also published by Addison-Wesley is a series of four programs of material for addition, subtraction, multiplication, and division. *Experiences with Geometry* by Eicholz and O'Daffer (1966) has been used mainly with older groups.

PLUS, published by Educational Service, Inc. (P.O. Box 112, Benton Harbor, Mich. 49023), is a book for teachers that gives a number of additional suggestions for supplementary activities in arithmetic.

Scholastic Book Services (904 Sylvan Avenue, Englewood Cliffs, N.J.), publishes five "self-teaching" arithmetic books for use as supplements to textbooks and courses of study designed for grades two, three, and four. They can also be used for remedial purposes and extra practice for children in more advanced groups. They cover basic concepts, facts, and processes of addition, subtraction, multiplication, and division. Because the books are programmed, children can work independently. A teacher's guide is included.

REFERENCES

Orton, June. *A Guide to Teaching Phonics*. Cambridge, Mass.: Educators Publishing Service, 1964.

RESOURCES

Addison-Wesley Publishing Company
School Division
3220 Porter Avenue
Palo Alto, California 94304
  Eicholz and O'Daffer. *Experiences with Geometry*, 1966
  Basic Modern Mathematics, First Course, 1965
  Basic Modern Mathematics, Second Course, 1965
  Modern General Mathematics, 1964.

American Printing House for the Blind
1859 Frankfort Avenue
Louisville, Kentucky

Benefic Press
1900 North Narragansett Avenue
Chicago, Illinois
Experimental Developmental Program

Continental Press, Inc.
Elizabethtown, Pennsylvania 17022

Cuisenaire Company of America, Inc.
9 Elm Avenue
Mt. Vernon, New York 10550

Educational Service, Inc.
P.O. Box 112
Benton Harbor, Michigan
SPARK
PLUS

Educators Progress Service
Randolph, Wisconsin 53956
Elementary Teachers Guide to Free Curriculum Materials, 24th Edition, 1967.

Educators Publishing Service
301 Vassar Street
Cambridge, Massachusetts
Orton. *A Guide to Teaching Phonics*, 1964.
Forbes. *Let's Start Phonics: Graded and Classified Spelling Tests for Teachers*, 1956.
Plunkett and Peck. *Spelling Workbook for Early Primary Corrective Work*, Book 1, Grade 2, 1960.
Childs and Childs. *Sound Spelling*, 1963.
Childs and Childs. *Spelling Rules*, 1965.
Plunkett. *Spelling Workbook for Corrective Drill*, 1961.
Helson. *A First Course in Phonic Reading*, 1965.
Helson. *A Second Course in Phonic Reading*, Books I and II, 1965.

Follett Publishing Company
1010 West Washington Blvd.
Chicago, Illinois 60607
Botel. *Spelling and Writing Patterns*, 1963.

Hayes School Publishing Company
Wilkinsburg, Pennsylvania

Houghton Mifflin Company
53 West 43rd Street
New York, New York
Stern, Stern, and Gould. *Structural Arithmetic Program*, 1965.

Scholastic Book Services
904 Sylvan Avenue
Englewood Cliffs, New Jersey
   Studebaker and Studebaker. *Self-teaching Arithmetic Books.*

Science Research Associates
259 East Erie Street
Chicago, Illinois 60611
   Cunningham. *Greater Cleveland Mathematics Program,* 1964.

Silver Burdett Company
Division of General Learning Corp.
Park Ave. and Columbia Rd.
Morristown, New Jersey 07960
   Pictures that Teach: Science for Beginners
   Pictures that Teach: Science I
   Primary Social Studies Picture Packets
   Families Around the World (Kindergarten)
   Families and Their Needs (Grade 1)

Teaching Aids
159 West Kinzie Street
Chicago, Illinois 60610
   Montessori Templates

University of the State of New York
State Education Department
Bureau of Elementary Curriculum Development
Albany, New York 12224
   Science for Children: K–3
   Science for Children: 4–6
   Social Studies: K–3

Webster Company
Manchester Road
Manchester, Missouri 63011
   Tannenbaum and Stillman. *Webster Beginner Science Series,* 1960.
   Webster Classroom Science Library
   It's Fun to Know Why
   The Wonderful World of Science
   Exploring Science

Zaner-Bloser Company
613 North Park Street
Columbus, Ohio 43215

17

Evaluation for Educational Programming

Many of the children experiencing learning problems in the regular classroom have been to reading or speech clinics and to rehabilitation centers. Most of them have received some kind of remedial or tutorial help in reading, spelling, and arithmetic but they still continue to have difficulties in their classrooms.

The various test results from psychologists, psychiatrists, neurologists, pediatricians, speech pathologists, reading specialists, tutors, and former teachers, usually contain relatively little information about how a child learns. Consequently, it is necessary for the teacher or language consultant to determine the specific language abilities and disabilities of a child before educational programming can be planned.

Although we realize the importance of the emotional aspects of behavior and their influence on learning, our experience has led us to believe that the learning problems we can identify are what we should focus on. We have found that the learning and/or behavioral problems of the children are usually due to a lack of, or a breakdown in, the development of one or more of the following areas:

1. sensorimotor processes
2. eye, hand, foot dominance
3. auditory processes
4. visual processes
5. associational processes.

The majority of the children we have seen not only have learning problems as such, but also need to learn how to learn. Learning disabilities are viewed in terms of gaps in the developmental sequence of those skills necessary for learning to take place.

Psychological Evaluations

Typically, we do not initiate an evaluation to determine if a child has a learning and/or behavioral problem. This already has been determined prior to placement into the special educational program.

Tests used most frequently by psychologists in initial evaluations are:

1. *Wechsler Intelligence Scale for Children*
2. *Bender Visual-Motor Gestalt Test*
3. *Goodenough Draw-A-Man Test*
4. *Wide Range Achievement Test.*

Educational Evaluations

Various formal evaluations are used to identify the specific abilities and disabilities of children after they have been placed into a special educational program and it becomes necessary to plan an individually designed curriculum experience. However, careful observation of a child's performance in his daily learning situation provides as much information about his problems as can be obtained from formal evaluations. As Getman (1965) observes, "It is now time to remember 'that the little child shall lead us'—if we adults can just be astute enough to let him do so" (p. 74).

What we want to observe about a particular child is: Through which channels can he learn and which of those channels need to be developed so he can learn more effectively? By "channels" are meant visual, auditory, and kinesthetic sensory areas. This is not to say that a program is planned to strengthen one channel by the use of the others. If we are going to strengthen the child's auditory skills, we must work on the auditory skills alone, because if we should use visual skills to try to strengthen auditory skills we are only affecting the stronger skill and not the weaker one. However, this applies to remedial training only and not to the learning situation in general. In addition to a weakness in a particular channel many children have even greater difficulties in transferring information from one sense modality to another.

Following is a summary listing of the devices used in performing a formal evaluation after a child is placed into a special program. Information obtained from this evaluation may indicate a need for further observations to determine specific problem areas.

1. *Durrell Analysis of Reading Difficulty*, used to determine a child's reading level, not for planning a retraining program.

2. *Frostig Test of Visual Perception*, used to evaluate visual perceptual skills: figure-ground perception, eye-hand coordination, position in space, spatial relationships, and form constancy.

3. *Informal Reading Inventory* (Temple University), to determine the four reading levels measured by this inventory: independent, instructional, frustration, and capacity levels. Also used to determine if there is a difference between oral and silent comprehension, to observe if a child can comprehend material read orally at grade level even though he cannot read it. Finally, the inventory is used to observe the types of reading errors made.

4. *Illinois Test of Psycholinguistic Abilities* (McCarthy and Kirk, 1961), used to measure language abilities as indicated on nine subtests.

5. An adaptation of Kephart's (1960) *Perceptual Survey Rating Scale*. An evaluation sheet has been devised that gives the test item, what to look for in responses, and then the training indicated from the results. Some of the areas included are gross motor coordination, laterality, directionality, form perception, and eye control.

6. Lateral dominance evaluations for preferred eye, hand, foot.

7. *Monroe Reading Aptitude Tests* (1963), primary form, includes tests for hand-eye preference and percentile scores for visual, auditory, motor, articulation, and general language skills.

8. *Peabody Picture Vocabulary Test* (Dunn, 1959), a general measure of a child's ability that does not require a verbal response.

9. *Picture Story Language Test* (Myklebust, 1965), used to evaluate a child's skill with written language.

10. *Screening Tests for Identifying Children with Specific Language Disability* (Slingerland, 1964). There are three sets of screening tests for use, designed to detect areas of specific language disabilities in children of average or above-average general intellectual abilities in grades one through four.

11. *Templin-Darley Test of Articulation* (1960), used to evaluate articulation ability. An oral peripheral examination also is given.

In summary, an educational evaluation should:

1. Determine the child's specific language abilities and disabilities;

2. Indicate the sensory-motor channels through which the child may receive maximum learning benefits;

3. Provide specific recommendations for training in those language areas where the child needs help;

4. Suggest a more general educational program;

5. List a variety of materials that will be suitable for the child.

The original plan is subject to change at any time. Data from continued re-evaluations in all areas should be noted on record cards.

The Language Consultant

The language consultant undertakes the following responsibilities in educational evaluation and programming areas:

1. Coordinates and interprets information in the child's permanent record folder;

2. Assists teachers in identifying the child's specific language abilities and disabilities;

3. Coordinates and supervises the periodic educational evaluations made by classroom teachers;

4. Helps teachers plan individualized educational programs;

5. Plans retraining or remedial programs in specific areas such as auditory perception and visual-motor coordination;

6. Assists in the selection of appropriate materials;

7. Undertakes continued diagnostic evaluations throughout the school year for the purpose of revising planning;

8. Performs speech and language training directly with children to strengthen areas basic to more general areas.

Following is a form (Form 1) used to gather information systematically on a child when he is first placed into a special education program.

FORM 1: GENERAL INFORMATION

Name of Child_____Birthdate_____Age_____

Evaluator_____Date_____

A. School History

    1. Age child entered school

    2. Has child repeated any grades?

    3. Has child been absent frequently?

    4. Has child transferred schools?

    5. Other pertinent information

B. School History of Family

    1. Schooling of parents

    2. Did parents have difficulty in school?

    3. School history of siblings:

        a. Present grade(s)

        b. Repeated any grades?

        c. Referred to psychologists or clinics?

        d. Any reading or speech problems?

        e. Other

C. Health Record

_____

D. Speech Correction

_____

E. Remedial Reading

_____

F. Tutoring

_____

G. Psychological Evaluation(s)
_____
    1. Results
_____
    2. Interpretations by psychologist

    3. Interpretations by language consultant
_____

H. Neurological Evaluation(s)
_____

I. Medical History, especially about medications
_____

J. School Performance (test result and teachers' comment(s))
    Kindergarten
_____
    First Grade
_____
    Second Grade
_____

Third Grade _____

Fourth Grade _____

Fifth Grade _____

Other Grades _____

K. Specific Information from Test Results or Teachers' Comments in: _____

    1. Reading _____

    2. Spelling _____

    3. Writing _____

    4. Arithmetic _____

    5. Science, social studies _____

    6. Behavior in the classroom _____

L. Suggested Evaluations for Educational Programming _____

M. Other Evaluations (speech, eye examinations, hearing) _____

N. Comments: _____

_____

Reviewing the permanent folder has been found useful in revealing various areas of difficulty children have had through the grades. Teachers' comments often suggest general areas of learning difficulty. For example, comments such as "he doesn't hear sounds," "poor coordination," "has difficulty copying from the board," "disorganized," "does not pay attention," "reverses letters" will be found. The problem now is to determine why he "isn't hearing sounds" and to plan a program to develop the skills necessary for doing so.

Samples of children's work are often included in the permanent record folder. An analysis of the kinds of errors made or the areas in which the child has experienced difficulties may give us information about the more specific types of evaluation that should be completed. For example, if a child reverses letters when he spells he may have difficulty in visual-motor sequencing. If he confuses short vowels when he spells, he may have difficulty in auditory perception or symbol-sound associations. If he cannot re-visualize, he may put down any combination of letters which have no connection with the word he tried to spell.

Thus, from careful analysis of the types of errors made in spelling we may learn the nature of the child's spelling problem. This enables planning for a retraining or training program in visual memory or symbol-sound associations that will help the child learn how to spell. More spelling exercises will not help and are of no assistance to the child whose perceptual problems interfere with his ability to spell. We must work with the perceptual problems first and then transfer the training into the actual spelling program. It is not enough to work with visual memory and then give the child a regular spelling program.

Similarly, a careful analysis of the errors made in arithmetic or in the types of problems a child cannot do often provides information about the type of perceptual or language training he needs before he will be able to master certain concepts or computations in arithmetic. For example, if a child can do computations, but has difficulty with word problems, he may have a receptive language deficit. That is, he has difficulty comprehending the meaning of words and so even if he is able to add and subtract he cannot understand the meaning of the problem. If he has difficulty with long division he may have a problem in sequencing or in spatial relationships.

The Child

Who is the child with a learning problem? He is the child who has a good vocabulary but cannot read. He is the child who reads well but cannot do simple arithmetic problems. He is the child who finds math easy, but his spelling is bizarre. He is the child whose finished written work looks beautiful but he has difficulty in directionality. He is the artist of the class but cannot write a sentence. He looks well coordinated on the playground but he has no balance. He is the child who talks continuously but is unaware of the speaker-listener relationship. He is the child who reads well but cannot follow oral directions.

These descriptive statements are only a few of the combinations of abilities and disabilities that can be found. Each child with language difficulties by definition has a breakdown in his communication system, the basis of all learning. The only thing a group of these children have in common is a need for training in learning *how to learn*.

Language

A study of language is necessary because we communicate by speaking, listening, reading, and writing. It is important to understand what is meant by language. We use the term to include the use of symbols. Reading is primarily a language-receptive process where combinations of letter symbols are translated into spoken words, either orally or in inner speech, or thought. Writing is considered a language-expressive process where the spoken or remembered sound of a word—an auditory stimulus—arouses the associated visual pattern of symbols (visual memory) and the kinesthetic memory of the written form of the symbols.

Both in reading and writing the meaning of the words has been learned from hearing them. A direct association of the pattern of language sounds in a spoken word is the basis for writing and spelling.

Following is a form used to record more specific data obtained after the general information has been collected and recorded on Form 1. Form 2 is used to provide a rapid view of a child's measured abilities and his needs for training in the general areas included.

FORM 2: FORMAL TEST SUMMARY

Name of Child_____ Birthdate_____·_____ Age_____

Evaluator_____ Date_____

Date Given	Training Needs	Adequate or Above	Subject Category	Test	
			Eye-Hand Coordination	I	Visual Perception
			Figure-Ground Perception	II	
			Form Constancy	III	
			Position in Space	IV	
			Spatial Relationships	V	
			Information	I	WISC
			Comprehension	II	
			Arithmetic	III	
			Similarities	IV	
			Vocabulary	V	
			Digit Span	VI	
			Picture Completion	VII	
			Block Design	VIII	
			Coding	IX	
			Object Assembly	X	

Comments

			Auditory Decoding	I	
			Visual Decoding	II	
			Auditory Vocal Association	III	
			Visual Motor Association	IV	
			Vocal Encoding	V	ITPA
			Motor Encoding	VI	
			Auditory Vocal Automatic	VII	
			Auditory Vocal Sequential	VIII	
			Visual Motor Sequential	IX	
			Auditory Synthesizing	I	
			Auditory Analyzing	II	
			Auditory Memory for Sentences	III	
			Reading Silent Oral		
			Arithmetic		
			Spelling		
			Written		

Summary Statement

Form 3 is the next formal record used. It is for making weekly reports of use to the language consultant and teacher.

FORM 3: TEACHER-LANGUAGE CONSULTANT
WEEKLY COMMENT SHEET

Name of Student_____ Age_____

Person Working with Student_____ Date_____

I. Major Areas of Difficulty:
Auditory Processes
Visual Processes
Sensorimotor Processes
Associational Processes
II. Specific Area or Areas for Additional Work:
III. Materials and Procedures:
IV. Summary of Results:
V. Recommendations for Work in the Classroom for the Week of _____

VI. Summary of the Work Done in the Classroom for the Previous Week of

VII. Teacher's Comments (regarding further evaluations, specific areas where the student needs help, etc.)

REFERENCES

Getman, G. N. The visuomotor complex in the acquisition of learning skills. In Hellmuth, J. (Ed.) *Learning Disorders.* Volume 1. Seattle, Wash.: Special Child Publications, 1965, pp. 49–76.

Kephart, N. C. *Perceptual Survey Rating Scale.* In *The Slow Learner in the Classroom.* Columbus, O.: Merrill, 1960.

Myklebust, H. R. *Development and Disorders of Written Language.* Volume 1 (*Picture Story Language Test*). New York: Grune & Stratton, 1965.

RESOURCES

American Guidance Services, Inc.
720 Washington Avenue, S.E.
Minneapolis, Minnesota 55414
    Dunn. *Peabody Picture Vocabulary Test,* 1959.

Bureau of Educational Research and Service
Extension Division
State University of Iowa
Iowa City, Iowa
    Templin and Darley. *Templin-Darley Test of Articulation: A Manual of Discussion of One Screening and Diagnostic Test,* 1960.

Consulting Psychologists Press
577 College Avenue
Palo Alto, California
    Frostig Test of Visual Perception and *Administration and Scoring Manual: Developmental Test of Visual Perception,* 1961. *Teacher's Guide,* 1964.

Educators Publishing Service
301 Vassar Street

Cambridge, Massachusetts
   Slingerland. *Screening Tests for Identifying Children with Specific Language Disability* (Grade 1 and beginning Grade 2; Grade 2 and beginning Grade 3; Grades 3 and 4), 1964.

Harcourt, Brace & World, Inc.
Tarrytown, New York
   Durrell. *Durrell Analysis of Reading Difficulty,* 1937, 1955.

Houghton Mifflin Company
53 W. 43rd Street
New York, New York 10036
   Monroe. *Monroe Reading Aptitude Tests,* 1963.

The Psychological Corporation
304 East 45th Street
New York, New York 10017
   Wechsler Intelligence Scale for Children, 1959.
   Wechsler Preschool and Primary Scale of Intelligence, 1967.

Reading Clinic
Department of Psychology
Temple University
Philadelphia, Pennsylvania
   Informal Reading Inventory

University of Illinois Press
Urbana, Illinois
   McCarthy and Kirk. *Illinois Test of Psycholinguistic Abilities,* 1961.

Western Psychological Services
12035 Wilshire Boulevard
Los Angeles, California 90025
   Bender Visual-Motor Gestalt Test for Children, 1962.
   Jastak and Bijou. *Wide Range Achievement Test,* 1965.

World Book Company
Yonkers-on-the-Hudson, New York
   Goodenough Draw-A-Man Test
   The Measurement of Intelligence by Drawings, 1962.

18

Visual Processes

Form 4 is used by the classroom teacher and/or language consultant to record information obtained from an evaluation of a child's visual processes. Questions and items to look for in a child follow the form and are related to the five major areas and the subareas on the form.

Following Form 4 is a more detailed outline of the various aspects of visual processes along with additional suggestions on how to conduct more detailed evaluations and provide training for areas of visual perception.

Following are two sections. The first is devoted to questions to ask and special areas to look for in using Form 4.

The second section outlines a training program that follows the special areas listed on Form 4.

EDUCATIONAL EVALUATION CHECK LIST
FORM 4: VISUAL PROCESSES

Name of Child_____ Birthdate_____ Age_____

Evaluated by_____ Date_____

COMMENTS

I. Visual Perception	
A. Figure-Ground	
B. Perceptual Constancy	

COMMENTS

C. Position in Space	
D. Spatial Relationships	
II. Visual Discrimination	
A. Objects	
B. Letters	
C. Words	
III. Visual Memory	
A. Designs	
B. Numbers	
C. Letters	
D. Words	
IV. Visual Sequencing	
A. Designs	
B. Numbers	
C. Letters	
D. Words	
V. Visual Decoding	
A. Pictures	
B. Words	

FORM 4: QUESTIONS AND EVALUATION AREAS

I. Visual Perception

Parts of the *Frostig Test of Visual Perception* are used. Observations often help the evaluator in planning an educational program for the child with visual perceptual problems.

A. Figure-Ground Perception.
1. Is the child inattentive?
2. Is the child disorganized?
3. Does he form letters correctly?
4. Does he have difficulty keeping his place while he reads or while he copies material?
5. Does he skip sections on tests or in his workbooks?
6. Is he unable to complete material presented on a crowded page?

B. Perceptual Constancy.
1. Does the child know a word in context, but if it is presented in a new situation he acts as if he had never seen it before?
2. Does he have difficulty matching letters, shapes?
3. Does he have difficulty recognizing letters?

C. Position in Space.
1. Is the child constantly bumping into things?
2. Are his body movements clumsy even though he appears to be fairly well coordinated?
3. Does he know the concepts of before, after, in, out, up, down, left, right?
4. Does he reverse letters, numbers, words?

D. Spatial Relationships.
1. Does the child perceive letters, numbers in the correct sequence? He may spell *bring* as *birng*, *first* as *frist*.
2. Does he have difficulty in math problems that require a sequence of processes, such as long division?
3. Does he have difficulty with measurement?
4. Does he have difficulty understanding graphs or maps?

II. Visual Discrimination

A. Does the child recognize similarities and differences among groups of objects (shape, color, size)?

B. Can he match letters, numbers? Does he confuse letters that look alike but do not depend on directionality as their difference (*m* for *n, n* for *h, r* for *n*)? Slingerland's Test Number 4 taps visual discrimination.

C. Observe the child when he reads to see if he confuses words that look alike. Look at the child's spelling papers; does he write *m* for *n, r* for *h, h* for *n*?

III. Visual Memory

EXPLANATIONS:

There are two types of memory problems that are frequently found:

Immediate—where the child is unable to store symbols. This type of memory problem is seen in the child who can recognize letters or numbers only momentarily.

Recall of what is learned—the child can recognize the symbol when given a model, but cannot recall it by himself. In other words, he has difficulty re-visualizing symbols.

The child with an immediate memory problem usually is a non-reader or reads at a pre-primer level. He has difficulty in spelling, writing, and arithmetic. The child with a recall memory problem usually can read fairly well. His reading level may be two to three years below grade level. He experiences more difficulty in spelling and writing than in reading.

A. Designs.
1. Put several objects on a table. Remove one of them. Ask the child to tell you what is missing.
2. *Graham-Kendall Memory for Designs.*
3. Slingerland's Subtest Number 5.

B. Numbers.
1. Slingerland's Subtests Numbers 3 and 5.
2. Construct your own test; on strips of tagboard write numbers beginning with one on a card and increasing the amount of numbers up to eight.

C. Letters.
1. Slingerland's Subtests Numbers 3 and 5.
2. Construct your own test; on strips of tagboard write

letters beginning with one and increasing the number to eight.

D. Words.
    1. Slingerland's Subtests Numbers 3 and 5.
    2. *Durrell Analysis of Reading Difficulty.*

IV. *Visual Sequencing*

Tasks that require a child to sequence also require memory. Here we are concerned with the child's ability to remember the correct order of the stimuli. We have found that children with sequencing problems have directionality problems or spatial relationship problems. They read *string* as *stirring* and spell *from* as *form.*

A. Designs.
    1. Visual-Motor Sequencing subtest of the ITPA.
    2. Slingerland's Subtest Number 5.

B. Numbers.
    1. Slingerland's Subtests Numbers 3 and 5.
    2. Note the type of errors made in arithmetic.

C. Letters.
    1. Slingerland's Subtests Numbers 3 and 5.
    2. Observe the types of reading errors made.
    3. Note the type of spelling errors made. Does he put down *any* combinations of letters when he spells, even if they do not make sense? If so, he probably has difficulty in re-visualizing what the word looks like. If he confuses the order of the letters he may have a problem in directionality, sequencing, or both.

D. Words.
    1. Slingerland's Subtests Numbers 3, 5, and 6.
    2. Observe the types of reading errors made. Does he reverse whole words or parts of words?
    3. See C, #3.

V. *Visual Decoding*

A. Pictures.
    1. Visual Decoding subtest of the ITPA.
    2. Show the child several pictures. Is he able to comprehend the meaning of the pictures?

B. Words.
1. Does the child have difficulty comprehending when he reads silently? A child who has a visual decoding problem may do better on comprehension when he reads aloud.
2. Have the child read a paragraph at his independent reading level silently; have him answer questions about the paragraph. Then, have him look at the paragraph while you read it to him; have him answer further questions about the paragraph. Use the same paragraph and the same questions for both tasks. If his comprehension improves when he hears the auditory with the visual stimulus, he probably has a visual decoding problem; if the reverse is true, he probably has an auditory-verbal language problem.

VISUAL PROCESSES TRAINING PROGRAM

I. Visual Perception: The Frostig Program.

During the first week in September the *Frostig Test of Visual Perception* is administered to all the younger children in the special education program. The language consultant administers the test and the classroom teacher proctors. The test is scored by the language consultant and the results are recorded on index cards kept in the teachers' files. At this time the child's record folder from previous years is reviewed by the language consultant to determine if there are any indications that would further substantiate results obtained on the test. On occasion, a child's performances on the test does not indicate a need for training in a specific area although his behavior otherwise gives indications of needs for training. For instance, if the child has difficulty keeping his place on a page when he is reading but his test performance showed no indications of difficulty he still may need training in figure-ground perception.

It is important to know how visual perception is defined in the Frostig *Administration Manual* and the *Teacher's Guide* because this definition is related to reading, writing, spelling, and arithmetic. The Frostig materials may be supplemented by three-dimensional materials and also integrated with other perceptual and motor development tasks.

The Frostig Program in the Classroom

Visual perceptual training is initially provided for all members of each class, especially for younger children, because of the almost universal occurrence of visual perceptual deficits among children who exhibit learning problems. There are some children who do not need this initial training, of course, and other provisions are made.

Generally, it has been found necessary to provide activities that precede the formal Frostig program. These "pre-program" activities may take as long as three or four months with some children. This is another way of saying that the Frostig program is not entirely suited for very young children or for those with more serious problems.

Following are some lessons to show how Frostig's suggestions can be used for developing various areas of visual perception *before* the worksheets are used. These sample lessons follow the format used in Form 4.

SAMPLE LESSON: A

A. *Figure-Ground Perception*

MATERIALS NEEDED:

Collective picture—many colors and objects.

1. Color

"I have a picture here. Look at it carefully.
Now I want you to find the

a. red things,

b. green things,

c. yellow things."

(Go outside and have children identify the same colors in the street, playground, etc.)

2. Shape

a. Round; property of roundness.

(Pass out balls.) "What is the shape of the thing you have in your hand? How do you know it is round? Move your hand around the ball, and now close your eyes and feel it. What things are round? (Have children roll the balls.) (Show two-dimensional circles.) Why is a circle round? Why and how is the circle like a ball?"

b. Squares; property of squareness.
(Pass out colored paper squares.) "What is this? How do you know? (lines and points) Let's all look carefully at this—it's a square. (Run two fingers around edges.) How many lines can your fingers tell you when you do this?"

c. Similar activities for triangles, rectangles, ovals. Use any that require the children to give their attention to a figure in a background. Sorting activities are useful.

SAMPLE LESSON: B

B. *Perceptual Constancy (Figure-Ground)*

1. Finding things of similar size.
    a. Give the child a paper plate with buttons of various sizes on it. In the beginning the sizes should be relatively easy to discriminate. Later, they should be more difficult. Hold up a large button; have the child find a button of similar size on the plate. (Buttons of different sizes should be of different colors.)
    b. Have the child sort colored sticks.
    c. Have the child sort nuts and bolts or nails and screws.
    d. Give each child an assortment of various objects and sort them according to size.
    e. Give the child triangles of various sizes and sort them according to size. Do the same for circles, squares, and rectangles.
    f. Give the child sticks of varying lengths and have them sorted according to long and short.
    g. *Stick-O-Mats* by Judy, for developing perception of size, shape, and color.
    h. *Color-Shapes* by Judy.

2. Finding things according to weight.
    a. Collect various objects that are heavy and light. Put a heavy toy in the child's one hand and a light one in the other hand. Talk about which one is heavier. Then give the child other objects that are heavy. When you give the objects to him say

"This is heavy." The child should respond verbally that it is heavy so he associates the feeling of heavy with the verbal symbol.

b. When the child has had several experiences with heavy objects repeat the procedure with light objects.

c. Comparing heavy and light objects. The child is now asked which object is heavier or lighter.

d. Have a large object which is actually lighter than a smaller one. Ask the child to look at the object and tell you which one is larger and which one is heavier. Then have him close his eyes. Put the two objects in his hands, one in each and have him tell you which one feels heavier.

e. After many varied experiences in feeling objects that are heavy and light, have the child look at everyday pictures of objects and see if he knows which ones are heavier than others.

SAMPLE LESSON: C

C. *Position in Space*

Introduction to Body Parts

MATERIALS NEEDED:

Filmstrips and record for *Look and Say,* Part I (first half; end at frame 23).

Theme: "Mystery"

Dialogue:

"You live with this thing and you think you know it very well. It has many parts. These parts do different things. It helps find out about things.

"Keep your answer to yourself and when I turn on the film and record you'll know more about it and you'll find out if you guessed what we're talking about."

(Show film)

"You may raise your hand if you guessed right. I know you learned much about yourself."

Part I—Naming Body Parts

"There are different parts of your body that tell you different things about the world. First let's find out how many parts we have that tell us things."

(Picture of whole body on tagboard)

"Come up and name the part and outline it with your finger."

arm	foot	ear	tongue
leg	toes	eye	head
hand	torso	nose	face
fingers	neck	mouth	wrist

Part II—Senses

(Picture of face on cardboard)

1. "What part helps you know that you're not in a dark room? Can you see in a dark room? Point to your eyes. How many do you have? What color are your eyes? Everyone turn to your neighbor; what color are his eyes? What other color eyes are there?"

2. "Close your eyes; I have a surprise. Don't tell us what it is when we come near you. (Pass paste on a paper plate.) Don't tell your neighbor. Open your eyes. Do you think you know what it is? Raise your hands; how did you know?" (The idea is that they can smell the paste.)

3. (Ears) "Close your eyes. (Use any record or noise; train whistle.) Raise your hand if you know. Tell what it is; how did you know?"

4. "Close your eyes. (Pass out some peppermint marshmallows.) I'm putting something on a plate on your desk. You find it. Don't tell me what it is. Raise your hand when you know what it is. Tell me: How did you know? How does it feel? Eat it."

5. "What told you how it tasted? (Tongue) What do you think it's going to taste like? Did this fool you? Why? What did you do to make sure you knew how it tasted?"

Part III

1. Have the children lie on the floor and make their shadow on paper and cut it out. Discuss the different parts of the body.

2. Make a ditto of the various parts of the body. Have the children cut them out and put the body together.

3. Have each child stand in front of a full-length mirror. Have them tell you the color of their hair and eyes. Have them point to the various body parts.

4. Blindfold one child. Have a boy and girl come to the front of the room and have the blindfolded child tell you which is the boy and which is the girl.

SAMPLE LESSON: D

D. *Spatial Relationships*

1. Give each child a small paper plate and have them put the plates on top of their heads. Ask them if the plate will stay there if they do not move. Why? (Because it is in the middle of the body.) We say it is balanced. Ask them again why the plate stays on their heads. Have them establish the idea of *middle* and that they have two sides to their bodies. What do we call the two sides? (Left and right.) What happens when we put the plate on one side? (The teacher does it. The children respond, "It fell off.") Now the children do it. Review the concepts of middle of the body and two sides. You may want to have the children look in the mirror and discover what is in the middle of their bodies and what they have two of.

2. Prior to undertaking these activities, several weeks of developing laterality (Kephart, 1960) and knowledge of the terms *left* and *right* for direction should be established.

   a. Positions.

     1. Have the child stand in back of his chair. Have him push the chair away and also toward him while he says "Push away" and "Pull toward." Do this with doors and other objects such as brooms, shovels, etc.

     2. Left and right.

       (a) Have the child lie on the floor on his stomach. Have him turn to the left, bend his left arm and leg. (The position should be like that described on p. 202 for "Crawl.") Do the same for the right. Have the child say *left* and *right* as he turns. Have him stand up and do the same.

       (b) Have the child stand in front of a chair and then move him to the left and right.

       (c) Have the child point to his left and right eyes, ears, etc. A game of *Simon Says* using left and right body parts can be used.

The above activities should be done several times a day. Also, the teacher should comment frequently about things being at the left or the right.

       (d) Give the child a green and a red block, the red one on the left and the green one on the right. Give directions such as "Move the green block to the right, the red one to the left."

       (e) Give pencil and paper tasks such as putting a red dot at the left of the paper.

b. Patterns. Models in three dimensions. The child should construct the pattern with concrete materials such as blocks.
 1. Simple designs with parquetry blocks.
 2. Simple patterns with beads.
 3. Simple patterns with pegboards.
 4. Teacher-made puzzles; can be used on flannel board.
 5. *Rig-A-Jig* construction sets (from Beckley-Cardy Company).

Informal Experiences

For each group of children there are many materials the children consider as games. The game-type material is carefully selected for the purpose of developing visual perceptual skills. Games can be used by the children during their free time periods. Many teachers have found it helpful to place a particular game or building type of activity on the child's desk in his study area before he enters the room in the morning. He then is free to do the activity by himself, but it has been selected for a purpose not made obvious to the child.

For example, if a child has difficulty with spatial relationships the teacher may give him some block problems with patterns or pegboard designs to work with. The teacher constructs the model so the child will succeed in building it. As the child is able to do simple patterns or designs, the teacher may give him more difficult ones. There is no limit to the activities an imaginative person can develop for visual perceptual training if it is understood how visual perception affects the child's ability to perform various tasks. If a child is observed to be having difficulty the teacher should ask himself, "Why is he having difficulty; am I asking him to do too much? If I changed the material would he be able to succeed?" The child should be the sole center of information for the teacher.

Frostig Worksheets

When a child is ready for the worksheets in a particular area of visual perception it is better to give him work on all five areas at the same time rather than ask him to do one area and then another. The child progresses at his own rate. If he has difficulty with a particular worksheet the teacher should develop other materials and activities similar to the Frostig worksheet. When the child is ready he may then be given the appropriate worksheet.

During the time a child is receiving the visual perceptual training he should also be receiving training in auditory perception, language, motor development, and other areas described in this book. If he enters the special educational program for children with learning problems and is able to read and do arithmetic, but has visual perceptual problems that are interfering with his success in academic subjects, the teacher should present the activities in a particular subject in such a manner that the child is not frustrated by his perceptual problems.

For example, if a child is known to have difficulty in figure-ground perception and therefore cannot tolerate a paper with ten arithmetic problems on it, the teacher can cut up the worksheet and give the child one problem at a time. As he is able to tolerate more than one problem the teacher may give him two problems on a page. If the child is unable to keep his place when he reads, a slotted marker can be used to help him.

II. Visual Discrimination

The child should receive pre-readiness activities in visual discriminations for perceptual constancy, such as in the Frostig program. After some training in perceptual constancy the activities from the following sources may be used for visual discrimination training for reading:

Cruickshank, W., et al. A Teaching Method for Brain-injured and Hyperactive Children, 1961, pp. 236–40.

Cruickshank, W. The Brain-injured Child in Home, School, and Community, 1967.

McLeod, P. H. Readiness for Learning, 1965, pp. xi–xiii in the teacher's edition.

Visual discrimination dottos from Continental Press.

Montessori materials from Creative Playthings or Teaching Aids.

Gotkin, L. G. Language Lotto, 1966.

Specific Discrimination Problems with Letters

Many children confuse m and n in reading and writing. Part of the confusion stems from learning that the printed m has two humps and the n has one hump. Children then learn cursive writing and the m has three humps and the n has two humps. It is helpful to discuss the differences in manuscript and cursive forms of the m and n at the beginning of the reading and writing programs so children are aware of the differences from the beginning. Color clues can be used for helping children to discriminate between *r* and *h,* and *h* and *n* in the manuscript form.

III. and IV. Visual-Memory Sequencing

A. Motor Sequencing—PART 1.

LEVEL I

1. Close your eyes
   Open your eyes
2. Sit down
3. Raise your arm
4. Stand up
5. Point to your nose
6. Touch your hand
7. Clap your hands
8. Tap your foot
9. Hold up your thumb
10. Hold up your index finger
11. Put your hand behind your neck

LEVEL II

1. Sit down; raise your arm
2. Bend your knees; touch your head
3. Stand up; touch your eyes
4. Clap your hands twice
5. Clap your hands; touch your head
6. Touch your head; your elbow
7. Touch your knee; nose; stomach; foot
8. Touch something

square	round
hard	soft
higher	lower

LEVEL III

1. Have the child touch two things and tell you what he touched.
2. Increase the number of items, repeating the procedure.

Motor Sequencing—PART 2.

MATERIALS: Collect small objects such as erasers, pencils, ball, string.

PROCEDURE: Seat a group of children in front of a table. Let the children feel each object, name the objects, and tell how they feel.

LEVEL I

1. Place two objects, starting at the left side of the table.
2. Emphasize left-to-right order.
3. Mix up objects.
4. Have children replace objects in the same order.

LEVEL II

Repeat the above procedure (Level I). This time use three objects. Increase the number of objects as the children are able to reproduce the correct sequences. When children can remember five or six objects the next stage should be introduced. Variation: bead stringing, animal pictures, colored blocks.

Motor Sequencing—PART 3.

LEVEL I

PROCEDURE: On flannel board place two cards, first one to the left. Emphasize left-to-right progression. Each child then begins with his two cards. Have the child trace the designs on each card with his finger. Talk about how they look and feel. Have each child then place the two designs on his desk in the same order as those on the flannel board. Repeat the procedure, placing the two cards on flannel board for 5–10 seconds. Remove them and have the children arrange their own designs in the same order. Put the design on the flannel board again and have the children compare their order with the model. (If a child reverses the pattern, discuss this with him and review left-right progression.)

LEVEL II

Repeat above procedures using four, five, six cards with various designs. It is suggested that Part 3 be carried out for one or two weeks. Some children will need more training and are themselves the best source for telling you how much training they need at what levels. For the child with severe visual memory problems, naming the designs out loud may help, although the auditory clues should be removed as soon as possible.

Motor Sequencing—PART 4.

Horizontal Plane—Near Point

MATERIALS: Dittos of figures, designs, for each child. Tachistoscopes for use with the ditto sheet, one for each child.

PROCEDURE: Have the children look at a figure, shape, etc. Cover it or move the tachistoscope so the figure is covered. Have children reproduce what they saw. Increase the difficulty of the design. As the child's memory improves, use figures that have parts in different colors.

Motor Sequencing—PART 5.

Vertical Plane—Far Point

MATERIALS: Master list of figures or visual memory slides from Getman and Kane's *Physiology of Readiness*. Transparencies with the figures on them. Overhead projector. Paper and crayons. Salt trays; place a sheet of colored paper on the tray and cover lightly with salt or sand.

LEVEL I

Eyes on model

Step 1. Have the child look at the design on the chalkboard or the overhead projector. Have him reproduce the design in the salt tray while he looks at the model (and not at his hand). This procedure is helpful in developing the kinesthetic feel for form.

Step 2. Have the child reproduce a design using paper and pencil or crayons, looking at a model and not at his hand.

Step 3. Have the child repeat steps one and two while looking at his tray or paper.

LEVEL II

Model is removed; repeat the three steps from Level I.

Motor Sequencing—PART 6.

Repeat the procedures of Parts 4 and 5, Levels I and II, using numbers instead of figures. Gradually increase the amount of numbers.

Motor Sequencing—PART 7.

Repeat the procedures of Parts 4 and 5, Levels I and II, using letters. Gradually increase the number of letters employed.

Motor Sequencing—PART 8.

Repeat the procedures of Parts 4 and 5, Levels I and II, using words the child has learned to read and spell. Gradually increase the number of words in the sequence.

Motor Sequencing—PART 9.

Repeat the procedures of Part 4, Level I, and Part 5, Level II, using sentences.

V. *Visual Decoding*

If a child has difficulty comprehending the meaning from pictures the following activities may be useful in developing his visual decoding ability:

1. Perceptual constancy and figure-ground "pre-activities" in the Frostig program.
2. Display pictures and ask the child to find certain things.
3. Display figures with parts missing and have the child tell you the missing parts. Then have him fill them in.
4. *Language Lotto.*
5. *Laugh and Learn with Julie and Jack.*
6. Ask the child to identify action in pictures. For example, "Show me the boy walking."

If the child has difficulty in comprehending the meaning of printed words, sentences, or paragraphs, the following activities may be useful:

A. Words.

1. Show the child the word cat. Have him select a cat

Sample Visual Memory Drawings: I

from three pictures. You say, "Find me the cat." Then put the picture of the cat next to the word *cat*. The child should then point to the word and say "cat." It is important that the child respond verbally to the spoken word with the printed word. Give the child many experiences with this type of activity. Begin with nouns, then verbs, then prepositions. With the verbs, the child can actually perform the actions when he is learning the word along with saying it.

Sample Visual Memory Drawings: II

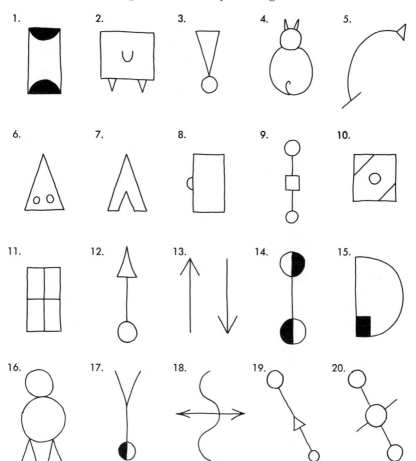

B. Sentences.
    1. Same as above only for sentences.
    2. Tape a series of sentences that correspond with pictures. The pictures and sentences in the *Julie and Jack* series "Sentence Sequence" section may be used or some can be made. The child listens to the sentence as he looks at the picture. After many experiences with this type of activity he may then be given two pictures

and told to circle the picture that denotes the action told by the sentence on the tape. Also, he may be given two verbal statements and one picture; he must then tell which sentence describes the action in the picture.

C. Paragraphs and stories.

   1. Use the stories in the "Story Sequence" section of the *Julie and Jack* series. Tape the story.

     a. Have the child look at the pictures as he listens to the story.

     b. Have the child look at the printed sentences as he listens to the tape.

     c. Ask the child oral questions about the story and have him respond verbally.

     d. When he is successful in his verbal responses to the stories give him similar kinds of stories but:

       (1) Give him multiple-choice questions where he circles the correct answer;

       (2) After he can do the multiple-choice questions, give questions requiring him to write a word or several words to answer the questions. The ability to do this writing activity will depend on the age of the child.

   2. Repeat "d" but do not use pictures. Use reading material at the child's independent reading level.

REFERENCES

Cruickshank, W. *The Brain-injured Child in Home, School, and Community.* Syracuse, N. Y.: Syracuse University Press, 1967.

Cruickshank, W., *et al.* *A Teaching Method for Brain-injured and Hyperactive Children.* Syracuse, N. Y.: Syracuse University Press, 1961.

Getman, G. N. & Kane, E. S. *Physiology of Readiness.* Minneapolis, Minn.: P.A.S.S., 1964.

Kephart, N. C. *Perceptual Survey Rating Scale.* In *The Slow Learner in the Classroom.* Columbus, O.: Merrill, 1960.

McLeod, P. H. *Readiness for Learning.* Teacher's Edition. Philadelphia, Pa.: Lippincott, 1965.

RESOURCES

Appleton-Century-Crofts
440 Park Avenue South

New York, New York
    Gotkin. *Language Lotto,* 1966.

Beckley-Cardy Company
1900 North Narragansett
Chicago, Illinois 60639
    Rig-A-Jig

Consulting Psychologists Press
577 College Avenue
Palo Alto, California
    Frostig Test of Visual Perception and *Administration and Scoring Manual: Developmental Test of Visual Perception,* 1961. *Teacher's Guide,* 1964.

Continental Press, Inc.
Elizabethtown, Pennsylvania 17022

Educators Publishing Service
301 Vassar Street
Cambridge, Massachusetts
    Slingerland. *Screening Tests for Identifying Children with Specific Language Disability* (Grade 1 and beginning Grade 2; Grade 2 and beginning Grade 3; Grades 3 and 4), 1964.

Harcourt, Brace & World, Inc.
Tarrytown, New York
    Durrell. *Durrell Analysis of Reading Difficulty,* 1937, 1955.

The Judy Company
310 North Second Street
Minneapolis, Minnesota
    Stick-O-Mats
    Color-Shapes

Psychological Test Specialists
Box 1441
Missoula, Montana
    Graham-Kendall Memory for Designs Test

St. John's School for the Deaf
Milwaukee, Wisconsin
    Sister Mary Walter. *Laugh and Learn with Julie and Jack,* 1964.

Teaching Aids
159 West Kinzie Street
Chicago, Illinois 60610
    Montessori Templates

University of Illinois Press
Urbana, Illinois
    McCarthy and Kirk. *Illinois Test of Psycholinguistic Abilities,* 1961.

19

Auditory Processes

Our understanding of auditory perception is relatively limited. Most of the information we have is based on hypothetical neurological explanations or observations of the auditory behavior of persons known to have damage in the auditory cortex. From this limited amount of information the following can be said.

Physiology

Auditory perception is largely governed by the temperoparietal area of the cortex especially along the fissure of Sylvius. According to Penfield and Roberts (1959) auditory perception is vital to learning and maintaining patterns of speech. Hardy (1956) feels that the transmissive and perceptive levels of auditory symbols may be closely related. He states that the functions of the auditory cortex are: (1) to decode the message; (2) to synthesize the information; (3) to project it in a pattern that can be related to other cortical functions (Hardy, 1956, p. 298).

The Nature of Perception

Hardy's description of auditory perceptual development is as follows: In the first year of life much of the child's time is spent in learning how to listen. Here the child is involved in the "construction of a detailed pattern of conditioning and inhibition, pertinent to numerous events of sound and their meanings in his daily life, and interrelated with the rest of his sensorium" (p. 298). After this stage the child is getting ready to speak. As his attention span increases and he is stimulated by his daily experiences, the child learns to decode and encode messages. At two years of age he develops "demonstrable speech," what linguists call the use of verbal symbols in reference to direct communication.

The major step in linguistic learning has occurred during the first two years of life. "Thereafter, his symbol-making and symbol-using activities are intimately connected with the experiences of every waking hour" (Hardy, p. 298).

Myklebust (1954) feels auditory perception is developmental, as is visual perception. Lewis (1951) divides auditory perceptual development into four stages:

1. The child distinguishes between two sounds, recognizing there is a difference.
2. The child recognizes similarities between two sounds.
3. The child begins to combine sounds that can be recognized and identified.
4. The child becomes aware of similarities and differences among combinations of sounds. He differentiates between finer differences and assigns meanings.

Cruickshank *et al.* (1961) state that "What the child perceives becomes a part of him and in terms of symbolic patterns becomes a memory and a model for the child. These models control the shifting phonetic events of his speaking; a feedback mechanism is set up, and the child is able to hear his own speech and compare what others say" (p. 435). Thus, the child learns to monitor himself.

The authors also state that auditory perception can be viewed as the ability "to select out of a total mass of auditory stimuli certain groups of sounds, each of which has a unique quality. These groups of sounds then become the symbols of the language" (p. 143). They go on to say that auditory memory is necessary to perceive patterns of speech. The recognition of individual speech sounds and series of sounds will be difficult if auditory memory span is poor.

Auditory perception can be viewed as the putting together of "pitch, intensity, and time characteristics so the combination becomes a recognizable sound" (Lewis, 1951, p. 81). We come to organize out of a mass of stimuli certain groups of sounds that have their own quality and are recognized by this quality. Just as we see a figure against a background so we hear known sounds against backgrounds.

In summary, auditory perception involves more than just recognizing certain sounds as speech sounds. It appears to be a complex process that is developmental and learned. By the end of the second year of life the child has developed and learned some of the major aspects of auditory perception. The early linguistic environment of the child is thus very significant in developing auditory perception.

Form 5 is used to record information obtained from an evaluation of a child's auditory processes. Questions and items to look for in a child follow the form. This form is similar in format to Form 4 on visual processes. Following the form are suggestions on how to conduct more detailed evaluations and provide training for areas of auditory perception.

Areas of Difficulty

Some explanations for the use of Form 5 may be helpful. We found that children have difficulty in one or more of the following auditory-verbal language areas:

1. Auditory discrimination—hearing differences and similarities between sounds.
2. Auditory memory—immediate and delayed recall of material presented aurally.
3. Auditory sequencing—recall of material that requires children to remember a particular order of sounds.
4. Auditory analyzing—identifying beginning, middle, and ending sounds.
5. Syllabication—dividing a word into syllables.
6. Vocal encoding—expressing oneself through the use of the spoken word.
7. Auditory Decoding—comprehending the spoken word.

Children also may have difficulty with auditory-vocal association tasks or in associating the visual symbol with the auditory symbol.

An evaluation of each child's auditory-verbal language problems should precede any use of the training programs suggested in this chapter. Some children will need work in all areas and others in only a few. The length of time needed to develop the various auditory skills will vary and no estimates can be made on a general basis.

EDUCATIONAL EVALUATION CHECK LIST
FORM 5: AUDITORY-VERBAL PROCESSES

Name of Child_____ Birthdate_____ Age_____

Evaluated by_____ Date_____

COMMENTS

I. Auditory Perception	
A. Recognition of Gross Sounds	
B. Auditory Discrimination	
C. Auditory Memory	
D. Auditory Sequencing	
E. Auditory Synthesizing	
F. Auditory Analyzing	
II. Auditory Reception	
A. Word Meaning	
B. Phrase Meaning	
C. Sentence Meaning	
D. Paragraph Meaning	
III. Expressive Verbal Language	
A. Auditory Recall for Words	
B. Vocal Encoding	
1. Phrases	
2. Sentences	
3. Stories	
C. Use of Grammar in Connected Speech	
IV. Speech	

EVALUATION MATERIAL
AUDITORY-VERBAL LANGUAGE

I. Auditory Perception

   A. Recognition of gross sounds. The ability to associate a sound with an object.
      1. Collect a group of objects (bell, whistle, noisemaker). Place the objects on a table. Have the child close his eyes. Ring the bell, etc.; have the child open his eyes and point to the correct object.
   B. Auditory Discrimination. Hearing similarities and differences between sounds.
      1. *Wepman Test of Auditory Discrimination* (1958).
      2. Look at the child's spelling errors; does he write *f/th, f/v, sh/ch*?
   C. Auditory Memory.
      1. For digits: Auditory-Vocal Sequencing subtest of the ITPA.
      2. For letters: Slingerland's subtest number 6.
      3. For words: Slingerland's individual auditory testing section.
      4. For sentences: Auditory Memory for Sentences, by E. M. Spencer (1958).
      5. Does the child's school record indicate difficulty in following oral directions?
   D. Auditory Sequencing. The child may be able to remember a series of digits, and thus indicate he has auditory memory; however, the concern here is with the child's ability to remember things in the correct order.
      1. Note the child's performance on the auditory memory tasks. Does he reverse the order of the stimuli?
      2. Can he produce tapped rhythms (see Kephart, 1960).
      3. On a toy xylophone play a series of melodies—for example, high, low, low, high. Can the child reproduce the melody?
      4. Present a short story in sequence. Can the child repeat back in the correct order?
   E. Auditory Synthesizing. Is the child able to blend sounds together so he knows the meaning of the word?

1. Use only auditory clues. Do not present a word visually and then ask him to sound it out.
2. *Roswell-Chall Auditory Blending Test* (1963).
3. Can he combine separate sounds into words?
4. Can he combine or blend syllables? Construct your own evaluation tasks using the Forbes graded spelling lists.

F. Auditory Analyzing. The ability to perceive the order in which sounds occur.
1. Use auditory stimuli and verbal responses.
2. Present words with two sounds. Can the child tell you how many sounds are in the word? Increase the number of sounds in the words gradually.
3. Does the child recognize beginning, middle, and ending sounds in words?
4. Can he analyze a word into several parts?

II. *Auditory Reception*

A. Word Meaning. *Peabody Picture Vocabulary Test.*
B. Phrases. Prepare a list of phrases that require motor responses. For example, "Jump up onto the chair." Some of the cards in the *Language Lotto* series may be adapted for evaluation purposes.
C. Sentences.
1. Auditory Decoding subtest of the ITPA.
2. Prepare your own list of questions that require "yes" and "no" responses.
3. Some of the cards in the *Language Lotto* series may be used here.
4. Can the child follow directions?
D. Paragraph.
1. Does the child comprehend oral reading material
   a. When he reads it?
   b. When you read it to him?
   (The questions asked should require "yes" or "no" answers as the child with an expressive language problem may understand the material but may be unable to respond to questions that require sentence structure.)
2. Does the child understand what you say to him?

III. Expressive Verbal Language

   A. Auditory Recall for Words. Is the child able to retrieve words for spontaneous speech?

   1. Ask the child to name various objects or pictures of objects.
      a. Collect your own pictures
      b. Use some of the cards in *Language Lotto*.
   2. Ask the child a series of questions requiring a one-word response. For example, "What do you cut meat with?"
   3. Ask the child to name all the objects found in a bathroom, kitchen, etc.
   4. Does he use nouns in his conversational speech?
   5. The Vocal Encoding subtest of the ITPA can be used.

NOTE: If a child cannot retrieve words for spontaneous speech usage, give him two choices for a response. For example, "What do you cut meat with?" If there is no response ask, "A knife or a fork?" The child having difficulty recalling nouns will be able to give the correct response when given a choice.

   B. Vocal Encoding. Does the child speak in sentences?

   1. Have the child describe a picture.
   2. Evaluate his responses on the Vocal Encoding subtest of the ITPA.
   3. The Slingerland test has a section for recording the child's expressive language.

   C. Use of Grammar in Connected Speech.

   1. Observe the child's use of grammar on the Auditory-Vocal Automatic and Vocal Encoding subtests of the ITPA.
   2. Have the child describe a picture. Observe his use of grammar.
   3. Is the child able to form the motor movements for speech?

IV. Speech

   1. *Templin-Darley Articulation Test.*
   2. Oral Peripheral examination.
   3. Sample of conversational speech (use tape recorder).

AUDITORY PROCESS TRAINING PROGRAM

I. Auditory Perception

The following activities are only a few suggestions for use in auditory perceptual training. For other activities refer to Cruickshank *et al.* (1961) *A Teaching Method for Brain-injured and Hyperactive Children,* pages 240–46, and Blessing's (1965) paper "Remediation of Psycholinguistic Deficits in Retarded Children."

A. Recognition of Gross Sounds.
1. Any activities requiring the child to attend to sound.
2. Activities that require the child to identify sounds such as bells, whistles, drums, horns, etc.

B. Auditory Discrimination.
1. Place several objects that make sounds on a table. The child looks at the objects and then turns his back. The teacher sounds a particular noisemaker. The child turns around and points to the object that made the sound.
2. Activities that require the child to discriminate pitch, intensity, and tempo.
3. The above activities should precede those that require the child to discriminate speech sounds, words that begin with the same sound, or words that sound alike.

C. Auditory Memory.
1. Have various instruments such as a bell, drum, whistle, horn. Play two instruments. The child then picks up the two he heard. At this stage the order he picks them up is not of interest. Increase the number of sounds gradually.
2. Tapping out patterns.
   a. Rhythm activities such as those in McLeod (1965), *Readiness for Learning,* p. 10.
   b. Also in Kephart (1960), *The Slow Learner in the Classroom,* pp. 235–9.
3. Repeating activities (begin with two and gradually increase):
   a. Numbers
   b. Individual speech sounds
   c. Syllables

      d. Words

      e. Phrases

      f. Sentences

    4. Sentence-completion activities.

    5. Dictation.

D. Auditory Sequencing (see Gillingham and Stillman, 1960, p. 145).

    1. Have the child reproduce a series of movements presented aurally. Examples: "run," "run, hop," "run, hop, skip." Gradually increase the number.

    2. Put several objects that produce sound on a table. Sound two of them. The child turns his back when you sound them. He then sounds the objects in the correct sequence.

    3. Have the child fill in the missing number. Example, "8, 9, —." The numbers are presented aurally. Increase the numbers gradually.

    4. Present a series of verbal commands. The child must do them in the correct order.

    5. Following oral directions: Prepare a ditto sheet with rows of numbers, pictures, or letters on it. Record the verbal directions on a tape recorder—"Listen" (pause) "Ready" (pause) "Put an X on the boy." In the beginning pause only for a fraction of a second but gradually increase the length of the pauses.

    6. Dictation. See Gillingham and Stillman (1960), p. 196.

    7. Melodies. An a toy xylophone play a three-note, four-note, etc., melody. Have the child imitate the melody.

    8. *See-Quees* by Judy, complete stories cut into separate episodes; also story sets by Judy.

E. Auditory Synthesizing.

    1. MATERIALS: flannel board and pictures. Have various items belonging to one category such as food or clothing. Put two pictures on the board. Say, "I am going to say the sounds that make up the name of one of the things on the board. I am going to say the sounds very *slowly.* You will have to put the sounds together to find out which one it is. Put on your listening ears." Give some examples before asking a child to do this. Any

variation of the above use of materials can be used. Do this activity every day during the auditory perceptual training period.

2. Give each child a picture or an object. The child holds up the object that has been sounded and gives the name.

3. After the group becomes familiar with synthesizing, have team games.

4. Have a ditto sheet with pictures. Say the sounds for a particular thing. The child circles the appropriate picture.

5. After many experiences with the above activities, give only an auditory clue, no visual clue. Say the sounds separately, for example, c-a-t. Have the child say the sounds separately and then have him blend them.

If a child has difficulty with synthesizing have him repeat the sounds after you, and then have him blend them for activities 1–4. The tape recorder and an *Echorder* can be used for synthesizing.

F. Auditory Analyzing.

1. Use instruments such as a bell, whistle, etc. Play two of them. Ask the child, "Which one did you hear first?" Do this until the child can identify the first sound consistently.

2. Use individual speech sounds. Ask the child, "Which sound did you hear first?" Repeat this until the child is able to identify the first sound easily and consistently.

3. Using words the children listened to for synthesizing, ask, "How many sounds do you hear in this word?" Say the word slowly at first so they can count the sounds as you make them. Or, have them put a mark on a paper or on the chalkboard for each sound they hear. After several days increase the rate at which the sounds are produced.

4. For older children: have them divide the words into syllables.

5. Introduce beginning sounds in words. Choose a sound, such as "p." Collect pictures of objects or things with "p." Have the child say the words. Ask the child, "What sound do you hear at the beginning of 'pig'?"

All these activities are done only with auditory stimuli. The visual symbols for the sounds are not presented during this period of auditory training.

II. Auditory Reception

We have found that a child with auditory receptive language problems often has auditory perceptual difficulties as well. The child's speech may be characterized by jargon or by echolalic speech —when he does not understand what you have said he repeats what you have said to him. Also, his verbal responses are sometimes delayed. Often, if a sentence is reworded for him he can understand what was said. A child with a receptive language problem may be able to do number computations but be unable to do word problems. The nature and degree of the auditory receptive problem can best be determined by working with the child.

Speaking in short phrases and/or simplifying the structure of the sentence, using verbal clues and gesture language, are some general ways the teacher can help the child gain information in the classroom.

Although most materials and procedures are developed by the person working with the child, the following sources have been found useful.

1. The *Echorder* and the accompanying *A Manual of Speech and Language Training Methods Using the Echorder,* by Ronald K. Sommers and Dorothy C. Brady (1964).
2. Continental Press publications such as *Useful Language* duplicating masters, and *Building Good English.*
3. *Language Lotto, by* Lassar G. Gotkin (1966).
4. *Laugh and Learn with Julie and Jack,* by Sister Mary Walter (1964) of St. John's School for the Deaf, Milwaukee, Wisconsin.
5. *Peabody Language Development Kits,* Level I and Level II, by Dunn *et al.*
6. *Steps in Language Development for the Deaf,* by Bessie L. Pugh (1955).
7. *Listening Aides Through the Grades, by* David H. and Elizabeth F. Russell (1966).
8. *Language Development Experiences for Young Children,* by Rose C. Engel *et al.* (1966).

III. Expressive Verbal Language

We have observed the following types of oral language problems in children:

1. Difficulties in remembering words for use in spontaneous speech;
2. Difficulty in expressing ideas in spoken words;
3. Difficulty with word order, verb tenses, prepositions, or word endings;
4. Difficulties in moving the articulators for speech (an inability to make the necessary motor movements).

Children with expressive language problems should not be held responsible for verbal responses. However, as they get older they can respond by writing their answers. The following activities are suggested for helping children express themselves more adequately.

A. Auditory Recall for Words.
1. Develop a useful vocabulary.
2. Multiple-choice activities. For example, "Do we cut with scissors or with a pencil?"
3. Rapid naming activities.
4. Sentence-completion activities.
5. Stories with pictures. For example, "This is a picture of a house."
6. Word pairs and associations.
7. Activities using the *Language Master.*
8. Lessons for auditory recall in *A Manual of Speech and Language Training Methods Using the Echorder,* by Sommers and Brady (1964), pp. 6–18.
9. Use visual clues to develop auditory recall. The child looks at a picture of a hat. The word is then presented by itself. The child names the object. Repeat, using the first two letters of the word, the first letter, and then with no visual clue have the child name the object.
10. Feeling objects and naming them.
11. Activities to help the child picture things in his mind (imagery).

B. Vocal Encoding.
1. The activities used for auditory recall may be used for developing vocal encoding.

2. Activities from the *Peabody Language Development Kit,* Levels I and II.

3. The vocal encoding activities mentioned by Blessing (1965) in "Remediation of Psycholinguistic Deficits in Retarded Children."

C. Use of Grammar in Connecting Speech.

The child may have difficulty in one or more of the following areas due to difficulty in retaining patterns: word order, word endings, verb tenses, prepositions, and articles. The training he needs will depend on what type of difficulty he has with the structure of the language. A trial period of training should be provided. If the child does not respond to the training after a reasonable amount of time, it may be necessary to discontinue the training until later. Some children "pick up" the syntax and are able to retain the patterns of our language and others seem relatively unable to do so.

The following materials are useful for those wanting more information about the structure of language:

1. *Psycholinguistics,* edited by Sol Saporta (1961).

2. *Certain Language Skills in Children* by Mildred Templin (1957).

3. *Language and the Discovery of Reality,* by Joseph Church (1961).

4. *The Process of Education,* by Jerome Brunner (1963).

5. *Toward a Theory of Instruction,* by Brunner (1966).

6. *Development and Disorders of Written Language,* by Helmer Myklebust (1965).

IV. Speech

In addition to auditory-verbal language problems, many children were slow in beginning to speak. Their speech may have been unintelligible in the pre-school and kindergarten years, or they had some articulation deviations, or their speech development progressed at a slower rate than would be expected. Although some children have unintelligible speech during their early years in school, the majority have what is usually considered a mild or moderate articulation problem. That is, they have a lisp or they substitute sounds ("w" for "r," "wabbit" for "rabbit").

Auditory perceptual training and language training should precede speech correction. Generally, many children show evidence of difficulty in auditory feedback. They lack an awareness of the speaker-listener relationship. Before speech correction can be started, in most instances the child must learn to decode and encode language. Many children have difficulty in figure-background, auditory memory, and other problems of audition that must be learned or developed before they can learn to monitor their speech. Once they are able to monitor what they hear and what they say, correction for their articulation deviations can be attempted.

REFERENCES

Blessing, K. Remediation of psycholinguistic deficits in retarded children. In Hellmuth, J. (Ed.) *Learning Disorders.* Volume 1. Seattle, Wash.: Special Child Publications, 1965.

Brunner, J. *The Process of Education.* New York: Vintage Press, 1963.

Brunner, J. *Toward a Theory of Instruction.* Cambridge, Mass.: Harvard University Press, 1966.

Church, J. *Language and the Discovery of Reality.* New York: Random House, 1961.

Cruickshank, W., *et al. A Teaching Method for Brain-injured and Hyperactive Children.* Syracuse, N. Y.: Syracuse University Press, 1961.

Dunn, L. M. *Peabody Picture Vocabulary Test.* Minneapolis, Minn.: American Guidance Service, 1959.

Dunn, L. M., Smith, J. O., & Horton, K. B. *Peabody Language Development Kits,* Levels I and II. 720 Washington Avenue, S. E., Minneapolis, Minn. 55014: American Guidance Service.

Duplicator Material for Special Education. Elizabethtown, Penn.: Continental Press.

Engel, Rose C., *et al. Language Development Experiences for Young Children.* Department of Exceptional Education, University of Southern California, Los Angeles, 1966.

Gillingham, A. & Stillman, B. *Remedial Training for Children with Specific Disability in Reading, Spelling, and Penmanship.* Cambridge, Mass.: Educators Publishing Service, 1966.

Gotkin, L. G. *Language Lotto.* New York: Appleton-Century-Crofts, 1966.

Hardy, W. Problems of audition, perception, and understanding. *Volta Review,* June 1956, 68, 289–300.

Kephart, N. C. *The Slow Learner in the Classroom.* Columbus, O.: Merrill, 1960.

Language Master. Bell and Howell Corp., 6800 McCormick Road, Chicago, Ill. 60645.

Lewis, R. S. *The Other Child.* New York: Grune & Stratton, 1951.

McCarthy, J., & Kirk, S. *Illinois Test of Psycholinguistic Abilities.* Urbana, Ill.: University of Illinois Press.

McLeod, P. H. *Readiness for Learning.* Philadelphia, Penn.: Lippincott, 1965.

Myklebust, H. *Auditory Disorders in Children.* New York: Grune & Stratton, 1954.

Myklebust, Helmer. *Development and Disorders of Written Language.* New York: Grune & Stratton, 1965.

Penfield, W., & Roberts, L. *Speech and Brain Mechanisms.* Princeton, N. J.: Princeton University Press, 1959.

Pugh, B. *Steps in Language Development for the Deaf.* 1537 35th Street, N. W., Washington, D. C.: The Volta Bureau, 1955.

Roswell, F. G., & Chall, J. S. *Auditory Blending Test.* P. O. Box 5, Planetarium Station, New York 24, N. Y.: The Essay Press, 1963.

Russell, D. H., & Russell, E. F. *Listening Aides Through the Grades.* New York: Teachers College Press, Columbia University, 1966.

St. John's School for the Deaf, Milwaukee, Wisc. *Laugh and Learn with Julie and Jack,* by Sister Mary Walter, 1964.

Saporta, S. (Ed.) *Psycholinguistics: A Book of Readings.* Philadelphia, Penn.: Holt, Rinehart & Winston, 1961.

See-Quees, by Judy. The Judy Company, 310 North Second Street, Minneapolis, Minn. 55401.

Slingerland, B. *Screening Tests for Identifying Children with Specific Language Disability.* Cambridge, Mass.: Educators Publishing Service, 1964.

Sommers, R. K., & Brady, D. *Echorder* and *A Manual of Speech and Language Training Methods Using the Echorder.* RIL Electronics, Southampton, Penn.

Spencer, E. M. Auditory Memory for Sentences. Doctoral dissertation, Northwestern University, 1958.

Templin, M. *Certain Language Skills in Children.* Minneapolis, Minn.: University of Minnesota Press, 1957.

Templin, M., & Darley, F. L. *Templin-Darley Test of Articulation: A Manual and Discussion of One Screening and Diagnostic Test.* Iowa City, Iowa: Bureau of Educational Research and Service, State University of Iowa, 1960.

Wepman, J. M. *Wepman Test of Auditory Discrimination.* Chicago, Ill.: 95 East 59th Street, Language Research Associates, 1958.

20

Non-Verbal Processes

The importance of non-verbal skills and their optimal development in the classroom cannot be overemphasized. As Kastein (1962) states, "Only when the child has developed an awareness of himself as an organism apart from the mother and apart from the physical world around him, only when he is able to focus on a stimulus and perceive it against the background of unstructured stimuli, will he be able to listen, look, touch, and react adequately to what he has so perceived. Sensations will then be followed by perception, perception leads to concept formation (symbol behavior) and language and speech result" (p. 158).

Thus, for children who have motor learning problems and who do not respond to sensory stimuli appropriately, we must, as Getman (1965) states, help the child "learn to act." Getman says "children must first learn to act, and when they have achieved magnitudes of skills in these actions, they will act to learn" (p. 74).

It is important to differentiate between motor training and the traditional physical education program in the schools. Generally, the physical education program emphasizes physical fitness. The perceptual-motor training program is concerned with developing motor coordination and utilization of motor patterns (Kephart, 1963). The physical education program is integrated with the motor training program.

Motor training programs are outlined by Kephart (1960) in *The Slow Learner in the Classroom,* and by Getman and Kane (1964) in *The Physiology of Readiness.*

With some children the teacher can outline a motor training program to be carried out at home by the parents. The teacher should outline the program and demonstrate it to the parents during individual parent conferences.

Many children do not respond adequately to sensory stimuli. In classes for younger children the focus is on the perceptual-motor aspects of development; these have been found to be basic to success in learning tasks of an "academic skill" nature, such as reading, writing, and spelling (Delacato, 1963; Dubnoff, 1966; Frostig, 1961; Getman, 1965; Kephart, 1960). A deficiency or lag in development in one or more aspects of visual-perceptual-motor growth has been found to affect other areas such as reading or writing.

For example, a child who has not developed laterality (an inner awareness of directionality, of the two sides of the body) usually has difficulty in seeing the difference between *b* and *d* in reading or in reproducing the *b* and *d* in writing. If laterality and directionality are developed the child typically does not have difficulty with those letters and numbers that commonly are reversed.

Form 6 is used to record information obtained from an evaluation of a child's visual-motor, perceptual-motor, and written language processes, and his "neurological organization." The form is similar in design to Forms 4 and 5. Questions and items to look for in a child follow the form along with suggestions on how to conduct more detailed evaluations and how to provide training for the areas covered.

<hr>

EDUCATIONAL EVALUATION CHECK LIST
FORM 6: NON-VERBAL PROCESSES

Name of Child_____ Birthdate_____ Age_____

Evaluated by_____ Date_____

COMMENTS

I. Visual-Motor	
A. Eye-Hand Coordination	
B. Copying	
C. Kinesthetic Feel for the Form of Letters and Numbers	

D. Ocular Control	
E. Left-Right Progression	
F. Small-Muscle Coordination	
II. Perceptual-Motor	
A. Control of Gross Musculature	
B. Balance	
C. Rhythm	
D. Laterality	
E. Directionality	
F. Crossing the Midline	
G. Body Image	
H. Performance with Bilateral Activities	
I. Splinter Skills	
J. Form Perception	
III. Neurological Organization	
A. Crawl	
B. Cross Pattern Creeping	
C. Cross Pattern Walking	
D. Handedness	
E. Footedness	
F. Eyedness	
IV. Tactile	
A. Objects	
B. Letters	
C. Numbers	
V. Written Language	

EVALUATION MATERIAL
NON-VERBAL PROCESSES

I. Visual-Motor

   A. Eye-Hand Coordination.
      1. Can the child catch a ball?
      2. "Imitation of Movements" (Kephart, 1960, p. 132). These tasks require the child to transfer a visual pattern into a motor pattern.
      3. Eye-hand coordination subtest of the *Frostig Test of Visual Perception* (1961).
      4. Writing
         a. Describe the posture of the child when he writes.
         b. How does the child position his paper?
         c. Does the child put his head close to the paper?
         d. Does his head tilt to the left or the right? If the child is right-eyed, he usually tilts his head to the left. If he is left-eyed, he usually tilts his head to the right. (Refer to Delacato, 1966, pp. 12–13; and Gillingham and Stillman, 1966, pp. 290–394 for descriptions of correct posture and position of paper.)
         e. How does the child hold his hand when he writes?
   B. Copying.
      1. Slingerland's (1964) test:
         a. Far point; subtest number 1.
         b. Near point; subtest number 2.
      2. Construct your own test.
      3. A child who has difficulty in copying because he:
         a. Is unable to read what he is copying;
         b. Does not see each word as a whole;
         c. Does not have the kinesthetic feel for the form of the letters;
         d. Has poor visual memory
  should be observed as he copies in order to determine the reason(s).
   C. Kinesthetic Feel for the Form of Letters and Numbers.
      1. Slingerland's (1964) test, subtests numbers one and two.

2. Have the child write the alphabet and numbers 1–10:
   a. Does he form the letters correctly?
   b. Does he have difficulty re-visualizing what the letter looks like?
3. Have the child write several letters without looking at the paper. Is he able to write the letters? If not, his kinesthetic feel for the form of the letters is weak.
4. Do the same for numbers.

D. Ocular Control.
   1. Kephart's (1960, pp. 147–9) *Perceptual Rating Survey Scale*.
   2. Refer to Delacato's (1966, pp. 7–9) pamphlet, *Neurological Organization in the Classroom*. If a child seems to have an eye problem a referral can be made to an optometrist or ophthalmologist to determine its significance; usually, ocular control problems can be handled in the classroom.

E. Left-Right Progression.
   1. Does the child begin to read at the left side of the page?
   2. Does he read words, phrases, in the reverse order?
   3. Put two dots on the blackboard. Does he connect them from left to right?
   4. Is he able to arrange a series of pictures in left-right sequence?
   5. When given paper and pencil tasks does he begin at the left side of the page?

F. Small-Muscle Coordination.
   1. At what age was the child able to tie his shoes?
   2. Observe the child as he colors a picture. Can he stay inside the lines?
   3. Observe the child stringing beads.
   4. Observe the child using a pegboard.
   5. Have the child cut out a figure.
   6. Review his school records. Did the kindergarten, first, or second grade teachers comment that he had poor small-muscle coordination?
   7. How does he hold his pencil? Usually, if he has not developed small-muscle coordination for writing but is

required to write in first grade, he will not use his fingers to control his pencil. Also, the writing will be quite large. Letters may be formed incorrectly. He may write very slowly for a child his age.

8. Collect samples of his writing and compare them with samples from other children his age.

II. Perceptual-Motor

Kephart's (1960, pp. 120–55) *Perceptual Rating Survey Scale* is used for evaluating the child's perceptual-motor development. This scale has been adapted for use as an evaluation sheet for teacher-use. The evaluation sheet enables teachers to record the child's performance, to know how to evaluate the performance, and to know what type of training will be needed. The user should be familiar with the original text by Kephart.

When the "Perceptual Rating Survey Scale" is complete the information can be transferred to Form 6, "Non-Verbal Processes."

PERCEPTUAL RATING SURVEY SCALE
(Adapted from Newell Kephart, *The Slow Learner in the Classroom.* Columbus, Ohio: Charles E. Merrill, 1960.)

Child's Name_____ Birthdate_____ Age_____

Teacher_____ Date_____

I. BALANCE
   A. *Walking Board*
      1. Forward
      2. Backward
      3. Sideways
         a. left to right (start with right)
         b. right to left (start with left).
  EVALUATION: (see pp. 123–9 of Kephart)
    #2 inadequate if he steps off more than twice.
    #3 Is there hesitation when movement must change from one foot to another? Observe which foot he starts with in (a) and (b) above.

Inadequate performance—failure to maintain balance.

Does he use one side of his body more consistently than the other?

Does he use his arm symmetrically during too much of his performance?

#3 identifies the child who is too one-sided; indicates a laterality problem if he goes better in one direction than the other.

B. *Jumping*
  1. Both feet
  2. Right
  3. Left

C. *Skipping*

D. *Hopping*
  1. 1/1 in place
     a. Right
     b. Left
     c. Alternate
  2. Hop 2/2 (twice on one foot, twice on other)
  3. Hop 2/1 (twice on right foot, once on left)
  4. Hop 1/2 (once on right foot, twice on left)

OBSERVE: Is behavior jerky or smooth? If jerky, he cannot shift from one postural orientation to another.

II. KNOWLEDGE OF BODY

A. *Identification of Body Parts*—children stand 10 ft. apart

Tester asks child to touch his

  1. shoulders   6. feet
  2. hips   7. eyes
  3. head   8. elbows
  4. ankles   9. mouth
  5. ears

OBSERVE:

Does child "feel around" for final target once he gets going in the general direction? If so, he is not aware of the exact location in space of the part.

  1. Hesitancy of response
  2. Paired parts, touches both

For complete evaluation, see p. 131.

TRAINING: angels in the snow; assembling body parts, etc.; drawing, coloring, etc. See p. 131.

B. *Imitation of Movements*

"Do whatever I do": see pp. 132 and 133 of Kephart

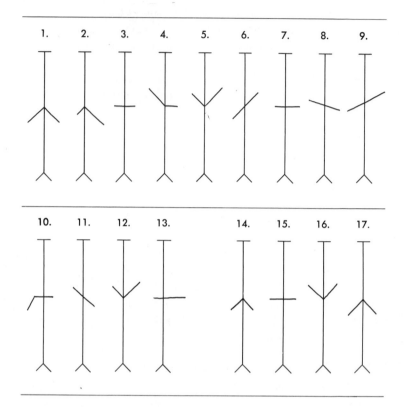

If the child does not perform correctly, the teacher may correct him.

OBSERVE:

1. It is desirable if child reverses laterality of examiner's movement. If not, let him parallel your movements. The consistency is what is important.
2. Movements should be prompt and definite. Look for abortive movements in the arm that should *not* move or a different direction in arm that *should* move.

EVALUATION AND TRAINING (see p. 133)

These tasks require the child to translate a visual pattern into a motor pattern. Use suggested chalkboard activities, p. 169; orientation activities, p. 180; and clock game, p. 171. This training is useful in filling the gap between visual-motor translation in a free situation and the more precise translation required for pencil and paper tasks.

C. *Obstacle Course*

> Materials: yardstick, 2 chairs
>> 1. Put yardstick across 2 chairs as high as child's knee. Ask him to step over it.
>> 2. Ask child to duck under an obstacle 2 in. lower than his shoulders without touching it.
>> 3. Ask him to squeeze through a narrow opening such as between the backs of 2 chairs facing each other without touching any part of the chair.

EVALUATION AND TRAINING (see p. 134)

Difficulty in these tasks indicates that the child's awareness of the space occupied by his body is not adequate. TRAINING: Part III in Kephart's book. Trampoline is especially useful. See Chapter 8, p. 217.

D. *Angels in the Snow*

> Child lies on back, arms at side, feet together.
> Preliminary exercises:
>> 1. Move arms over head, along floor until the hands touch.
>> 2. Move feet apart, keep heels on floor.

EVALUATION ITEMS:

> 1. Move just this arm (right). Put it back. Repeat for left arm.
> 2. Move just this leg (right). Now back. Repeat for left leg.
> 3. Move both arms. Now back.
> 4. Move both legs. Now back.
> 5. Move this arm and this leg (left arm and left leg). Now back. Repeat, using right arm and right leg. Next, try the exercise with right arm and left leg. Repeat for left arm and right leg. In each case point to the limb; do not say "left" or "right."

EVALUATION (see p. 136)

> 1. Smooth or jerky movements
> 2. Hesitation in beginning movements
> 3. Maximum extension of limb movements
> 4. Overflow of movements to limbs not required
> 5. Inability to initiate movement on basis of visual clues
> 6. Inability to carry out any patterns.

TRAINING (p. 230)

In case of severe failure, go back to the walking board, develop laterality concepts.

E. *Stepping Stones*

> Materials needed are 6" cardboard squares—10 black and 10 red. Place them around the room as described on p. 138.

OBSERVE:

Length of step demanded varies—does he have trouble adjusting? Look for false starts; crossing one foot over the other; does right or left foot lead?

EVALUATION (see p. 139)

F. *Chalkboard*

 1. "Draw a circle."

OBSERVE:

 1. Preferred hand
 2. Size of drawings
 3. Position of drawing with reference to midline
 4. Accuracy of production
 5. Direction

EVALUATION (p. 142)

TRAINING (pp. 161–8)

If gross motor is poor also, go back to walking board, other activities.

If poor only on the chalkboard, do scribbling, finger painting for directionality.

 2. Double Circles

OBSERVE:

 1. Relative size of drawings (two different size circles indicate inadequately correlated movement patterns of the two sides).
 2. Position of drawings with reference to each other (small circles that are wide apart indicate inadequate patterns of wrist and forearm; one circle on top of the other indicates avoidance of bimanual activity).
 3. Direction of movement of the two hands (right-handed child should draw the right circle counterclockwise, the left circle clockwise; left-handed child does the opposite).
 4. Relative accuracy of the two drawings (circles flat on the inside indicate a problem of laterality and midline; non-parallel distortions indicate inadequate correlation between the sides of the body).
 5. Attention (if child watches performance of one hand and disregards the other, he is avoiding laterality by making one hand so dominant the other merely follows along).

EVALUATION (p. 144)

If one circle is smaller than the other, there is difficulty matching activities on two sides of the body. If the problem is motor, bilateral activities, such as the walking board, are needed. If the problem is perceptual-motor, chalkboard activities of a bimanual nature are required. Difficulty with positioning the circles or common distortion of shape indicates a problem with perceptual-motor translation at the midline. Use training for difficulty in positioning one circle. Inconsistency or indecision in determining the direction of movement of circles or circles drawn with parallel movements indicate a need for orientation training. If the child gives all his attention to one hand, the perceptual-motor match is restricted; he may profit from bimanual training.

TRAINING (p. 165)

> 3. Lines
>   Lateral lines. The child is to connect two points, 18 inches apart on the chalkboard.

OBSERVE:

Use of the body (walking across indicates difficulty crossing the midline).

Use of the hand (inaccurate production across the midline or changing hands indicates difficulty crossing the midline).

Vertical lines. The child is to draw two parallel lines. Notice any distortions. If they are due to laterality, laterality training and perceptual-motor translation are indicated. If it is due to perceptual-motor translation, chalkboard orientation (Lazy 8) is needed.

EVALUATION (p. 146)

TRAINING (p. 182)

G. *Ocular Pursuits*

> 1. Lateral (use pencil with thumbtack in eraser). Follow an arc of 18 inches.
> 2. Vertical. Follow an 18-inch vertical arc. OBSERVATIONS: same as in #1.
> 3. Diagonal, from lower left to upper right; then reverse directions. Evaluate the poorer of the two performances.
> 4. Rotary. Radius of 18-inch arc.
> 5. Monocular—Right eye. Cover left eye and repeat #1–4.
> 6. Monocular—Left eye. Cover the right eye and repeat #1–4. Note the diagonal movements, especially "stair-stepping" at the midline (see p. 150.)

OBSERVE:

> 1. Smooth or jerky movements, indicating the degree of control
> 2. Relationship of the two eyes
> 3. Are the eyes always on target?
> 4. Performance across the midline

TRAINING (see Part III, Chapter 9, p. 241)

EVALUATION (see pp. 146–50)

H. *Visual Achievement Forms*

Present the forms in a straight vertical and horizontal orientation. Instruct the children to "make one like this." Notice if they turn the paper. Present forms according to this scale.

Chronological age of 7 years—all forms
6 years—first 5 forms
5 years—first 4 forms
4 years—first 3 forms

Do not present forms to children under 4 years of age.

OBSERVE:

Form of drawings. Is the form completed as a whole, or one piece at a time? The child should use one continuous line.

Size should be same as that of the form presented.

Divided rectangle. The diagonals and bisecting lines should be seen as parts of the total figure.

Diamond. Notice "ears" on the form.

EVALUATION (p. 154)

If the child cannot make a recognizable form in one or more drawings or there is gross segmenting, this indicates form-perception weakness. Training includes chalkboard activities, especially drawing and copying. Minor segmenting of "dog ears" indicates difficulty in maintaining a constructive form. Form-perception training is indicated (see Part III). The child who makes the figures too small or cramps them into a restricted area is demonstrating a splinter skill.

TRAINING (see p. 183)

III. *Neurological Organization*

A. Crawl.

    1. Stationary

    2. Moving

"The child lies on his stomach with his head turned to the right, his right arm flexed with his hand at eye level. His right leg should be flexed with the knee level with his left hip. The child's left arm and left leg should be extended. The child then reverses this arrangement alternately in a rhythmic manner . . ." (McLeod, 1965, p. iv).

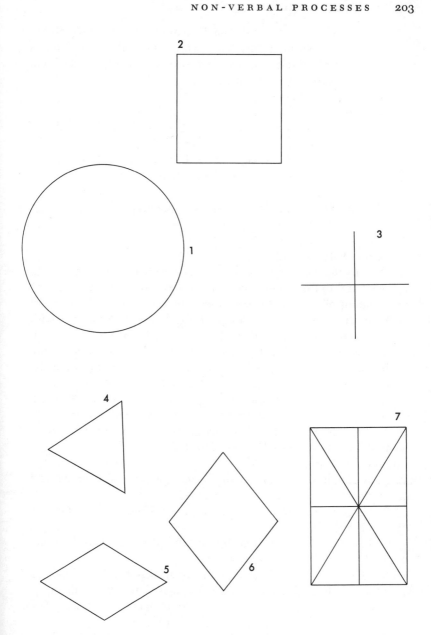

This activity gives an indication of the child's ability to coordinate his body. Have the child do the crawl several times so that he knows what is expected of him before evaluating his ability.

B. Cross Pattern Creeping.

"The specific aspects of creeping to notice are these:

1. Is the pattern proper—that is, do the right hand and left knee touch the floor at the same time, and do the left hand and right knee touch at the same time?
2. Is the rhythm good? Does it seem like a smooth, easy motion?
3. Are the hands and fingers in the proper position?
4. Do the toes drag along on the floor?"

(Delacato, 1966, p. 7).

C. Cross Pattern Walking.

"Say to the student, 'Watch me walk. Notice that I point with one hand to the opposite foot as I walk.' Now demonstrate, stepping off with your right foot, pointing to it with your left hand, then stepping forward with the left foot, point to it with your right hand. After you have taken eight or nine steps, turn around and say, 'Now watch me again—I am pointing to the opposite foot.' Walk back to your starting position and tell the child, 'You do it.' Watch him as he walks to see if the opposite arm and leg move at the same time. Negative indications are a lack of rhythm, improper pattern (using both sides of the body at the same time), crossing over of the feet, loss of balance, or inability to get started" (Delacato, 1966, pp. 8–9).

Before evaluating handedness, eyedness, and footedness, the evaluator should be familiar with the various writers' opinions and the studies done in the area of dominance:

1. *Speech and Brain Mechanisms,* by Penfield and Roberts (1959), Chapter VI.
2. *Reading, Writing, and Speech Problems in Children,* by S. Orton (1937), pages 48–60.
3. "The Needs of Teachers for Specialized Information on Handedness, Finger Localization, and Cerebral Dominance," by Gaddes, pages 209–21, in Cruickshank, W. (Ed.) *The Teacher of Brain-injured Children* (1966).
4. *The Diagnosis and Treatment of Speech and Reading Problems,* by Delacato (1963).

D. Handedness.
    1. Case history of handedness.
    2. Does anyone in the family use his left hand? Are they all left- or right-handed?
    3. Keep a record of the activities he uses his right or left hands for.
    4. Ask the child to pretend he is
        a. Eating
        b. Brushing his teeth
        c. Throwing a ball
        d. Writing.
    Then have him actually do these things with the appropriate utensils. A child will often use his dominant hand for the pretended activities and his non-dominant hand that he was forced to use for the real activity in instances where the child was switched.
    5. Observe the child in the classroom and have the mother keep a record at home of which hand he prefers for
        a. Throwing a ball
        b. Picking up objects
        c. Coloring
        d. Cutting
        e. Writing.

E. Footedness.
    1. Have the child kick a ball across the room.
    2. Have him pretend he is kicking a football.
    3. Have him move a small object across the floor.
    4. Have him step on a chair. Which foot does he use to step up with?

F. Eyedness.
    1. Fold a 9x12-inch paper in half two times. Tear off a corner for a peephole. Have the child hold it in both hands at waist level, arms outstretched. Tell him to fixate on a small object on eye level at midline. Then have the child lift the paper, look through the peephole at target, pulling the peephole closer to his eyes. Do this several times. The eye with which he looks through the peephole may be said to be dominant.
    2. "Have the child sit at his desk and mark an 'X' about a

quarter of an inch high on a sheet of paper. Give him a small tube, three or four inches long, made of a rolled sheet of paper. Have him hold the tube in both hands and look at the 'X' through the tube. Then ask him to bring the tube slowly back closer to his eye without losing sight of the 'X.' Notice to which eye he brings the tube" (Delacato, 1966, p. 12). Do this several times.

IV. Tactile

A. Objects.

Collect several objects. Put them in a bag. Ask the child first to tell you what shape, size, or other characteristics the objects have and then to tell you what they are. Objects may be a cup, spoon, fork, eraser, pencil, plastic fruit.

B. Letters.

Use sandpaper letters. Place several in a bag. Ask the child to feel each letter very carefully and tell you what they are.

C. Numbers.

Same as with letters.

V. Written Language

A. Use *Picture Story Language Test* (Myklebust, 1965).
B. Evaluate the quality of the child's written work.
1. Can he write letters?
2. Can he connect the letters to form a word?
3. Can he write a sentence?
4. Can he express a thought in writing?
5. Can he copy?

C. Spelling.
1. Do the errors show lack of knowledge of certain spelling rules?
2. Does the child write any combination of letters for words, even though they may not make sense? If so, he may have difficulty in re-visualizing.
3. Does the child confuse short vowels or other sounds,

for example *s* for *sh*? If so, he may have difficulty in symbol-sound association.

4. Dictate phonetic nonsense syllables such as *nif, taf*. The child who uses auditory clues when he spells will be able to write one nonsense syllable after several practice syllables. The child who is unable to write what he hears is not using auditory clues for spelling.

5. Can the child spell words of more than one syllable? If not, he may have difficulty in syllabication.

D. Grammar.

Does the child leave out certain parts of speech such as prepositions, verbs, nouns, endings of words?

NON-VERBAL PROCESSES TRAINING PROGRAM

The materials that follow do not adhere to the order listed on Form 6, but are presented in Levels I, II, and III. The reason for this is that the activities, as separate from the evaluation processes, should be carried out in an integrated manner.

LEVEL I

All the activities of this level should be carried out at approximately the same time rather than scheduling different ones for different blocks of time.

A. Motor.
   1. Crawl (McLeod, 1965, p. xi).
      a. Stationary
      b. Moving.
   2. Creeping (Delacato, 1966, p. 7).
   3. "Angels in the Snow" (Kephart, 1960, pp. 132–3).
B. Laterality.
   1. Trampoline activities (Kephart, 1960, pp. 224–33).
   2. Balance on toes
      a. Both feet
      b. Right foot
      c. Left foot.
   3. Tape walking
      a. Forward

      b. Backward
      c. Sideways.
    4. Balance beam (Getman and Kane, 1964, pp. 36–9).
      a. Forward
      b. Backward
      c. Sideways.

C. Visual.
    1. Have the child hold an object at arm's length. He moves the object and follows it with his eyes. His head should remain stationary.
    2. Child tosses balls and beanbags in the air.

D. Visual-Motor.
    1. "Imitation of Movements" (Kephart, 1960, p. 133).
    2. "Simon Says"
    3. "Experimenting with Motor Patterns" (See Level I of the Writing Program, p. 217).
    4. Small-muscle coordination
      a. Montessori templates
      b. Simple cutting, placing, pasting activities
      c. Parquetry blocks
      d. Bead stringing
      e. Pegboard activities
      f. Montessori button, lacing frames.

E. Body Image.
    1. Unit on the body (see activities for Position in Space, p. 163).
    2. Learning more about our bodies.
      a. Have the children roll across the floor. Talk about the various parts of the body. As children roll, ask them to name the part of the body they are on.
      b. Experiencing how the various body parts move. Have the children lie on mats. Have them stretch their arms and then their legs. Have them open and close their hands. Have them do all this with their eyes closed. Talk about the feelings of stretching and relaxing.
      c. Activities in Group I, "Basic Songs for Exceptional Children," Concept Records, Volume I.
      d. Concept Records, Volume II: "Shiver and Shake,"

"Arms Up, Arms Down," "Hands on My Head," "The Toe Song," "Fingers, Fingers," "Up, Up, Up, Down, Down."

3. Learning about moving the body through space.
   a. Have the children lie on the floor and then sit up.
   b. Have the children sit and then stand up.
   c. Have the children stand and then sit.
   d. Have the children kneel and then stand.
4. Moving in space.
   a. Have the children jump over a yardstick placed between two chairs at the appropriate height for each child.
   b. Put circles on the floor, using masking tape. Have the circles of different sizes. Have the children walk over them without touching the sides; then have them jump over. (Squares, triangles, and rectangles may also be used. These may also be used for training in perceptual constancy and form perception by having children walk around the forms and describe the movements they make to get around them.)

The preceding activities help the child make the necessary perceptual-motor matches that are the foundation for the visual perception skills needed for reading, writing, and other "academic" skills.

F. Tactile.
   1. The child should be given many experiences in just feeling objects. The teacher says, "This is smooth; this is rough; this is round; this is light." The child should repeat after the teacher.
   2. Experiences in feeling objects should be provided every day. A corner of the room can be set aside where children can go during their free time and manipulate the various objects.

LEVEL II

A. Motor.
   1. Gross pattern walking (Delacato, 1966, pp. 8–9).
   2. Control of gross musculature.
B. Laterality.
   1. Continue on trampoline, balance beam.

  2. Introduce left and right sides of the body.

  3. Concept Records, Volumes II and III.

C. Visual.

  1. The teacher holds an object and the child follows it
   a. Left to right
   b. Up and down
   c. Diagonally.

  2. Ocular-control training in Part III of Kephart's *The Slow Learner . . .* (1960).

D. Visual-Motor.

  1. Continue small-muscle coordination activities of Level I.

  2. Frostig worksheets for developing eye-hand coordination.

E. Body Image.

  Continue Level I activities.

F. Tactile.

  1. Using the objects of Level I, the teacher should direct the child's experiences in comparing the feelings of rough, smooth, etc.

  2. The child should be given activities where he is expected to discriminate between two objects by feel.

  3. Ask the child to sort all the rough things from the smooth by feel.

  4. Have the child walk, run, skip; begin the development several objects in a bag. The child describes them, he doesn't just name them.

LEVEL III

A. Motor.

  1. Continue with gross motor coordination activities.

  2. "Jumping Jacks."

  3. "Bilateral action" activities (Getman and Kane, 1964, pp. 19–21).

  4. Have the child walk, run, skip; begin the development of "motor patterns" and "motor generalizations" (Kephart, 1963). For example, have the child run to a certain point and skip back. Have him walk around a circle and then run on command. Have an obstacle

course where the child must jump over things, hop to a certain point, run back to the starting point, etc.

B. Directionality.
1. Have the child experiment with his body going up, down, left, right, under, on top of; standing beside, next to, etc.
2. Chalkboard activities such as random dot games, the clock game, the lazy eight (Kephart, 1960, pp. 169, 171, 182).

C. Left-Right Progression.
1. Make the child conscious of left and right in all classroom activities.
2. Use color cues for beginnings of words, sentences, so the child's attention is drawn to the left.
3. Do picture stories, and stress that we begin at the left.
4. Bead-stringing, block patterns that require the child to go from left to right.
5. Eye movement exercises in the Frostig *Teacher's Guide,* p. 18.

D. Visual.
1. Continue with Level II activities.
2. Eye pursuit movements (Getman and Kane, 1964, p. 65).

E. Neurological Organization.
Before starting these activities the child's sidedness for eye, hand, and foot should be determined.
1. Handedness.
a. Picking up objects with the preferred hand.
b. Gesturing with the preferred hand.
c. Activities such as tossing a ball with the preferred hand, catching a beanbag with one hand, badminton, or ring toss games that require the use of only the preferred hand.
d. Encourage the child to use his preferred hand.
e. Discuss with the parents the importance of the child's using the preferred hand for eating, combing hair, etc.
f. Feeling objects—this activity will help develop the tactile-kinesthetic abilities. Describing the object

felt without naming it will help develop ability to express ideas.

2. Footedness.
   a. Games that require the child to use one foot (practice in kicking a ball, hopping relays).
   b. Stepping up onto chairs or other high places with the preferred foot.
3. Eyedness.
   a. Far-point sighting:
      (1) Have the child sight things through a cardboard tube.
      (2) Sight things using telescope, microscope.
   b. Head position for writing:
      (1) Right-handed—head rotated to the left, tilted slightly to left.
      (2) Left-handed—head rotated to right, tilted slightly to the right.
   c. Use of the preferred eye in reading. Delacato (1966, pp. 18–19) recommends the following techniques for reinforcing the use of the preferred eye in reading:
      (1) Filtering process—materials needed are one sheet of green cellophane and one sheet of red. Put the green cellophane over the non-dominant eye. Do this five minutes the first day; continue the training twice a day for two- or three-minute periods. Gradually increase the time to twenty minutes a day.
      (2) Have the child hold a piece of cardboard a short distance in front of the non-dominant eye so that it blocks this eye from seeing the reading material.

Visual perceptual, visual discrimination, visual memory, and auditory skill training as well as language development activities should be integrated with the non-verbal skill training. When the child is ready for reading readiness work he should begin with the activities outlined below. In arithmetic, social studies, science, and other "academic" subjects auditory and visual aids are used if the child is unable to read the material but is able to comprehend the concepts.

Written Language

A child may be able to write one-word responses, but not sentences. Any testing should then require only one-word responses. The child may be tested for comprehension of the material by an oral examination or on multiple-choice type tests.

Activities for writing:

1. The material in the *Laugh and Learn with Julie and Jack* series can be adapted for work in developing written language.
2. Chapter VI, "Expressing Ideas in Writing," in *Remedial Training for Children with Specific Disability in Reading, Spelling, and Penmanship,* Seventh Edition, by Gillingham and Stillman (1966).
3. Show the child a picture. The child recites a sentence that describes the picture into the tape recorder. On the playback he writes the sentence as he hears it. He then reads the sentence.
4. Teach the child how to write in short sentences. We have found this rather simple technique has helped many children.

Many of the children having problems in non-verbal processes will exhibit these problems when they write. Since the basis of learning to write is the pre-learning of other non-verbal skills, these are presented first. The writing program itself follows in detail in Chapter 21.

Use the following form, adopted from Myklebust (1965, p. 308), to obtain a general picture of a child's level of motor development.

FORM 7: SCHEDULE OF MOTOR DEVELOPMENT

Name of Child＿＿＿＿＿＿＿＿＿＿ Birthdate＿＿＿＿＿ Age＿＿＿

Evaluated by＿＿＿＿＿＿＿＿＿＿ Date＿＿＿＿＿＿＿＿

Item	Expected Age of Occurence (in months)	Comments
Holds head erect and steady	2.9	
Sits with support	3.5	

Sits unsupported	7.5
Pulls to standing position	10.5
Walks with help	11.6
Stands alone	12.5
Walks alone	13.0
Stands on right or left foot with help	19.9
Tries to stand on walking board	22.5
Stands momentarily on right foot or left without assistance	29.3
Walks on tip-toe	30.0
Stands on walking board with both feet	31.0
Walks on a line (10 ft.) in general direction and stepping on line	31.3
Walks on board with two or more alternating steps	38.0
Hops on right foot two or three hops	49.3
Walks downstairs alternating foot forward	50.0
Stands with one foot before the other with eyes closed	48.0

Touches the nose with forefinger
with eyes closed   48.0   _____

Makes circles with forefinger,
arms extended outright from
sides   48.0   _____

Balances on tip-toe   60.0   _____

Hops 15 feet on one foot   60.0   _____

Rolls a small piece of thin paper
into a ball using the fingers of
one hand only   60.0   _____

Balances on one foot for ten
seconds   72.0   _____

Throws ball at a target five feet
away   72.0   _____

Jumps over a rope (20 cm. high) 72.0   _____

General Comments:

REFERENCES

Concept Records, North Bellmore, Long Island, N. Y. *Basic Songs for Exceptional Children*, Volumes I and II.

Delacato, C. H. *The Diagnosis and Treatment of Speech and Reading Problems*. Springfield, Ill.: Charles C Thomas, 1963.

Delacato, C. H. *Neurological Organization in the Classroom* (Pamphlet). Chicago, Ill.: Systems for Education, 1966.

Dubnoff, B. Perceptual training as a bridge to conceptual ability. In Hellmuth, J. (Ed.) *Educational Therapy*. Volume I. Seattle, Wash.: Special Child Publications, 1966, pp. 317–49.

Frostig, M., & Horne, D. *Frostig Test of Visual Perception* and *Administration and Scoring Manual: Developmental Test of Visual Perception*. Palo Alto, Calif.: Consulting Psychologists Press, 1961.

Gaddes, W. H. The needs of teachers for specialized information on handedness, finger localization, and cerebral dominance. In Cruickshank, W. (Ed.) *The Teacher of Brain-injured Children*. Syracuse, N.Y.: Syracuse University Press, 1966, pp. 207–18.

Getman, G. N. The visuomotor complex in the acquisition of learning skills. In Hellmuth, J. (Ed.) *Learning Disorders*. Volume I. Seattle, Wash.: Special Child Publications, 1965, pp. 49–76.

Getman, G. N., & Kane, E. R. *The Physiology of Readiness*. Minneapolis, Minn.: P.A.S.S., 1964.

Gillingham, A., & Stillman, B. *Remedial Training for Children with Specific Disability in Reading, Spelling, and Penmanship*. Cambridge, Mass.: Educators Publishing Service, 1966.

Kastein, S. Cerebral palsy: Current problems of diagnosis and assessment—language and speech. In Michal-Smith, H. & Kastein, S. *The Special Child: Diagnosis, Treatment, Habilitation*. Seattle, Wash.: Special Child Publications, 1962, pp. 155–62.

Kephart, N. C. *The Slow Learner in the Classroom*. Columbus, O.: Merrill, 1960.

Kephart, N. C. *The Brain-injured Child in the Classroom*. Chicago, Ill.: National Society for Crippled Children and Adults, 1963.

McLeod, P. H. *Readiness for Learning*. Philadelphia, Penn.: Lippencott, 1965.

Myklebust, H. *Development and Disorders of Written Language*. Volume I *(Picture Story Language Test)*. New York: Grune & Stratton, 1965.

Orton, S. T. *Reading, Writing, and Speech Problems in Children*. New York: W. W. Norton, 1937.

Penfield, W. & Roberts, L. *Speech and Brain Mechanisms*. Princeton, N. J.: Princeton University Press, 1959.

St. John's School for the Deaf, Milwaukee, Wisc. *Laugh and Learn with Julie and Jack*, by Sister Mary Walter, 1964.

Slingerland, B. H. *Screening Tests for Identifying Children with Specific Language Disability*. Cambridge, Mass.: Educators Publishing Service, 1964.

21

Non-Verbal Processes: Writing (Continued)

What follows is to be used as a general outline for a writing program. Most children in primary-level classes have had little or no cursive writing experience. In general, their writing habits are poor. The program can be used with the majority of the children in most primary-level classes.

In intermediate-level classes, approximately three-fourths of the children will need to go through the writing program. The other children will need retraining, or their writing is satisfactory. The retraining program for handwriting as outlined on pages 289–307 in Gillingham and Stillman's (1966) book, *Remedial Training for Children with Specific Disability in Reading, Spelling, and Penmanship*, can be used.

WRITING PROGRAM

Pre-Readiness

LEVEL I
1. See the Level I activities of the Non-Verbal Processes Training program (p. 207). Laterality and directionality training should be carried out prior to and along with the writing program.
2. Experimentation with motor patterns.
   a. Scribbling (Kephart, 1960, p. 161), using chalkboard, finger painting, and large newsprint with magic marker or large crayon.
   b. Directionality—visual orientation toward a goal. Use the chalkboard: random dot games, clock game, lazy eight (Kephart, 1960, pp. 160, 171, 182).

LEVEL II

1. See #4 under Level III in the section on Non-Verbal Processes (p. 210).

2. To help the child become aware of where his body parts are when he is unable to see them: Demonstrate to the child that he knows where all his body parts are, even in the dark. Help the child realize that if his arm, hand, or foot is placed in a certain position, he can move it and return it to the same position without looking. Show the child that he does not have to look at his hands when he catches a ball.

3. Developing a kinesthetic awareness for the feel of form.
Note: It is important that the child's eyes be turned away from the paper for the following activities. The child should not close his eyes, as the whole body becomes tense when the eyes are closed (Gillingham and Stillman, 1966, p. 301).

   a. Dots. Place a dot on the chalkboard, and ask the child to draw a line without looking. He then is to retrace the line and stop on the dot. See if he can estimate the direction and distance through feel. Variations: vary the distance; vary the direction.

   b. Shapes. Circle, cross, square, triangle, rectangle, diamond (to be presented in this order). Put the model of the shape on the chalkboard, or give the child a large piece of newsprint and a crayon. The child looks at the model, with eyes *on* the model and not on his paper; he attempts to make a circle, etc. Tell him he is to try to return to the starting point by feeling, not looking. Do this as many times as needed for all the shapes.

   Repeat. The child looks at the board or his paper but there is *no* model. He tries to make the shapes.

LEVEL III

Copying shapes. Constant visual control over a motor pattern, using chalkboard. See Kephart (1960), pp. 185–210. Children six years of age or older should be able to do all the forms.

LEVEL IV

Copying shapes, using large newsprint. Procedures are the same as in Level III, or as outlined by Getman and Kane (1964, p. 84), using desk templates.

Children having difficulty expressing shapes in writing will also experience similar difficulty with numbers. Activities specifically designed for acquainting the child with number forms may be necessary. It is suggested that the child be given as many experiences in number concepts as is feasible. One example might be presenting the names of the numbers when the visual symbols themselves are presented. Another example is using sandpaper numbers to develop the child's kinesthetic feel for the form of the number. Other procedures are:

1. Writing Numbers Using an Overhead Projector.

    MATERIALS: Use overlays with each number made on a separate transparency. Make the different parts of the numbers in various colors. To show direction of the numbers, "technamation" materials are used. A polaroid filter mounted on a clear plastic wheel that is motorized is placed over the transparency when the teacher wishes to show the direction in which the number is to be made.

PROCEDURE:

    (a) Name the number. Have the child say the name.
    (b) Discuss the form of the number as he looks at it on the screen.
    (c) On a blank overlay, make the number for the child.
    (d) Using the polaroid filter wheel, show the child the direction of the number.

2. Using a "Number Clock."

    VERBAL EXPLANATIONS: All numbers should be the same height. Numbers 1, 4, 5, and 6 begin with a line and start at the top. For 4 and 5 the left-hand vertical line on the left side is drawn first. The horizontal line of the 5 is drawn from the left to the right. Using a circle with dots in place of numbers on the clock: a green dot where the 10 would be on a clock, a red dot at 2, a blue dot where 8 would be, and a yellow dot at 4. The teacher then can say: "Numbers two and three begin on the green dot on the circle. No other numbers begin this way. Numbers eight, nine, and zero begin on the red dot. They are made by going up and around." The circle with dots may be called the "number clock."

All numbers except 8, 9, and 0 start close to the preceding

number. This hint may be used when the children have learned all the numbers and are now writing several numbers on a line.

PROCEDURE:

(a) Each number is introduced on the overhead projector or on the chalkboard.

(b) The "number clock" is used for introducing the number.

(c) Numbers should be introduced one at a time.

(d) Give the child experiences in re-visualizing the number. For example, ask him to describe the number before he writes it. Having the child make the number in the air also sometimes helps.

Readiness

LEVEL I—Introductory Movements for Cursive Writing.

1. On Chalkboard.

   a. Discuss how the movement is made. For example, ∧∨∨∧ . "First we go up and then we go down." Teacher demonstrates on the board. Or, say, "We go away from our body and then toward our body."

   b. Have the children make the movement at the board while they look at the model but not at the board. Have them say "up" when they are going up and "down" when they are going down. The movements should be rhythmic and free-flowing. Have the children stand at least six inches from the board.

   c. After the child has had several days of doing the movement on the board following the above procedure, eliminate the auditory clue and have him make the movement on the board while he looks at the model but not at his hands.

   d. Remove the model and have the child make the movement from memory. However, do not let him look at his hands.

2. On large newsprint with crayon.

   Repeat the procedures outlined in b and c above, this time on paper.

Suggested movements:

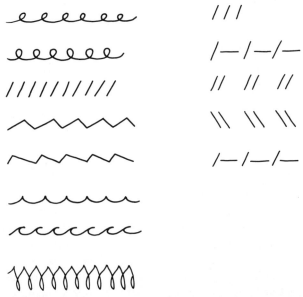

Introduce one or two movements a week. If a child has difficulty with any movements, give him additional practice as often as possible. Before introducing a new movement, review the previous ones.

LEVEL II—Introducing Movements on Chalkboard (Eyes on the Movement).

1. Repeat #1 and 2 as outlined for Level I, but allow the child to look at the paper. The following are important: (a) The child should have correct posture when he does the movements; (b) The slant of the paper should be correct, depending on the hand used; (c) The hand position should be proper. Refer to Gillingham and Stillman (1966), pages 290–97 for descriptions of the proper positions for writing.

The movements on paper should be done first on paper with one-inch spaces; the letters should be three spaces high initially, then two spaces, and finally one space high. The teacher can line the paper with magic markers, using blue for the top line, green for the middle line, and red for the bottom line. This helps the children stay on and within the lines.

LEVEL III—Movements for Cursive Writing (Eyes Averted).

On chalkboard.

1. The movements adapted from Cruickshank *et al.* (1961) can be used:

a. ⌒	f. ((	k. U
b. C	g.))	l. ʔʔ
c. ⋏	h. ∩	m. ⌒~
d. ⌣	i. O	n. ((
e.))	j.)⟩	o. ⊃

Repeat the procedures outlined in #1 a–d of Level I.

    2. On newsprint with crayon or magic marker.
Repeat procedures outlined in #1 a–d of Level I (Introductory Movements).

LEVEL IV—Movements for Writing (Eyes on Movement).

    1. On chalkboard; repeat procedures used in #1 a–d of Level I.

    2. On one-inch-lined paper, make three lines with red, green, and blue magic markers; the letters are three spaces high. Do letters two spaces high, then one space high. Finally, use regular lined paper.

    3. Introducing the letter.

MATERIALS:

(a) Overlays with each letter made on the transparency with magic marker. Blank overlays. Overhead projector. (b) The different parts of the letter are made in different colors to show the various movements of the letter. Magic markers are used for the colors. (c) To show the direction of the letters, such as *s*, *z*, and others, "technamation" materials are used. A polaroid filter mounted on a clear plastic wheel that is motorized is placed over the transparency. The letters then move from left to right, or right to left, to show the child the direction of the letter.

PROCEDURE:

(a) Name the letter.
(b) Discuss the form of the letter while the child looks at it.
(c) On a blank overlay, make the letter for the children.
(d) Using the polaroid filter wheel, show the children the direction of the letter.
(e) Develop the kinesthetic feel for the form of letters with

use of script letterboards, sunken, and script letterboards, raised (may be purchased from the American Printing House for the Blind).

4. Writing the letter.

    a. The child makes the letter while he looks at the model. His eyes are on the model, not on his hand.

    b. Help him compare his work with the model.

Auditory clues may be given to help the child who has difficulty with the letter, or the child's hand may be held as he makes the letter. Some children may need to write the letter in salt or sand (on a salt tray).

    c. Have the child write the letter on the chalkboard without the model. Eyes averted.

Repeat the procedure outlined in Level I; the child now does not have a model to look at.

    d. Have child write the letter on newsprint with a model. Eyes averted.

    e. Have child write the letter on newsprint without a model. Eyes averted. The procedure is the same as that on Level I #1 b and c; magic markers and crayons are used.

    f. Have child write on paper with eyes on the paper.

Use one-inch-lined paper. The space is divided into three parts using magic markers. If the top line is always blue, the middle line green, and the bottom line red, the teacher can then say to the child, "Start on the red line, go up to the blue line, come down to the red line," depending on the letter. The lines should be dark and heavy so the child will be able to stay within them.

PROCEDURE: The teacher puts a model of the letter on the child's paper. The letter form and direction are discussed. The position of the paper for the left- and right-handed children is demonstrated. Each child's paper is checked for proper positioning. Masking tape or marks on the desk are used to show the child how he should position the paper.

The writing posture is discussed and demonstrated: Elbow on desk, non-writing hand holding the paper, fingers on the pencil correctly, feet on floor, proper head tilt (McLeod, 1965). The distance between the eye and the hand should be about the same distance as that between the elbow and first knuckle (Delacato, 1966). Before each writing assignment the correct habits for writing should be reviewed. A bulletin board may be put up at writing time and taken away if the children are distracted by it during other lessons.

The child traces the model of the letter. He makes a row of his own. The teacher should watch him carefully to determine his success with the letter and to decide where he needs help.

Have the child write on two-inch-lined paper, then use one-inch-spaced lines, and finally on regular primary paper, following the same procedures as above.

The following order for presentation of the letters is from Cruickshank *et al.*, 1961, p. 198:

Step I: m, i, u, w, t, e.
Step II: s, n, h, k, b, o, a.
Step III: r, c, v, x.
Step IV: l, d, f.
Step V: j, p, q, g, y, z.

When the child can write *m* and *i*, he can then connect the letters.

The time of the writing period should vary. If one child can tolerate writing only one line he should write only that much. If another child can write a whole page, he should be allowed to do so.

REFERENCES

Cruickshank, W., *et al. A Teaching Method for Brain-injured and Hyperactive Children.* Syracuse, N.Y.: Syracuse University Press, 1961.

Delacato, C. *Neurological Organization in the Classroom* (Pamphlet). Chicago: Systems for Education, 1966.

Getman, G. N., & Kane, E. R. *The Physiology of Readiness.* Minneapolis, Minn.: P.A.S.S., 1964.

Gillingham, A., & Stillman, B. *Remedial Training for Children with Specific Disability in Reading, Spelling, and Penmanship.* Cambridge, Mass.: Educators Publishing Service, 1966.

Kephart, N. C. *The Slow Learner in the Classroom.* Columbus, O.: Merrill, 1960.

McLeod, P. H. *Readiness for Learning.* Philadelphia, Penn.: Lippincott, 1965.

22

Associational Processes

In the preceding chapters we have been concerned primarily with the auditory, visual, and non-verbal processes necessary for learning the spoken, read, and written forms of language. A child may have difficulty in one or more of these areas. He may also have difficulty in transferring information from one sense modality to another.

According to Myklebust (1965), children with learning difficulties have problems not only in obtaining information through one sense modality, "but also in being able to convert that which is learned through other channels. It is such transmodal learning which often is deficient in children with learning disabilities" (p. 5). He has found persons who could learn *intra*sensorially but could not learn *inter*sensorially. For example, a child may learn the visual aspects of words but may be unable to transfer these visual components into motor patterns.

Work continues on developing detailed programs for the various types of transmodal learning problems that we have observed in children. A brief list of activities found helpful in developing transmodal learning will be presented.

Attempts should be made to determine the channels through which the child learns most efficiently. Some children can learn when visual, auditory, and kinesthetic stimuli are used. Other children cannot tolerate having these three senses stimulated at the same time. Some children are able to make the necessary auditory-visual associations needed for reading; others have difficulty making the transfer from the auditory to the visual, or the other way around. Still other children, who are able to read, are unable to make the auditory-visual-kinesthetic associations needed for writing, and consequently have difficulty with spelling as well. Some children cannot follow an oral direction requiring a motor response; they have to be shown what to do.

The evaluation tasks presented in this chapter are used in determining the channels through which a child can learn and in determining the type of associational difficulties he may have. Observation in the classroom is, however, still the most reliable source of information.

We are reprinting here Form 8: Associational Processes of the Educational Evaluation Check List. We shall provide additional information on the items of the form, and in a separate section offer suggestions for training.

EDUCATIONAL EVALUATION CHECK LIST
FORM 8: ASSOCIATIONAL PROCESSES

Name of Child_____ Birthdate_____ Age_____
Evaluated by_____ Date_____

	Comments
I. Visual-Motor Associations	
II. Auditory-Visual Associations	
III. Auditory-Vocal Associations	
IV. Visual-Vocal Associations	
V. Auditory-Motor Associations	

Form 8: Evaluation Items

I. Visual-Motor Associations

A. Administer Visual-Motor Association subtest of the ITPA.

B. Have the child pair concrete objects according to their use or function.

C. Determine if the child is able to place objects in position. For example, place pictures of people and objects so they are facing left and right. Have cutouts of the same pictures. Let the child place the cutouts in the same positions as the models. Note whether he is able to place the cutouts without using a trial-and-error method.

D. Is the child able to construct what he perceives? Prepare a series of figures graded in difficulty. For example, a circle; square; triangle; a figure made up of curves to the top right, left, and bottom; geometric figures made up of curves and straight lines (Harrison, 1965). Have the child construct these figures using small sticks or pieces of cardboard. Use different colors for the parts of the contour lines.

E. Is the child able to construct a figure when given parts?
   1. "Picture Completion" subtest of the WISC.
   2. Puzzles.
   3. Have the child construct a house, a cat, or a person.

F. Is the child able to perceive whole-part relationships?
   1. *Bender Visual-Motor Gestalt Test.*
   2. *Graham-Kendall Memory for Designs Test.*

II. Auditory-Visual Associations

A. Does the child get meaning from the printed word?
   1. Have him read a story silently. (A paragraph from the *Durrell Analysis of Reading Difficulty* may be used.)
   2. Have him answer questions orally about the paragraph.
   3. At what grade level is his sight vocabulary? Did he read the paragraph and have little or no comprehension for the material? If so, he may have difficulty making the visual-auditory association needed.

B. Does he get meaning from the printed word when the auditory stimulus is presented?

1. Have him read aloud the same story or paragraph used already.
2. Ask him questions about the paragraph. Is his comprehension better when he reads it aloud? If his comprehension improves with auditory clues, he may have difficulty in visual decoding. If his silent reading is better than his oral reading, he may have an auditory-verbal language problem. In other words, he may know the meaning of the word when he sees it, but he cannot transfer what he sees into an auditory-motor pattern.

C. Does he remember the names of letters when the visual stimulus is presented?
1. Print each letter of the alphabet on a card.
2. Show the child the card.
3. Ask him the *name* of the letter.

D. Does the child remember the name of the letter when the auditory stimulus is presented with the visual stimulus?
1. Present the consonants.
2. Present the short vowels and long vowel sounds.
3. Present the digraphs.

E. Have a collective picture. Name a specific object. Have the child find it.

F. Does the child get meaning from the printed word when you read a paragraph to him while he looks at it?
1. Use the same paragraph used earlier.
2. Have him follow along as you read the paragraph to him.
3. Have him answer questions about the paragraph. If his comprehension is better than it was for sections A or B, he may have a visual decoding problem.

G. Does the child remember the sound of a letter when it is presented visually?
1. Present the consonants.
2. Present the vowels and ask for the short and long sounds.
3. Present the digraphs.
4. Present words at grade level that can be sounded out. Graded spelling lists may be used. Is he able to sound them out?
5. Present nonsense syllables that can be sounded out. Some children will be able to synthesize auditory units when

they are presented orally, but when the visual stimulus is presented and they are asked to transfer the visual stimulus into the auditory they are unable to do so.

III. Auditory-Vocal Associations

A. Auditory-Vocal Association subtest of the ITPA.
B. If the child has difficulty with oral reading, he may have an auditory-verbal language problem. See II, B.

IV. Visual-Vocal Associations

A. Present a picture of an object. Have the child describe what he sees.
B. Present a picture that tells a story. (For example, a picture of a family at a picnic.) Have the child describe what he sees.

V. Auditory-Motor Associations

A. When given a verbal direction requiring a motor response, can the child carry out the motor act? For example, can he put an "X" on a picture, draw a line under a word, etc. If you ask him to jump over a stick, run to the door, can he do this? Give him a piece of chalk in each hand; have him move his hands to the left, right, up and down. It is important with these tasks that you determine if he knows where *up* and *down* are on the blackboard, as he may be having difficulty with directionality rather than with auditory-motor transfer.
B. See Section II (Auditory-Visual), B #2.

Training in Associational Abilities

If a child does not have any visual or auditory perceptual difficulties, but is having difficulty in reading and in other "academic" areas, his problem may lie in transferring information from one sense modality to others. Many children seem to have such problems. Following is a brief outline of training activities which follows the format of Form 8.

I. Visual-Motor Associations

  A. Activities.

    1. "Imitation of Movements" (Kephart, 1960, p. 131).

    2. Activities in the *Peabody Language Development Kits,* Levels I and II.

    3. Sorting and matching similar objects (color to color, shape to shape).

    4. Show a picture of a girl with a comb in her hand. Ask the child to show you what the girl will do next.

    5. Make patterns on paper. Have the child construct the patterns with pegboards, *Rig-A-Jig* construction sets, beads, or blocks.

    6. Grouping pictures belonging to the same category.

    7. Reading-readiness activities such as those that require drawing a connecting line from a number to a group of pictures of the same number, or from a word to a matching picture.

    8. Reading and answering written comprehension questions.

    9. Matching concrete objects to their pictures.

    10. Matching word to word.

    11. Reproducing (with paper and pencil) shapes, figures, etc.

  B. Ability to manipulate spatial relationships.

    1. "Pre-activities" for spatial relationships in the teacher's guide to the Frostig program.

    2. The evaluation tasks described above may be adapted for training activities.

    3. For constructing what is perceived: Use colored sticks all of the same length and in different colors; straight and curved pieces of felt in different sizes and colors for use on a flannel board; or pieces of tagboard may be used. The figures should be graded in difficulty. First, the child should have a three-dimensional model to copy from. Second, he should copy the figure from a model made on paper. He should copy contour lines of a whole where the parts are in different colors, and then all of one color; he

should construct parts of a whole and parts within a whole.

4. For placing objects in relation to each other, evaluation tasks earlier described may be adapted for training. Prior to this training the child should be given many concrete experiences moving his body first from in front of something to behind, and then in manipulating concrete objects in front of him and behind him, etc. *Language Lotto* may be used.

5. Teacher-made puzzles, and cutout pictures.

II. Auditory-Visual Associations

A. Tape sentences, for example, "The boy saw a bird." Prepare a ditto sheet with the same sentences that are on the tape. The child listens to the tape and reads along silently. After each sentence on the tape ask a question such as "What did the boy see?" On the ditto sheet have pictures from which the child can choose an answer. He circles the picture that will answer the question. After he is able to respond correctly by circling pictures, words may be used on the ditto sheet instead of pictures, and oral or written responses may be given. Repeat the procedure for paragraphs and short stories.

B. Present a picture of a rabbit. Give the child three auditory choices, such as "This is a rabbit; it is a dog; it is a cat." The choices are repeated and the child raises his hand when he hears the correct phrase. Increase the difficulty of the choices; "This is a brown rabbit; this is a blue rabbit; this is a white rabbit." Increase the difficulty by using verb tenses, vocabulary, and concepts derived from auditory clues that describe the picture.

C. Present a collective picture. Describe something in the picture. The child is asked to find the object.

D. Tape some sentences. On a ditto sheet have corresponding sentences that differ in some way. The child has to tell if the auditory and visual sentences are the same or different.

E. Dictate sounds. The child holds up the letter that goes with the sound. Do the same for words.

F. Dictate nonsense syllables. Have the child write them.

G. The evaluation tasks may be used for training purposes.

III. *Auditory-Vocal Associations*

A. *Language Lotto.*

B. *Laugh and Learn with Julie and Jack.*

C. Activities with the *Language Master,* using teacher-made cards with auditory clues.

D. *Peabody Language Development Kits,* Levels I and II.

E. Analogies, such as "Day is to night as top is to _____."

F. Completing sentences presented orally.

G. Describing objects after having felt them without looking at them.

H. Describe an object and have the child choose the correct one by naming and pointing to it.

I. Have the child name all the things he can think of when you say "cold."

J. Ask the child verbal absurdities, such as "Do birds bark?"

K. Record sounds such as those made by a horn, bell, whistle; the child names the thing that produces the sound.

L. Associating sounds with visual clues.

1. Present the sound visually (e.g., the word "toot" written on the chalkboard); the child says the sound.

2. Present the sound and have the child write it or point to a visual symbol of what makes the sound.

IV. *Visual-Vocal Associations*

A. Place several objects on a table and describe one of them. Have the child point to the object. Then, describe parts of the object and have the child point to them.

B. Repeat the above procedure for geometric shapes, designs, pictures, numbers, letters, words, etc.

C. Show part of an object; have the child identify it as quickly as he can.

V. *Auditory-Motor Associations*

A. Games, such as "Simon Says."

B. Activity records: "Hokey Pokey," "Eency Weency Spider,"

"Songs from Early Childhood," "Singing Games," and others. (These can be obtained from Children's Reading Service, 1078 St. John's Place, Brooklyn 13, New York.)

C. Finger plays with singing games.

D. Rhythm band activities.

E. Following oral directions that require a motor response. For example, "Jump over the rope," "Go to the door."

F. Chalkboard activities that require the child to transfer an auditory clue into a motor pattern. For example, "Draw a straight line; a curved line," "Make a jerky movement; a smooth movement," "With both hands draw a straight line up, down, to the side." Do the same activities on paper.

G. Pencil and paper activities that require the child to draw lines under things, around things, put "Xs" on, and others.

REFERENCES

Harrison, E. M. The brain-damaged child and writing problems. *Occupational Therapy* (Australian), November 1965, pp. 5–10.

Kephart, N. C. *The Slow Learner in the Classroom*. Columbus, O.: Merrill, 1960.

Myklebust, H. *Auditory Disorders in Children*. New York, N. Y.: Grune & Stratton, 1954.

23

Illustrative Studies of Individual Children

Three children are discussed in this chapter. Andy, Betty, and Charles represent children from primary-level, intermediate-level, and junior-high-level classes. Their problems are reviewed, the evaluations made of their problems are presented, and the appropriate programming for them is outlined.

ANDY
Seven years, eleven months old.

Andy is a twin. His identical twin brother also is in a primary-level special class. He has a younger sister and an older sister, both known not to have difficulty in school. He has an interdental lisp. There is no significant information in his home history that can be related to his learning problems.

School History

According to the kindergarten teacher's report, there was no evidence that Andy was experiencing difficulty in kindergarten. However, the mother states she did not feel Andy was ready for first grade. Andy transferred to another school for first grade. The records from the first grade only indicate that he received a "D" in reading and in spelling. Because he was experiencing difficulty in reading and his parents thought he would get more attention in the smaller classes of his first school, he returned there. He was placed into the second grade for two months and then returned to the first grade. Andy continued to have difficulty in reading, phonics, and spelling. The teacher commented that he had poor visual and auditory memory. He was referred to an optometrist because he seemed to have poor eye control. The optometrist agreed that he had poor eye control but there was no pathology.

Andy had difficulty following a moving object and was unable to shift his "regard" from point to point. The optometrist also stated that Andy's span and speed of visual recognition were poor. He also indicated that Andy had confusion in working with parts to the whole, figure-ground perception, and auditory memory. Andy did not receive any training in these areas in first grade. He was promoted to second grade and was referred for special class placement in November of that year. His second-grade teacher commented that he "lacked the ability to sound out words, cannot organize ideas, needs many concrete experiences in math, has short attention span, tires easily, very immature socially and emotionally."

Psychological Test Results

WISC (*Wechsler Intelligence Scale for Children*)

Verbal Scale IQ	96
Performance Scale IQ	96
Full Scale IQ	96

SUBTESTS	SCALED SCORES
Verbal Scale	
Information	9
Comprehension	13
Arithmetic	7
Similarities	7
Vocabulary	7
Digit Span	7
Performance Scale	
Picture Completion	9
Picture Arrangement	13
Block Design	9
Object Assembly	8
Coding	7

Instruments Used in the Educational Evaluation

1. *Illinois Test of Psycholinguistic Abilities* (ITPA).
2. Slingerland's *Test for Identifying Children with Specific Language Disabilities.*
3. Temple University's *Informational Reading Inventory.*
4. *Templin-Darley Articulation Test.*

5. *Memory for Sentences.*
6. Kephart's *Perceptual Rating Survey Scale* (adaptation).
7. Evaluation as outlined in previous chapters.

Summary of the Educational Evaluation

Visual Processes. The *Frostig Test of Visual Perception* indicated a need for training in perceptual constancy, figure-ground relationships, position in space, and spatial relationships. Andy preferred to position his booklet so he did not have to cross his midline on the eye-hand coordination subtest. He also wanted to draw his lines from right to left. His visual discrimination ability appeared to be adequate, although he had difficulty with discrimination tasks involving direction (for example, *b* and *d*, *p* and *q*).

Andy's visual memory for shapes, designs, and numbers was poor. He was able to remember only two items on the subtest. Reversals were frequent in visual discrimination, memory, and visual sequencing tasks. Andy had difficulty with whole-part relationships, especially in working from parts to the whole. He had no apparent difficulty comprehending the meaning in pictures. Because of his limited sight vocabulary it was difficult to determine whether he had difficulty understanding the printed word.

Auditory Processes. Andy had difficulty in tasks requiring auditory memory, synthesizing, and analyzing. He also had difficulty in auditory sequencing, along with organizing his thoughts for oral expression. His receptive language abilities were significantly above his auditory perceptual abilities. His lisp has become inconsistent.

Non-Verbal Processes. Andy was unable to maintain his balance while walking forward and backward on a tape line on the floor and on the balance beam. When he walked sideways his right side was stiff, suggesting he was too one-sided. He had difficulty jumping and hopping. He was unable to catch a ball. His ocular control was poor for both eyes. His right eye tears and blinks when he follows a moving target. He avoids crossing his midline. He had not yet established handedness but was beginning to prefer his left hand. He is left-eyed and left-footed. He was unable to coordinate his arms and legs for the stationary crawl and for cross pattern creeping. His small-muscle coordination for writing was adequate. His kinesthetic feel for the form of shapes, numbers, and letters was satisfactory. He had difficulty copying due to his poor visual memory and figure-ground perceptual problems.

Associational Processes. He had difficulty associating the sound of a word with the visual symbol. When he attempted to sound out a word, he began at the end of the word. He did not have the concepts of *beginning* and *end.* He had difficulty placing objects in position and in relation to one another. His auditory-motor, visual-vocal, and auditory-motor associational abilities were adequate. He comprehended material presented orally.

The Educational Program

Reading

1. Visual perceptual, visual memory, and visual sequencing training.
2. Auditory perceptual training for discrimination.
3. The materials and procedures suggested by Gillingham and Stillman (1966).
4. The *Merrill Linguistic Readers, Sullivan Programmed Reading,* and the *Stern Structural Reading* series.

Spelling

The spelling program is part of the reading program.

Arithmetic

The *Stern Structural Arithmetic* series.

Science and Social Studies

Visual aids such as filmstrips, and oral discussion along with oral rather than written tests.

Non-Verbal Processes

Emphasis on developing laterality and directionality, ocular control, bilateral motor skills, left-right progression.

BETTY

Eleven years and two months old.

History

The mother reported that labor lasted for eleven hours and instruments were used during delivery. The parents were concerned about Betty's slowness to walk and consulted a chiropractor when she was two. It is their impression that this helped the child to begin to walk, at approximately three years of age. She was unable to run well until she was about five. Her gait was awkward.

A pediatric neurologist stated that Betty's "learning and language difficulties were based on organic cerebral disease which is probably of metabolic nature but which we have not been able to pinpoint etiologically." He goes on to say "the cerebral dysfunction manifests itself as minor motor difficulties with significant language and learning problems." His recommendations were "Individual educational methods and carefully detailed understanding of the child possibly together with casework for the parents and the child herself, are the only specific therapeutic measures which I can think of." The child had a history of severe articulation problems and difficulty in expressing herself verbally.

Betty repeated first grade three times. She was promoted to second and third grades on the basis of her age and not her performance. In spite of her poor performance she was said to be a happy child who got along well with her companions. Her grades were below average in all subjects. The teachers report that she did not do written work and could not work independently.

On the Scott, Foresman *Basic Reading Test* which accompanies *Roads to Follow,* given when she was in third grade, Betty's lowest scores were in sensory images, relationships, sentence meaning, phonetic analysis, and structural analysis. Her over-all rank was very low (1-4 percentile). She received her highest scores on emotional reactions, scrutiny context, and dictionary skills.

There was little attempt on the part of teachers to describe Betty's learning problems. She was able to do simple arithmetic with the use of a counting rod. On the *Stanford Achievement Test* given at the end of the third grade her scores were 1.9 on Word Meaning; 1.8 on Paragraph Meaning; 1.4 on Science and Social Studies; 0 on Spelling; 1.4 on Word Study Skills; 2.2 on Language; 0 on Arithmetic; and 2.2

on Arithmetic Concepts. The over-all reading average was 1.7. At the end of the third grade, Betty was referred to the special education program.

Psychological Test Results

The school psychologist stated that because of Betty's "mutism" and "deep emotionality," the *Kent B. G. Y. Scales* were administered. The pro-rated results indicated an over-all I.Q. score of 77. Betty was eight years and two months old at that time. According to the psychologist, Betty's major problems were in the areas of similarities and contrasts, simple mathematical calculations, and reading comprehension. The psychologist stated that although her performance indicated a need for placement in an ungraded class she should stay in her regular class so that she might grow socially and emotionally and because she had a positive relationship with her teacher.

At the end of the second grade Betty was referred to a private institution for neurological and speech and language evaluations. The results of the neurological examination have been mentioned; the speech examination indicated a moderate to severe articulation problem, poor use of syntax, difficulty in auditory recall and expressive language. No formal tests of language were given. It was recommended that a reading evaluation and the ITPA be given at a future time.

Instruments Used in the Educational Evaluation

1. *Illinois Test of Psycholinguistic Abilities.*
2. *Frostig Test of Visual Perception.*
3. Slingerland's *Test for Identifying Children with Language Disabilities.*
4. *Peabody Picture Vocabulary Test.*
5. *Wepman Auditory Discrimination Test.*
6. *Memory for Sentences.*
7. *Templin-Darley Articulation Test.*
8. Temple University's *Informal Reading Inventory.*
9. Kephart's *Perceptual Survey Rating Scale* (adaptation).
10. Evaluations as outlined in previous chapters.

Summary of the Educational Evaluation

Visual Processes. Betty's performance on the Frostig test indicated a need for training in eye-hand coordination and figure-ground perception. For her language difficulties, it was recommended that she receive training in all areas of visual perception, to help her develop such concepts as left and right, self-concept, and motor sequence. Her visual memory is better than her auditory memory although not adequate enough to compensate for the lack of auditory ability. Additional visual memory training would help her to remember words for a sight vocabulary and for spelling. Training in re-visualizing and visual sequencing also was recommended.

Auditory Processes. Betty's inner and receptive language appears to be adequate. Her auditory memory, discrimination, synthesizing, and analyzing abilities were poor. She had difficulty recalling nouns for use in spontaneous speech. If given a multiple-choice question, she was able to give an answer; however, if she had to recall the information she had much difficulty. She had trouble with syntax and with expressing herself. When talking about something she was able to express herself, but when asked a question requiring a specific answer she had difficulty recalling the information requested.

The articulation test showed the following speech errors: substitution of k for g in the initial position, w for r in the initial position, s for sh in the final position, k for tr, p for bl; omissions of l in the final position, th in the medial position; s is inconsistently omitted in the initial position, l is omitted in blends; distortions of r in the final position. Her articulation deviations are inconsistent in conversational speech.

Non-Verbal Processes. Betty was unable to maintain her balance on the balance beam. Her body movements were jerky. She had difficulty catching a ball. Her ocular control was poor. She had difficulty crawling and creeping. She did not cross pattern when she walked. Her gait was awkward. She lost her balance when she jumped or hopped. Her form perception was adequate for her age. She had poor eye-hand coordination ability. She had difficulty copying. She had poor kinesthetic feel for the form of letters. She was right-handed, -eyed, and -footed. She had not developed laterality. She had difficulty with tasks involving direction. She was unable to write a sentence or a story.

Associational Processes. Betty was able to associate words in a meaningful way until the sentence structure and vocabulary were above a second-grade level. Her visual-motor associational skills were adequate and perhaps her strongest. She was unable to make the necessary auditory, visual, and motor associations for spelling. She had difficulty in symbol-sound associations needed for reading, especially in recalling the sound when the visual stimulus is presented. Her difficulty in auditory recall affects her ability to associate sounds with letters. When given a choice, she was usually able to give the correct responses; but when the sound was given, and she was required to name the letter, she had difficulty recalling it. She had even more difficulty in writing the letter when the sound was given orally. She had difficulty making visual-vocal associations.

THE EDUCATIONAL PROGRAM

Reading

1. Visual perceptual training.
2. Visual memory training.
3. Auditory perceptual training.
4. Language training: auditory recall and expressive language training.
5. *Stern Structural Reading* series with supplementary reading in the *Merrill Linguistic Readers* and the *Sullivan Programmed Reading* series along with *The Bank Street Readers*.

Spelling

A Guide to Teaching Phonics (Orton, 1964) should be used. The Forbes (1959) *Graded Spelling Lists* may be helpful in planning a spelling program.

Arithmetic

Montessori materials and the *Stern Structural Arithmetic* series should be used. Betty will need many concrete experiences.

Science and Social Studies

The material should be presented orally. Visual aids should be used. Tests should be oral rather than written.

Non-Verbal Processes

Because of her auditory recall and expressive language problems, Betty should be given multiple-choice questions as a means of determining whether she comprehends material. She should be given more time than usual to answer a question.

CHARLES

Twelve years and eleven months old.

History

A review of Charles's records leads to no clues for understanding why he has had learning problems. The kindergarten teacher reported that his work in number readiness, reading readiness, and language was unsatisfactory; there were no further comments. He repeated first grade and second grade, continuing to fail in all subjects in third grade and fourth grade. There were no detailed reports from teachers as to the nature of the difficulties he was having in the "tool" subjects. The comments in the folders were that he was "apathetic, unreliable, lazy, careless, mind wanders, untidy." He was referred to the psychologist at the end of his second year in the second grade. There were no specific recommendations or descriptions of his apparent reading problem and other learning problems. He attended a summer reading program during the summer of the third grade but it was not a remedial program. There were no evaluations in the folder to indicate the specific problems or what was done to help the boy.

Psychological Test Results

WISC (*Wechsler Intelligence Scale for Children*)

Verbal Scale IQ	91
Performance Scale IQ	99
Full Scale IQ	94

SUBTESTS	SCALED SCORES
Verbal Scale	
Information	8
Comprehension	10
Arithmetic	7
Similarities	11
Vocabulary	9
Digit Span	5
Performance Scale	
Picture Completion	12

Picture Arrangement 9
Block Design 9
Object Assembly 10
Coding 9

On the *Bender Visual-Motor Gestalt Test,* Charles had to recount the units (dots, lines, etc.) several times and often referred back to the stimulus card. The drawings were poorly executed.

On the *Draw-A-Man Test,* Charles protested about having to draw a figure. Results on the *Rorschach Ink Blot Test* suggested "poor inner judgment, poor contact with reality . . ." It was the opinion of the psychologist that Charles was of average intelligence but had "severe aphasic disorders" and would need psychiatric help.

Instruments Used in the Educational Evaluation

1. *Frostig Test of Visual Perception.*
2. Slingerland's *Tests for Identifying Children with Specific Language Disabilities.*
3. *Memory for Sentences.*
4. Temple University's *Informal Reading Inventory.*
5. Kephart's *Perceptual Rating Survey Scale* (adaption).
6. Evaluations as outlined in previous chapters.

Summary of the Educational Evaluation

Visual Processes. Charles's performance on the Frostig test indicated a need for training in all five areas: eye-hand coordination, perceptual constancy, figure-ground, position in space, and spatial relationships. On the eye-hand coordination tasks that required him to draw lines from left to right, he wanted to draw his lines from right to left.

Charles's visual discrimination was poor. He reverses *b, d, p, q, u* and *n* when he reads and writes. He confuses letters such as *m* and *n, r* and *h.* His visual memory is poor. His visual decoding ability was adequate. He was easily distracted by visual stimuli. He had difficulty in re-visualizing letters and words.

Auditory Processes. Charles had difficulty with auditory synthesizing, analyzing, and memory tasks. His receptive and expressive language was adequate. He was easily distracted by auditory stimuli. He was able to deal with abstract verbal concepts.

Non-Verbal Processes. Charles was unable to maintain his balance on a balance beam. He was right-handed, -footed, and -eyed. His eye-hand coordination was poor for his age. He had difficulty copying due to poor visual memory, figure-ground perceptual problems, and poor kinesthetic feel for the form of letters. He reversed whole words when he copied. He read words from the right to the left. He was unable to write the alphabet in sequence and could not remember the form of many of the letters.

Associational Processes. Charles had difficulty making symbol-sound associations. He had particular difficulty with the short vowels. He had difficulty placing objects in position, constructing what he perceived, and placing objects in relation to each other. He got meaning from the printed word when he read orally and silently. His visual-vocal, auditory-vocal associational abilities were adequate. He had some difficulty transferring information presented orally that required a motor response. He comprehended material at grade level that was read aloud to him but his reading level as indicated by formal testing was first-grade.

Arithmetic

Charles was able to do arithmetic material presented at a third-grade level. He had difficulty with subtraction and had little concept of multiplication.

THE EDUCATIONAL PROGRAM

Reading

1. Visual perceptual training.
2. Visual memory and sequencing training.
3. Auditory perceptual training: synthesizing, analyzing, and memory.
4. The program outlined by Gillingham and Stillman (1966).
5. The *Merrill Linguistic Readers.*

Spelling

The spelling program is part of the reading program; the Forbes *Graded Spelling Lists* may be helpful.

Arithmetic

Any word problems should be read to him.

Writing

Training with sandpaper letters and numbers, along with various other kinesthetic experiences such as feeling rough and smooth objects should precede the formal writing program. Charles has a typewriter available for his use in the classroom and is learning to type.

Science and Social Studies

The material should be presented orally. Visual aids such as movies, filmstrips should be used.

In addition to those activities, Charles should receive:

1. Eye-hand coordination training.
2. Balance beam and trampoline activities to develop laterality.
3. Activities to develop directionality.
4. Activities to develop left-right progression.
5. Activities to develop kinesthetic feel for the form of numbers and letters.

REFERENCES

Forbes, C. T. *Let's Start with Phonics*. Weston, Mass.: Forbes, 1956.

Gillingham, A., & Stillman, B. *Remedial Training for Children with Specific Disability in Reading, Spelling, and Penmanship*. Cambridge, Mass.: Educators Publishing Service, 1966.

Orton, J. L. *A Guide to Teaching Phonics*. Cambridge, Mass.: Educators Publishing Service, 1964.

Index